BLOOM'S

HOW TO WRITE ABOUT

Nathaniel Hawthorne

LAURIE A. STERLING

BLOOM'S
LITERARY CRITICISM
An imprint of Infobase Publishing

Chelsea House, Inc
An imprint of Infobase Publishing
132 West 31st Street
New York NY 10001

Library of Congress Cataloging-in-Publication Data

Sterling, Laurie A.
   Bloom's how to write about Nathaniel Hawthorne / Laurie A. Sterling ; introduction by Harold Bloom.
      p. cm.
   Includes bibliographical references (p.) and index.
   ISBN 978-0-7910-9481-5 (hc: alk. paper) 1. Hawthorne, Nathaniel, 1804–1864—Criticism and interpretation. 2. Criticism—Authorship. 3. Report writing. I. Bloom, Harold. II. Title. III. Title: How to write about Nathaniel Hawthorne.
   PS1888.S5775 2008
   813'.3—dc22   2006101324

Text design by Annie O'Donnell
Cover design by Ben Peterson

Printed in the United States of America

Bang CGI 10 9 8 7 6 5 4 3 2 1

This book is printed on acid-free paper.

CONTENTS

SERIES INTRODUCTION

BLOOM'S How to Write about Literature series is designed to inspire students to write fine essays on great writers and their works. Each volume in the series begins with an introduction by Harold Bloom, meditating on the challenges and rewards of writing about the volume's subject author. The first chapter then provides detailed instructions on how to write a good essay, including how to find a thesis; how to develop an outline; how to write a good introduction, body text, and conclusions; how to cite sources; and more. The second chapter provides a brief overview of the issues involved in writing about the subject author and then a number of suggestions for paper topics, with accompanying strategies for addressing each topic. Succeeding chapters cover the author's major works.

The paper topics suggested within this book are open-ended, and the brief strategies provided are designed to give students a push forward on the writing process rather than a roadmap to success. The aim of the book is to pose questions, not answer them. Many different kinds of papers could result from each topic. As always, the success of each paper will depend completely on the writer's skill and imagination.

HOW TO WRITE
ABOUT HAWTHORNE

by Harold Bloom

H AWTHORNE'S NOVELS and tales are at the canonical center of American literature. Emerson's silent walking companion in Concord, Hawthorne was the closest friend of Herman Melville, and became the dominant native influence upon the fiction of Henry James. No reader attempting to understand the American people can avoid the author of *The Scarlet Letter, The Marble Faun,* and such tales as "My Kinsman, Major Molineux," "Young Goodman Brown," "Wakefield," "Rappaccini's Daughter," "Ethan Brand," and "Feathertop."

How *not* to write about Hawthorne? Do not make easy assumptions. He was *not* a Puritan, nor was he an anti-Emersonian, as in the Southern American tradition that extends from Poe to the followers of T. S. Eliot, including Allen Tate and Robert Penn Warren. Like Melville and Emily Dickinson, Hawthorne had a dialectical relationship to Emerson's prophetic thought. These three were not the Seer of Concord's disciples, who included Thoreau, Walt Whitman, Margaret Fuller, Robert Frost, and Hart Crane. As with Wallace Stevens long after them, Hawthorne, Melville, and Dickinson struggled to evade Emerson, yet they all understood implicitly that he was the Mind of America. They became Emersonians with a difference, but then so was Emerson himself. Hawthorne's great heroine, Hester Prynne in *The Scarlet Letter,* and Melville's Captain Ahab in *Moby-Dick* are Emersonians of the wild side, as was "Walt Whitman," the grand fiction of *Leaves of Grass.* Henry James, who subtly misrepresented both Hawthorne and Emerson (for defensive reasons), gave us a fourth major Emersonian figure in Isabel Archer, heroine of *The Portrait of a Lady.*

My initial suggestion is therefore that an excellent preparation for writing about Hawthorne is to read carefully at least a handful of Emerson's most crucial essays: "Self-Reliance," "Experience," "Fate," "Power," and "Illusions." If you have not read Emerson before, these may surprise you. The young Henry James, despite a condescending tone in his book *Hawthorne*, was able to characterize accurately some of the main tenets of Emersonianism:

> Emerson expressed . . . the value and importance of the indi-
> vidual . . . He reflected with beautiful irony upon the exquisite
> imprudence of those institutions which claim to have appropri-
> ated the truth and to dole it out . . .

Good enough, but hardly the total Emerson: Henry James avoids the sage's darker ironies, which are manifested in Hester, Ahab, and Walt. Emerson was not a Christian but an American heretic, who hoped for an American Eve and an American Adam, free from the European and the biblical past. "There is no history, only biography," is Emerson's point of departure from which he set forth to explore the spiritual shores of America. Hester Prynne, the American Eve, fails only because the weak Dimmesdale is anything but an American Adam, though Chillingsworth admirably incarnates the American Satan. Walt proclaims himself "Adam early in the morning," and like a god can send forth sunrise from himself. Ahab is an Emersonian-Promethean when he cries out: "I'd strike the sun if it insulted me." These are all Emerson's progeny. He urged us to escape from time.

That Hawthorne is in love with Hester Prynne is palpable. Flaubert loved his Emma Bovary even as Tolstoy loved his Anna Karenina, and both great novelists murdered their beloveds. Hawthorne, aided by the form of the romance or visionary narrative, would not countenance killing the American Eve. Hester survives, though I (at least) chafe at her lost potential. Like the heroines of George Eliot, Hester lives on in expectation of a better time to come for elite Western women. In their very contrary ways, the female protagonists of Virginia Woolf and D. H. Lawrence, and of Willa Cather in America, live on as Hester does, in anticipation of futurity. Emerson, in the words of the great Rabbi Hillel, always asks: "If I am not for me, then who will be for me? And if I am for myself only, then what am I? And if not now, when?" Hester Prynne implicitly endures all of that, yet makes no attempt to answer the final question.

HOW TO WRITE
A GOOD ESSAY

WHILE THERE are many ways to write about literature, most assignments for high school and college English classes call for analytical papers. In these assignments, you are presenting your interpretation of a text to your reader. Your objective is to interpret the text's meaning in order to enhance your reader's understanding and enjoyment of the work. Without exception, strong papers about the meaning of a literary work are built upon a careful, close reading of the text or texts. Careful, analytical reading should always be the first step in your writing process. This volume provides models of such close, analytical reading, and these should help you develop your own skills as a reader and as a writer.

As the examples throughout this book demonstrate, attentive reading entails thinking about and evaluating the formal (textual) aspects of the author's works: theme, character, form, and language. In addition, when writing about a work, many readers choose to move beyond the text itself to consider the work's cultural context. In these instances, readers might explore the historical circumstances of the time period in which the work was written. Alternatively, they might examine the philosophies and ideas that a work addresses. Even in cases where a work's cultural context is explored, papers must still address the more formal aspects of the work itself. A good interpretative essay that evaluates Charles Dickens's use of the philosophy of utilitarianism in his novel *Hard Times,* for example, cannot adequately address the author's treatment of the philosophy without firmly grounding the discussion in the book itself. In other words, any analytical paper about a text, even one

1

that seeks to evaluate the work's cultural context, must also have a firm handle on the work's themes, characters, and language. You must look for and evaluate these aspects of a work, then, as you read a text and as you prepare to write about it.

WRITING ABOUT THEMES

Literary themes are more than just topics or subjects treated in a work; they are attitudes or points about these topics that often structure other elements in a work. Writing about theme therefore requires that you not just identify a topic that a literary work addresses but also discuss what that work says about that topic. For example, if you were writing about the culture of the American South in William Faulkner's famous story "A Rose for Emily," you would need to discuss what Faulkner says, argues, or implies about that culture and its passing.

When you prepare to write about thematic concerns in a work of literature, you will probably discover that, like most works of literature, your text touches upon other themes in addition to its central theme. These secondary themes also provide rich ground for paper topics. A thematic paper on "A Rose for Emily" might consider gender or race in the story. While neither of these could be said to be the central theme of the story, they are clearly related to the passing of the "old South" and could provide plenty of good material for papers.

As you prepare to write about themes in literature, you might find a number of strategies helpful. After you identify a theme or themes in the story, you should begin by evaluating how other elements of the story—such as character, point of view, imagery, and symbolism—help develop the theme. You might ask yourself what your own responses are to the author's treatment of the subject matter. Do not neglect the obvious either: What expectations does the title set up? How does the title help develop thematic concerns? Clearly, the title "A Rose for Emily" says something about the narrator's attitude toward the title character, Emily Grierson, and all she represents.

WRITING ABOUT CHARACTER

Generally, characters are essential components of fiction and drama. (This is not always the case though; Ray Bradbury's "August 2026: There

Will Come Soft Rains" is technically a story without characters, at least any human characters.) Often, you can discuss character in poetry, as in T. S. Eliot's "The Love Song of J. Alfred Prufrock" or Robert Browning's "My Last Duchess." Many writers find that analyzing character is one of the most interesting and engaging ways to work with a piece of literature and to shape a paper. After all, characters generally are human, and we all know something about being human and living in the world. While it is always important to remember that these figures are not real people but creations of the writer's imagination, it can be fruitful to begin evaluating them as you might evaluate a real person. Often you can start with your own response to a character. Did you like or dislike the character? Did you sympathize with the character? Why or why not?

Keep in mind, though, that emotional responses like these are just starting places. To truly explore and evaluate literary characters, you need to return to the formal aspects of the text and evaluate how the author has drawn these characters. The 20th-century writer E. M. Forster coined the terms *flat* characters and *round* characters. Flat characters are static and one-dimensional. They frequently represent a particular concept or idea. In contrast, round characters are more fully and realistically drawn, and they usually develop over the course of a work. Are the characters you are studying flat or round? What elements of the characters lead you to this conclusion? Why might the author have drawn characters like this? How does their development affect the meaning of the work? Similarly, you should explore the techniques the author uses to develop characters. Do we hear a character's own words, or do we hear only other characters' assessments of him or her? Or, does the author use an omniscient or limited omniscient narrator to allow us access to the workings of the characters' minds? If so, how does that help develop the characterization? Often, you can even evaluate the narrator as a character. How trustworthy are the opinions and assessments of the narrator? You should also think about characters' names. Do they mean anything? If you encounter a hero named Sophia or Sophie, you should probably think about her wisdom (or lack thereof), since *Sophia* means "wisdom" in Greek. Similarly, since the name *Sylvia* is derived from the word *sylvan,* meaning "of the wood," you might want to evaluate that character's relationship with nature. Once again, you might look to the title of the work. Does Herman Melville's "Bartleby, the Scrivener" signal anything about Bartleby himself? Is Bartleby adequately defined by his job as scrivener? Is this part of Melville's point? Pursuing questions like these can help you develop thorough papers about characters from psychological, sociological, or more formalistic perspectives.

WRITING ABOUT FORM AND GENRE

Genre, a word derived from French, means "type" or "class." Literary genres are distinctive classes or categories of literary composition. On the most general level, literary works can be divided into the genres of drama, poetry, fiction, and essays, yet within those genres there are classifications that are also referred to as genres. Tragedy and comedy, for example, are genres of drama. Epic, lyric, and pastoral are genres of poetry. *Form*, on the other hand, generally refers to the shape or structure of a work. There are many clearly defined forms of poetry that follow specific patterns of meter, rhyme, and stanza. Sonnets, for example, are poems that follow a fixed form of 14 lines. Sonnets generally follow one of two basic sonnet forms, each with its own distinct rhyme scheme. Haiku is another example of poetic form, traditionally consisting of three unrhymed lines of five, seven, and five syllables.

While you might think that writing about form or genre leaves little room for argument, many of these forms and genres are very fluid. Remember that literature is evolving and ever changing, and so are its forms. As you study poetry, you may find that poets, especially more modern poets, play with traditional poetic forms, bringing about new effects. Similarly, dramatic tragedy was once quite narrowly defined, but over the centuries playwrights have broadened and challenged traditional definitions, changing the shape of tragedy. When Arthur Miller wrote *Death of a Salesman*, many critics challenged the idea that tragic drama could encompass a common man like Willy Loman.

Evaluating how a work of literature fits into or challenges the boundaries of its form or genre can provide you with fruitful avenues of investigation. You might find it helpful to ask why the work does or does not fit into traditional categories. Why might Miller have thought it fitting to write a tragedy of the common man? Similarly, you might compare the content or theme of a work with its form. How well do they work together? Many of Emily Dickinson's poems, for instance, follow the meter of traditional hymns. While some of her poems seem to express traditional religious doctrines, many seem to challenge or strain against traditional conceptions of God and theology. What is the effect, then, of her use of traditional hymn meter?

WRITING ABOUT LANGUAGE, SYMBOLS, AND IMAGERY

No matter what the genre, writers use words as their most basic tool. Language is the most fundamental building block of literature. It is essential that you pay careful attention to the author's language and word choice as you read, reread, and analyze a text. Imagery is language that appeals to the senses. Most commonly, imagery appeals to our sense of vision, creating a mental picture, but authors also use language that appeals to our other senses. Images can be literal or figurative. Literal images use sensory language to describe an actual thing. In the broadest terms, figurative language uses one thing to speak about something else. For example, if I call my boss a snake, I am not saying that he is literally a reptile. Instead, I am using figurative language to communicate my opinions about him. Since we think of snakes as sneaky, slimy, and sinister, I am using the concrete image of a snake to communicate these abstract opinions and impressions.

The two most common figures of speech are similes and metaphors. Both are comparisons between two apparently dissimilar things. Similes are explicit comparisons using the words *like* or *as;* metaphors are implicit comparisons. To return to the previous example, if I say, "My boss, Bob, was waiting for me when I showed up at work five minutes late today—the snake!" I have constructed a metaphor.

Writing about his experiences fighting in World War I, Wilfred Owen begins his poem "Dulce et Decorum Est," with a string of similes: "Bent double, like old beggars under sacks, / Knock-kneed, coughing like hags, we cursed through sludge." Owen's goal was to undercut clichéd notions that war and dying in battle were glorious. Certainly, comparing soldiers to coughing hags and beggars underscores his point.

"Fog," a short poem by Carl Sandburg, provides clear example of a metaphor. Sandburg's poem reads:

The fog comes
on little cat feet.

It sits looking
over harbor and city
on silent haunches
and then moves on.

Notice how effectively Sandburg conveys surprising impressions of the fog by comparing two seemingly disparate things—the fog and a cat.

Symbols, by contrast, are things that stand for, or represent, other things. Often they represent something intangible, such as concepts or ideas. In everyday life we use and understand symbols easily. Babies at christenings and brides at weddings wear white to represent purity. Think, too, of a dollar bill. The paper has no value in and of itself. Instead, that paper bill is a symbol of something else, the precious metal in a nation's coffers. Symbols in literature work similarly. Authors use symbols to evoke more than a simple, straightforward, literal meaning. Characters, objects, and places can all function as symbols. Famous literary examples of symbols include Moby Dick, the white whale of Herman Melville's novel, and the scarlet *A* of Nathaniel Hawthorne's *The Scarlet Letter.* As both of these symbols suggest, a literary symbol cannot be adequately defined or explained by any one meaning. Hester Prynne's Puritan community clearly intends her scarlet *A* as a symbol of her adultery, but as the novel progresses, even her own community reads the letter as representing not just *adultery,* but *able, angel,* and a host of other meanings.

Writing about imagery and symbols requires close attention to the author's language. To prepare a paper on symbolism or imagery in a work, identify and trace the images and symbols and then try to draw some conclusions about how they function. Ask yourself how any symbols or images help contribute to the themes or meanings of the work. What connotations do they carry? How do they affect your reception of the work? Do they shed light on characters or settings? A strong paper on imagery or symbolism will thoroughly consider the use of figures in the text and will try to reach some conclusions about how or why the author uses them.

WRITING ABOUT HISTORY AND CONTEXT

As noted above, it is possible to write an analytical paper that also considers a work's context. After all, the text was not created in a vacuum. The author lived and wrote in a specific time period and in a specific cultural context and, like all of us, was shaped by that environment. Learning more about the historical and cultural circumstances that surrounded the author and the work can help illuminate a text and provide you with productive material for a paper. Remember, though, that when you write analytical papers, you should use the context to illuminate the text. Do not lose sight of your goal—to interpret the meaning of the literary work. Use historical or philosophical research as a tool to develop your textual evaluation.

Thoughtful readers often consider how history and culture affected the author's choice and treatment of the subject matter. Investigations into the history and context of a work could examine its relation to specific historical events, such as the Salem witch trials in 17th-century Massachusetts or the restoration of Charles to the British throne in 1660. Bear in mind that historical context is not limited to politics and world events. While knowing about the Vietnam War is certainly helpful in interpreting much of Tim O'Brien's fiction, and some knowledge of the French Revolution clearly illuminates the dynamics of Charles Dickens's *A Tale of Two Cities,* historical context also entails the fabric of daily life. Examining a text in light of gender roles, race relations, class boundaries, or working conditions can give rise to thoughtful and compelling papers. Exploring the conditions of the working class in 19th-century England, for example, can provide a particularly effective avenue for writing about Dickens's *Hard Times.*

You can begin thinking about these issues by asking broad questions at first. What do you know about the time period and about the author? What does the editorial apparatus in your text tell you? These might be starting places. Similarly, when specific historical events or dynamics are particularly important to understanding a work but might be somewhat obscure to modern readers, textbooks usually provide notes to explain historical background. These are a good place to start. With this information, ask yourself how these historical facts and circumstances might have affected the author, the presentation of theme, and the presentation of character. How does knowing more about the work's specific historical context illuminate it? To take a well-known example, understanding the complex attitudes toward slavery during the time Mark Twain wrote *Adventures of Huckleberry Finn* should help you begin to examine issues of race in the text. Additionally, you might compare these attitudes to those of the time in which the novel was set. How might this comparison affect your interpretation of a work written after the abolition of slavery but set before the Civil War?

WRITING ABOUT PHILOSOPHY AND IDEAS

Philosophical concerns are closely related to both historical context and thematic issues. Like historical investigation, philosophical research can provide a useful tool as you analyze a text. For example, an investigation into the working class in Dickens's England might lead you to a topic on the philosophical doctrine of utilitarianism in *Hard Times*. Many other works explore philosophies and ideas quite explicitly. Mary Shelley's famous novel *Frankenstein,* for example, explores John Locke's tabula rasa theory of human knowledge as she portrays the intellectual and emotional development of Victor Frankenstein's creature. As this example indicates, philosophical issues are somewhat more abstract than investigations of theme or historical context. Some other examples of philosophical issues include human free will, the formation of human identity, the nature of sin, or questions of ethics.

Writing about philosophy and ideas might require some outside research, but usually the notes or other material in your text will provide you with basic information and often footnotes and bibliographies suggest places you can go to read further about the subject. If you have identified a philosophical theme that runs through a text, you might ask yourself how the author develops this theme. Look at character development and the interactions of characters, for example. Similarly, you might examine whether the narrative voice in a work of fiction addresses the philosophical concerns of the text.

WRITING COMPARE AND CONTRAST ESSAYS

Finally, you might find that comparing and contrasting the works or techniques of an author provides a useful tool for literary analysis. A compare and contrast essay might compare two characters or themes in a single work, or it might compare the author's treatment of a theme in two works. It might also contrast methods of character development or analyze an author's differing treatment of a philosophical concern in two works. Writing compare and contrast essays, though, requires some special consideration. While they generally provide you with plenty of material, they also come with a built-in trap: the laundry list. These papers often become mere lists of connections between the works. As this chapter will discuss, a strong thesis must make an assertion that you want to prove or validate. A strong compare and contrast thesis, then, needs to comment on the significance of the similarities and differences you observe. It is not enough merely to assert that the works contain similarities and differences. You might, for example, assert why the similarities and differences are important and explain how they illuminate the works' treatment of theme. Remember, too, that a thesis should not be a statement of the obvious. A compare/contrast paper that focuses only on very obvious similarities or differences does little to illuminate the connections between the works. Often, an effective method of shaping a strong thesis and argument is to begin your paper by noting the similarities between the works but then developing a thesis that asserts how these apparently similar elements are different. If, for example, you observe that Emily Dickinson wrote a number of poems about spiders, you might analyze how she uses spider imagery differently in two poems. Similarly, many scholars have noted that Hawthorne created many "mad scientist" characters, men so devoted to their science or their art that they lose perspective on all else. A good thesis comparing two of these characters—Aylmer of "The Birth-Mark" and Dr. Rappaccini of "Rappaccini's Daughter," for example—might initially identify both characters as examples of Hawthorne's mad scientist type but then argue that their motivations for scientific experimentation differ. If you strive to analyze the similarities or differences, discuss significances, and move beyond the obvious, your paper should move beyond the laundry list trap.

PREPARING TO WRITE

Armed with a clear sense of your task—illuminating the text—and with an understanding of theme, character, language, history, and philosophy, you are ready to approach the writing process. Remember that good writing is grounded in good reading and that close reading takes time, attention, and more than one reading of your text. Read for comprehension first. As you go back and review the work, mark the text to chart the details of the work as well as your reactions. Highlight important passages, repeated words, and image patterns. "Converse" with the text through marginal notes. Mark turns in the plot, ask questions, and make observations about characters, themes, and language. If you are reading from a book that does not belong to you, keep a record of your reactions in a journal or notebook. If you have read a work of literature carefully, paying attention to both the text and the context of the work, you have a leg up on the writing process. Admittedly, at this point, your ideas are probably very broad and undefined, but you have taken an important first step toward writing a strong paper.

Your next step is to focus, to take a broad, perhaps fuzzy, topic and define it more clearly. Even a topic provided by your instructor will need to be focused appropriately. Remember that good writers make the topic their own. There are a number of strategies—often called "invention"—that you can use to develop your own focus. In one such strategy, *freewriting*, you spend 10 minutes or so just writing about your topic without referring back to the text or your notes. Write whatever comes to mind; the important thing is that you just keep writing. Often this process allows you to develop fresh ideas or approaches to your subject matter. You could also try *brainstorming*. Write down your topic and then list all the related points or ideas you can think of. Include questions, comments, words, important passages or events, and anything else that comes to mind. Let one idea lead to another. In the related technique of *clustering*, or *mapping*, write your topic on a sheet of paper and write related ideas around it. Then list related subpoints under each of these main ideas. Many people then draw arrows to show connections between points. This technique helps you narrow your topic and can also help you organize your ideas. Similarly, asking journalistic questions—Who? What? Where? When? Why? and How?—can inspire ideas for topic development.

Thesis Statements

Once you have developed a focused topic, you can begin to think about your thesis statement, the main point or purpose of your paper. It is imperative that you craft a strong thesis; otherwise, your paper will likely be little more than random, disorganized observations about the text. Think of your thesis statement as a kind of road map for your paper. It tells your reader where you are going and how you are going to get there.

To craft a good thesis, you must keep a number of things in mind. First, as the title of this subsection indicates, your paper's thesis should be a statement, an assertion about the text that you want to prove or validate. Beginning writers often formulate a question that they attempt to use as a thesis. For example, a writer exploring the character of Aylmer in Hawthorne's "The Birth-Mark" might ask, Aylmer's name means "noble," but is Aylmer really noble? While a question like this is a good strategy to use in the invention process to help narrow your topic and find your thesis, it cannot serve as the thesis statement because it does not tell your reader what you want to assert about Aylmer. You might shape this question into a thesis by instead proposing an answer to the question: Although Aylmer's name means "noble," he is not an entirely noble character. His science and his learning are admirable, but his obsession with his scientific experiments is a flaw in his character. Notice that this thesis provides an initial plan or structure for the rest of the paper, and notice, too, that the thesis statement does not necessarily have to fit into one sentence. After establishing the meaning of Aylmer's name, you could examine the ways in which Aylmer is presented as a noble character and then show how Hawthorne casts Aylmer's relationship with science as obsessive, thereby presenting him as flawed.

Second, remember that a good thesis makes an assertion that you need to support. In other words, a good thesis does not state the obvious. If you tried to formulate a thesis about Aylmer by simply saying, Hawthorne's Aylmer in "The Birth-Mark" is a man who is dedicated to science, you have done nothing but rephrase the obvious. Since Hawthorne's first paragraph calls Aylmer "a man of science," there would be no point in spending three to five pages to support that assertion. You might try to develop a thesis from that point by asking yourself some further questions: What does it mean to be a "man of science"? Does the story seem to indicate that to be a man of science is a positive thing? Does it praise Aylmer for his scientific propensities, or does it criticize him because of them? Such a line of questioning might lead you to a more viable thesis, such as the one in the preceding paragraph.

As the comparison with the road map also suggests, your thesis should appear near the beginning of the paper. In relatively short papers (three to six pages), the thesis almost always appears in the first paragraph. Some writers fall into the trap of saving their thesis for the end, trying to provide a surprise or a big moment of revelation, as if to say, "TA-DA! I've just proved that Hawthorne uses color in 'Young Goodman Brown' to reflect his belief that humans are neither evil nor pure but a mixture of both." Placing a thesis at the end of an essay can seriously mar the essay's effectiveness. If you fail to define your essay's point and purpose clearly at the beginning, your reader will find it difficult to assess the clarity of your argument and understand the points you are making. When your argument comes as a surprise at the end, you force your reader to reread your essay in order to assess its logic and effectiveness.

Finally, you should avoid using the first person ("I") as you present your thesis. Though it is not strictly wrong to write in the first person, it is difficult to do so gracefully. While writing in the first person, beginning writers often fall into the trap of writing self-reflexive prose (writing *about* their paper *in* their paper). Often this leads to the most dreaded of opening lines: "In this paper I am going to discuss . . ." Not only does this self-reflexive voice make for very awkward prose, it frequently allows writers to boldly announce a topic while completely avoiding a thesis statement. An example might be a paper that begins as follows: The Scarlet Letter, Hawthorne's most famous novel, follows the life of Hester Prynne, who has committed adultery and is forced by Puritan leaders to wear a scarlet A. In this paper I am going to discuss the significance of the scarlet A in the novel. The author of this paper has done little more than announce a topic for the paper (the significance of the scarlet A). While the last sentence might have been intended as a thesis, the writer fails to present an opinion about the significance of the scarlet letter. To improve this thesis, the writer would need to back up a couple of steps. First, the announced topic of the paper is too broad; literary scholars have discussed the symbolism of Hester's A for more than 100 years without yielding any one, definitive interpretation. The writer should first consider some of the many functions of the A within Hawthorne's text. From here, the author could select the function that seems most appealing and then begin to craft a specific thesis. A writer who chooses to explore the relationship between Pearl and the scarlet letter might, for example, craft a thesis that reads, As a reflection of Hester's scarlet letter, Pearl challenges the Puritans' worldview. We see this in her play, her language, and her social interaction.

Outlines

While developing a strong, thoughtful thesis early in your writing process should help focus your paper, outlining provides an essential tool for logically shaping that paper. A good outline helps you see—and develop—the relationships among the points in your argument and assures you that your paper flows logically and coherently. Outlining not only helps place your points in a logical order but also helps you subordinate supporting points, weed out any irrelevant points, and decide if there are any necessary points that are missing from your argument. Most of us are familiar with formal outlines that use numerical and letter designations for each point. However, there are different types of outlines; you may find that an informal outline is a more useful tool for you. What is important, though, is that you spend the time to develop some sort of outline—formal or informal.

Remember that an outline is a tool to help you shape and write a strong paper. If you do not spend sufficient time planning your supporting points and shaping the arrangement of those points, you will most likely construct a vague, unfocused outline that provides little, if any, help with the writing of the paper. Consider the following example.

Thesis: As a reflection of Hester's scarlet letter, Pearl challenges the Puritans' worldview. We see this in her play, her language, and her social interaction.

  I. Introduction and thesis

 II. Pearl
      A. Play
      B. Language
      C. Social interaction
      D. The scarlet A

```
III. Hester

 IV. The Puritans
     A. Their worldview

  V. Dimmesdale

 VI. Conclusion
     A. Pearl challenges Puritans' worldview
```

This outline has a number of flaws. First, the major topics labeled with the Roman numerals are not arranged in a logical order. If the paper's aim is to show how Pearl functions as a challenge to Puritan attitudes, the writer should define those attitudes before presenting Pearl as a challenge to them. Similarly, the thesis makes no reference to Hester herself or to Dimmesdale, but the writer includes each of them as major sections of this outline. As Pearl's biological parents, they may well have a place in this paper, but the writer fails to provide detail about their place in the argument. Third, the writer includes the scarlet *A* as one of the lettered items in section II. Letters A, B, and C all refer to ways Pearl challenges Puritan society; the scarlet *A* does not belong in this list. The writer could argue that it is, like Pearl, a challenge to Puritan attitudes, but unlike the other items, it is not one of Pearl's challenges. A fourth problem is the inclusion of a letter A in sections IV and VI. An outline should not include an A without a B, a 1 without a 2, and so forth. The final problem with this outline is the overall lack of detail. None of the sections provide much information about the content of the argument, and it seems likely that the writer has not given sufficient thought to the content of the paper.

A better start to this outline might be the following:

```
Thesis: As a reflection of Hester's scarlet letter,
Pearl challenges the Puritans' worldview. We see this
in her play, her language, and her social interaction.

   I. Introduction and thesis

  II. The Puritans' worldview
```

```
    III. Parallels between Pearl and the scarlet A

     IV. The A's challenges to Puritan attitudes

      V. Pearl's challenges to Puritan attitudes
         1. Play
         2. Language
         3. Social interaction

    VI. Conclusion
```

This new outline would prove much more helpful when it came time to write the paper.

An outline like this could be shaped into an even more useful tool if the writer fleshed out the argument by providing specific examples from the text to support each point. Once you have listed your main point and your supporting ideas, develop this raw material by listing related supporting ideas and material under each of the main headings. From there, arrange the material in subsections and order the material logically.

For example, you might begin with one of the theses cited above: Although Aylmer's name means "noble," he is not an entirely noble character. His science and his learning are admirable, but his obsession with his scientific experiments is a flaw in his character. As noted above, this thesis already gives you the beginning of an organization: Start by supporting the notion that Aylmer is in some ways a noble character and then explain how Hawthorne casts his relationship with science as obsessive and therefore flawed. You might begin your outline, then, with three topic headings: (1) Aylmer as noble; (2) Aylmer's relationship with science as obsessive; and (3) the proof that Aylmer is therefore flawed. Under each heading you could list ideas that support the particular point. Be sure to include references to parts of the text that help build your case.

An informal outline might look like this:

```
Thesis: Although Aylmer's name means "noble," he is not
an entirely noble character. His science and his learn-
ing are admirable, but his obsession with his scien-
tific experiments is a flaw in his character.
```

1: **Aylmer as noble**
- Name means "noble"
- Narrator refers to him as a "man of genius"
- Georgiana's response to Aylmer
  - She falls in love with him
  - Georgiana loves him despite, or because of, his failures. After reading his journal, she says, "It made me worship you more than ever. . . ."
  - Georgiana: "You have aimed loftily—you have done nobly! Do not repent. . . ."

2: **Aylmer's relationship with science as obsessive**
- First note the conflict that the beginning of the story sets up: whether Aylmer's love of science or his "love for his young wife might prove the stronger of the two"
  - Note the narrator's language: Aylmer had "devoted himself . . . *too unreservedly* to scientific studies, ever to be weaned from them by any *second passion*"
- Aylmer's attitude toward the birthmark. The narrator tells us that people's responses to the birthmark "varied exceedingly, according to the difference of temperament in the beholders. . . ."
  - "Aylmer's somber imagination was not long in rendering the birthmark a frightful object, causing him more trouble and horror than ever Georgiana's beauty, whether of soul or sense, had given him delight.

    At all the seasons which should have been their happiest, he invariably, and without intending it—nay, in spite of a purpose to the contrary—reverted to this one disastrous topic."

- Aylmer says the birthmark "shocks" him
- The narrator speaks of "the tyrannizing influence acquired by one idea over his mind, and . . . the lengths which he might find in his heart to go, for the sake of giving himself peace"

3: **Proof that Aylmer is, therefore, flawed**

- Aylmer's motivations for removing the birthmark seem self-centered
  - Aylmer says to Georgiana: "Doubt not my power. . . . What will be my triumph, when I shall have corrected what Nature left imperfect, in her fairest work! Even Pygmalion, when his sculptured woman assumed life, felt not greater ecstasy than mine will be."
  - "I rejoice in this single imperfection, since it will be such rapture to remove it."
- Effects of Aylmer's attitude about the birthmark on his relationship with Georgiana
  - A mistrust grows between them
  - Georgiana grows to dislike the birthmark herself because she understands how much Aylmer hates it. This affects her sense of self.
- Effects of Aylmer's experiment
  - It kills Georgiana, "the best thing that earth could offer"
- The language of fire and smoke that surrounds Aylmer's laboratory—reminiscent of hell?

Conclusion

- According to Georgiana, Aylmer had "aimed loftily," and she tells him not to repent
- In the final paragraph, the narrator gives us a sense of just what Aylmer's flaw is: He had not reached "a profounder wisdom." Explain what that "profounder wisdom" is.

You would set about writing a formal outline with a similar process, though in the final stages you would label the headings differently. A formal outline for a paper that argues the thesis about "Young Goodman Brown" cited above—that Hawthorne uses color in the story to reflect his belief that humans are neither evil nor pure but a mixture of both— might look like this:

Thesis: Hawthorne uses color in "Young Goodman Brown" to reflect his belief that humans are neither evil nor pure but a mixture of both.

   I. Introduction and thesis

  II. Hawthorne's theology (humanity as fallen, neither wholly good nor evil)
     A. The devil: "Evil is the nature of mankind"
     B. The narrator's treatment of characters
       1. Faith's allegorical name
       2. The minister as a "venerable saint"
       3. Goody Cloyse as "an excellent old Christian"

 III. The colors of the forest (the devil's space)
     A. Darkness/gloom/ "deep dusk"—
       1. Particular uses in the story
         a. "He had taken a dreary road, darkened by all the gloomiest trees of the forest, which

barely stood aside to let the narrow path creep through, and closed immediately behind."

    b. "The road grew wilder and drearier and more faintly traced, and vanished at length, leaving him in the heart of the dark wilderness, still rushing onward, with the instinct that guides mortal man to evil."

  2. Metaphorical and literal meanings

B. Black

  1. Particular uses in the story

    a. "his staff, which bore the likeness of a great black snake"

    b. "black pines"

  2. Associations with death

  3. Associations with the devil

C. Red

  1. Particular uses in the story

    a. "red light" (of the fire)

    b. "lurid blaze"

  2. Associations with fire and hell

  3. Connections with the devil

IV. The colors of humanity

A. Brown (Young Goodman Brown)

  1. Common name—marks him as a sort of everyman

  2. Brown as a mixture of all three primary colors; neither white (purity) nor black (evil, demonic)

  3. Color marks Brown as earthy/of earth

B. Pink (Faith)

  1. Allegorical significance—humanity's faith, Brown's faith

> 2. Pink as a blending of white (purity)
>   and red (sensuality)
>
> V. Conclusion
>   A. How this comments on Young Goodman Brown's
>   attitudes at the end of the story
>   B. Connections to other Hawthorne characters
>   1. Giovanni from "Rappaccini's Daugh-
>   ter"
>   2. Aylmer from "The Birth-Mark"

As in the previous example, the thesis provided the seeds of a structure, and the writer was careful to arrange the supporting points in a logical manner, showing the relationships among the ideas in the paper.

Body Paragraphs

Once your outline is complete, you can begin drafting your paper. Paragraphs, units of related sentences, are the building blocks of a good paper, and as you draft you should keep in mind both the function and the qualities of good paragraphs. Paragraphs help you chart and control the shape and content of your essay, and they help the reader see your organization and your logic. You should begin a new paragraph whenever you move from one major point to another. In longer, more complex essays you might use a group of related paragraphs to support major points. Remember that in addition to being adequately developed, a good paragraph is both unified and coherent.

Unified Paragraphs

Each paragraph must be centralized around one idea or point, and a unified paragraph carefully focuses on and develops this central idea without including extraneous ideas or tangents. For beginning writers, the best way to ensure that you are constructing unified paragraphs is to include a topic sentence in each paragraph. This topic sentence should convey the main point of the paragraph, and every sentence in the paragraph should relate to that topic sentence. Any sentence that strays from the central topic does not belong in the paragraph and needs to be revised or deleted. Consider the following paragraph about Aylmer's obsession with Georgiana's birthmark. Notice how the paragraph veers away from the main point that Aylmer's love of science has become an obsession:

> The story's opening paragraph introduces the conflict that will drive the story's plot, Aylmer's love of science versus his love for his wife, and it asks whether his "love for his young wife might prove the stronger of the two." It does not take long for the reader to see that Aylmer's love for science has become an obsession. Even the narrator's word choice in the story's first paragraph hints that Aylmer's love of science goes a bit too far: "He had devoted himself . . . too unreservedly to scientific studies, ever to be weaned from them by a second passion." The phrase "too unreservedly" implies excess, as does labeling Aylmer's love of his wife a "second passion." The narrator also says that people view the birthmark differently, depending on their own temperament. Before their marriage Aylmer did not think much of the birthmark, but after the marriage he wished it away and tells Georgiana that the birthmark "shocks" him. But Georgiana calls the birthmark a "charm." Aylmer's assistant, Aminadab, says, "If she were my wife, I'd never part with that birth-mark."

Although the paragraph begins solidly and the second sentence provides the central theme, the author soon goes on a tangent. If the purpose of the paragraph is to demonstrate that Aylmer is obsessed with Georgiana's birthmark, the sentences about Georgiana and Aminadab's attitudes toward the birthmark are tangential here. They may find a place later in the paper, but they should be deleted from this paragraph.

Coherent Paragraphs

In addition to shaping unified paragraphs, you must also craft coherent paragraphs, paragraphs that develop their points logically with sentences that flow smoothly into one another. Coherence depends on the order of your sentences, but it is not strictly the order of the sentences that is important to paragraph coherence. You also need to craft your prose to help the reader see the relationship among the sentences.

Consider the following paragraph about Aylmer's obsession with science. Notice how the writer uses the same ideas as the paragraph above yet fails to help the reader see the relationships among the points.

> The story's opening paragraph introduces the conflict that will drive the story's plot, Aylmer's love of science versus his love for his wife. It asks whether Aylmer's "love for his young wife might prove the stronger of the two." It does not take long for the reader to see that Aylmer's love for science has become an obsession. The narrator says that Aylmer "had devoted himself . . . too unreservedly to scientific studies, ever to be weaned from them by a second passion." The narrator also says that people view the birthmark differently, depending on their own temperament. Aylmer tells Georgiana that the birthmark "shocks" him. Before their marriage Aylmer did not think much of the birthmark, but after the marriage he wished it away. The narrator says, "Aylmer's somber imagination was not long in rendering the birth-mark a frightful object, causing him more trouble and horror than ever Georgiana's beauty, whether of soul or sense, had given him delight."

This paragraph demonstrates that unity alone does not guarantee paragraph effectiveness. The argument is hard to follow because the author fails both to show connections between the sentences and to indicate how they work to support the overall point.

A number of techniques are available to aid paragraph coherence. Careful use of transitional words and phrases is essential. You can use transitional flags to introduce an example or an illustration (*for example, for instance*), to amplify a point or add another phase of the same idea (*additionally, furthermore, next, similarly, finally, then*), to indicate a conclusion or result (*therefore, as a result, thus, in other words*), to signal a contrast or a qualification (*on the other hand, nevertheless, despite this, on the contrary, still, however, conversely*), to signal a comparison (*likewise, in comparison, similarly*), and to indicate a movement in time (*afterward, earlier, eventually, finally, later, subsequently, until*).

In addition to transitional flags, careful use of pronouns aids coherence and flow. If you were writing about *The Wizard of Oz*, you would not want to keep repeating the phrase *the witch* or the name *Dorothy*. Careful substitution of the pronoun *she* in these instances can aid coherence. A word of warning, though: When you substitute pronouns for proper names, always be sure that your pronoun reference is clear. In a paragraph that discusses both Dorothy and the witch, substituting *she* could lead to confusion. Make sure that it is clear to whom the pronoun refers. Generally, the pronoun refers to the last proper noun you have used.

While repeating the same name over and over again can lead to awkward, boring prose, it is possible to use repetition to help your paragraph's coherence. Careful repetition of important words or phrases can lend coherence to your paragraph by reminding readers of your key points. Admittedly, it takes some practice to use this technique effectively. You may find that reading your prose aloud can help you develop an ear for effective use of repetition.

To see how helpful transitional aids are, compare the paragraph below to the preceding paragraph about Aylmer's relationship with science. Notice how the author works with the same ideas and quotations but shapes them into a much more coherent paragraph whose point is clearer and easier to follow.

```
Aylmer's most significant failure, the death of Geor-
giana, shows the reader his most significant flaws.
His love of science becomes an obsession. The story's
opening paragraph introduces the conflict that will
drive the story's plot, Aylmer's love of science versus
his love for his wife, and it asks whether his "love
for his young wife might prove the stronger of the
two." It does not take long for the reader to see that
Aylmer's love for science has become an obsession. Even
the narrator's word choice in the first paragraph hints
that Aylmer's love of science goes a bit too far: "He
had devoted himself . . . too unreservedly to scien-
tific studies, ever to be weaned from them by a second
```

passion." The phrase "too unreservedly" implies excess, as does labeling Aylmer's love for his wife a "second passion." Similarly, it is helpful to chart Aylmer's changing attitude toward the birthmark. Although he did not think of the birthmark much before their marriage, afterward Aylmer wishes the mark away and tells Georgiana that it "shocks" him. Soon this shock grows into an obsession. The birthmark is all that Aylmer can think of. It overshadows his love for Georgiana, and it consumes his thoughts.

Similarly, the following paragraph from a paper on the use of color in "Young Goodman Brown" demonstrates both unity and coherence. In it, the author argues that Hawthorne saw humanity as neither purely good nor evil but a mixture of both.

In "Young Goodman Brown" Hawthorne argues that humanity is neither wholly good nor wholly evil. The devil tells Brown, "Now are ye undeceived! Evil is the nature of mankind," but there is enough evidence in the story to show that this statement does not represent the author's belief. Brown's wife, Faith, is one example. As a character, Faith is described in positive terms. She is Brown's "dear Faith," and Brown says, "after this one night, I'll cling to her skirts and follow her to Heaven." Clearly, Hawthorne also means her to be an allegorical character. Brown loses his faith on his trip into the forest to meet the devil. Had Goodman Brown not left his faith, Hawthorne seems to indicate that he might have "followed her to Heaven." Additionally, when Brown returns to the village, the narrator's descriptions of the townspeople emphasize the contrast between the Browns' opinions and the narrator's. The narrator tells of Brown's meeting with "the good old minister" who "bestowed a blessing, as he passed, on Goodman Brown." Brown, however, "shrank from the venerable saint, as if to avoid an anathema." Similarly, the

narrator calls Goody Cloyse an "excellent old Christian." But as she "stood in the early sunshine . . .
catechizing a little girl," Brown "snatched away the
child, as from the grasp of the fiend himself."

Introductions

Introductions present particular challenges for writers. Generally, your
introduction should do two things: capture your reader's attention and
explain the main point of your essay. In other words, while your introduction should contain your thesis, it needs to do a bit more work than
that. You are likely to find that starting that first paragraph is one of
the most difficult parts of the paper. It is hard to face that blank page or
screen, and as a result, many beginning writers, in desperation to start
somewhere, start with overly broad, general statements. While it is often
a good strategy to start with more general subject matter and narrow
your focus, do not begin with broad sweeping statements such as, Color
is important to everyone or Throughout the history of
literature, many authors have used color to express
their points. Such sentences are nothing but empty filler. They begin
to fill the blank page, but they do nothing to advance your argument.
Instead, you might try to gain your readers' interest. Some writers like
to begin with a pertinent quotation or with a relevant question. Or you
might begin with an introduction of the topic you will discuss. If you are
writing about Hawthorne's use of color in "Young Goodman Brown," for
instance, you might begin by talking about color symbolism in Western
culture. Another common trap to avoid is depending on your title to
introduce the author and the text you are writing about. Always include
the work's author and title in your opening paragraph.

Compare the effectiveness of the following introductions.

1) Throughout history, colors have had significance.
   For example, think about red, white, and black.
   In this story, Hawthorne uses color to reflect
   his belief that humans are a mixture of evil and
   purity.
2) In many cultures, particular colors carry specific
   meanings. Western culture is no exception. Colors

convey meaning to us even though we are often not consciously aware of these meanings. White signals purity. Brides and babies wear white. Red signals danger or sexuality. Think about bullfighters' capes or Little Red Riding Hood's cloak. Often writers incorporate these color codes into their works to reinforce their meanings. In "Young Goodman Brown," Nathaniel Hawthorne uses these color codes to reflect his belief that humans are neither evil nor pure but a mixture of both.

The first introduction begins with a boring, overly broad sentence; cites unclear, undeveloped examples; and then moves abruptly to the thesis. Notice, too, how a reader deprived of the paper's title does not know the title of the story that the paper will analyze. The second introduction works with the same material and thesis but provides more detail and is consequently much more interesting. It begins by discussing cultural uses of color, gives specific examples, and then speaks briefly about the use of color symbolism in literature. The paragraph ends with the thesis, which includes both the author and the title of the work to be discussed.

The paragraph below provides another example of an opening strategy. It begins by introducing the author and the text it will analyze, and then it moves on by briefly introducing relevant details of the story in order to set up its thesis.

In "The Birth-mark," Nathaniel Hawthorne first introduces his main character as "a man of science." In the second paragraph we learn the name of the man of science: Aylmer. Scholars have noted that Aylmer's name means "noble," and it does seem that there is much that is noble about him. At first, the narrator seems to admire Aylmer's scientific abilities. But the story pits Aylmer's love of science against his love for his wife, Georgiana. In the second paragraph the narrator tells us that this struggle has "a deeply impressive moral." This moral seems to be revealed in Aylmer's determination to remove a birthmark from Georgiana's face. Sadly,

this experiment ends in Georgiana's death. This outcome
seems to show that although Aylmer's name means "noble,"
he is not an entirely noble character. His science and
his learning are admirable, but his obsession with his
scientific experiments is a flaw in his character.

Conclusions

Conclusions present another series of challenges for writers. No doubt
you have heard the old adage about writing papers: "Tell us what you
are going to say, say it, and then tell us what you've said." While this
formula does not necessarily result in bad papers, it does not necessarily
result in good ones either. It will almost certainly result in boring papers
(especially boring conclusions). If you have done a good job establishing your points in the body of the paper, the reader already knows and
understands your argument. There is no need to merely reiterate. Do not
just summarize your main points in your conclusion. Such a boring and
mechanical conclusion does nothing to advance your argument or interest your reader. Consider the following conclusion to the paper about
color in "Young Goodman Brown."

In conclusion, Hawthorne uses the colors brown, pink,
black, and red to tell his reader about humanity. Faith's
ribbons are pink, a mixture of red and white. They
indicate that even at our best, humanity is not wholly
good. Young Goodman Brown's last name, Brown, indicates
the same about him.

Besides starting with a mechanical and obvious transitional device, this
conclusion does little more than summarize the main points of the outline (and it does not even touch on all of them). It is incomplete and
uninteresting.

Instead, your conclusion should add something to your paper. A good
tactic is to build upon the points you have been arguing. Asking "why?"
often helps you draw further conclusions. For example, in the paper discussed above, you might speculate or explain why color symbolism is
effective in "Young Goodman Brown." Since scholars often discuss this
story as an allegory, you could discuss the allegorical use of color. Another

method of successfully concluding a paper is to speculate on other directions in which to take your topic by tying it into larger issues. You might
do this by envisioning your paper as just one section of a larger paper.
Having established your points in this paper, how would you build upon
this argument? Where would you go next? In the following conclusion to
the paper on "Young Goodman Brown," the author reiterates some of the
main points of the paper but does so in order to amplify the discussion of
the story's theological message.

> In the end, neither Faith nor Young Goodman Brown is
> completely pure. Hawthorne's use of pink and brown
> emphasizes this. But Hawthorne's point is larger.
> Brown's real problem is not that he contains both good
> and evil, faith and doubt, but that he has let doubt
> prevail. Once he returns to the village he believes
> himself faithful, while he doubts every other member
> of his community. The narrator describes Faith as joy-
> ful, the minister as "venerable," and Goody Cloyse as
> an "excellent old Christian," yet Brown "shrank" from
> them. In losing faith in others, Brown denies himself
> one good and necessary thing: human community. Finally,
> as if to emphasize that Brown's lost faith has taught
> him incorrectly, the narrator refers to Brown as "a
> stern, a sad, a darkly meditative, a distrustful, if not
> a desperate man."

Similarly, in the following conclusion to the paper on Aylmer's flawed
character, the author draws a conclusion about what can be learned from
Aylmer's obsession with science. Notice, too, how the author moved
some material from its original place in the outline. Instead of discussing
the language of fire and Aylmer's laboratory in the preceding paragraph,
the writer moves that material to the conclusion, using it as transitional
material.

> To emphasize that Aylmer's relationship with science
> is fanatical, Hawthorne uses fire, smoke, and soot to

characterize Aylmer's laboratory. When Georgiana first enters the laboratory, the scene reminds the reader of hell: "The first thing that struck her eye was the furnace, that hot and feverish worker, with the intense glow of its fire." Aylmer is "pale as death, anxious, and absorbed." In spite of this imagery, Georgiana's final words to her husband are positive, as if to emphasize what is good about him: "You have aimed loftily!—you have done nobly! Do not repent, that, with so high and pure a feeling, you have rejected the best that earth could offer." Georgiana's words seem to convey the moral of the story, and the narrator echoes them at the end of the story. He says, "Yet, had Aylmer reached a profounder wisdom, he need not thus have flung away the happiness, which would have woven his mortal life of the self-same texture with the celestial." "Profounder wisdom" would have told Aylmer that perfection does not exist on earth. Just as Georgiana loved him for his imperfections, Aylmer should have been content with Georgiana and her birthmark. Instead, Aylmer's obsession with science and obtaining perfection on earth led him to destroy "the best that earth could offer."

Citations and Formatting

Using Primary Sources

As the examples included in this chapter indicate, strong papers on literary texts incorporate quotations from the text in order to support their points. It is not enough for you to assert your interpretation without providing support or evidence from the text. Without well-chosen quotations to support your argument, you are, in effect, saying to the reader, "Take my word for it." It is important to use quotations thoughtfully and selectively. Remember that the paper presents *your* argument, so choose quotations that support *your* assertions. Do not let the author's voice overwhelm your own. With that caution in mind, there are some guidelines you should follow to ensure that you use quotations clearly and effectively.

Integrate Quotations:

Quotations should always be integrated into your own prose. Do not just drop them into your paper without introduction or comment. Otherwise, it is unlikely that your reader will see their function. You can integrate textual support easily and clearly with identifying tags, short phrases that identify the speaker. For example:

```
The narrator calls Young Goodman Brown "a stern, a sad,
a darkly meditative, a distrustful, if not a desperate
man."
```

While this tag appears before the quotation, you can also use tags after or in the middle of the quoted text, as the following examples demonstrate:

```
"Evil is the nature of mankind," claims the devil.
```

```
"I helped your grandfather, the constable, when he
lashed the Quaker woman so smartly through the streets
of Salem," the devil tells Brown. "And it was I that
brought your father a pitch-pine knot, kindled at my
own hearth, to set fire to an Indian village, in King
Philip's war."
```

You can also use a colon to formally introduce a quotation:

```
Aylmer's conceit is clear: "Doubt not my power."
```

When you quote brief sections of poems (three lines or fewer), use slash marks to indicate the line breaks in the poem:

```
As the poem ends, Dickinson speaks of the power of the
imagination: "The revery alone will do, / If bees are
few."
```

Longer quotations (more than four lines of prose or three lines of poetry) should be set off from the rest of your paper in a block quotation. Double-space before you begin the passage, indent it 10 spaces from your

left-hand margin, and double-space the passage itself. Because the inden-
tation signals the inclusion of a quotation, do not use quotation marks
around the cited passage. Use a colon to introduce the passage:

```
Aylmer soon becomes obsessed with the birthmark:

    At all the seasons which should have been their hap-
    piest, he invariably, and without intending it—nay,
    in spite of a purpose to the contrary—reverted to
    this one disastrous topic. Trifling as it at first
    appeared, it so connected itself with innumerable
    trains of thought, and modes of feeling, that it
    became the central point of all.

By now, the reader should not have any doubts about
Aylmer's obsession.
```

```
The  whole  of  Dickinson's  poem  speaks  of  the
imagination:

    To make a prairie it takes a clover and one bee,
    One clover, and a bee,
    And revery.
    The revery alone will do,
    If bees are few.

Clearly, she argues for the creative power of the
mind.
```

It is also important to interpret quotations after you introduce them
and explain how they help advance your point. You cannot assume that
your reader will interpret the quotations the same way that you do.

Quote Accurately:

Always quote accurately. Anything within quotations marks must be the
author's exact words. There are, however, some rules to follow if you need
to modify the quotation to fit into your prose.

1. Use brackets to indicate any material that might have been added to the author's exact wording. For example, if you need to add any words to the quotation or alter it grammatically to allow it to fit into your prose, indicate your changes in brackets:

    ```
    As a result of his encounter in the woods,
    Brown becomes "more conscious of the secret
    guilt of others, both in deed and thought, than
    [he] could now be of [his] own."
    ```

2. Conversely, if you choose to omit any words from the quotation, use ellipses (three spaced periods) to indicate missing words or phrases:

    ```
    Soon, Aylmer becomes obsessed with the birth-
    mark: "Trifling as it at first appeared . . .
    it became the central point of all."
    ```

3. If you delete a sentence or more, use the ellipses after a period:

    ```
    The narrator indicates that "Jollity and gloom
    were contending for an empire. . . . But May,
    or her mirthful spirit, dwelt all the year round
    at Merry Mount."
    ```

4. If you omit a line or more of poetry, or more than one paragraph of prose, use a single line of spaced periods to indicate the omission:

    ```
    To make a prairie it takes a clover and one bee,
    . . . . . . . . . . . . . . . . . .
    And revery.
    The revery alone will do,
    If bees are few.
    ```

Punctuate Properly:

Punctuation of quotations often causes more trouble than it should. Once again, you just need to keep these simple rules in mind.

1. Periods and commas should be placed inside quotation marks, even if they are not part of the original quotation:

   ```
   Aylmer's   conceit   is   clear:   "Doubt   not   my
   power."
   ```

   The only exception to this rule is when the quotation is followed by a parenthetical reference. In this case, the period or comma goes after the citation (more on these later in this chapter):

   ```
   Aylmer's conceit is clear: "Doubt not my power"
   (264).
   ```

2. Other marks of punctuation—colons, semicolons, question marks, and exclamation points—go outside the quotation marks unless they are part of the original quotation:

   ```
   Why does the narrator say that Brown "was him-
   self the chief horror of the scene"?
   ```

   ```
     Hawthorne  asks,  "Had  Goodman  Brown  fallen
   asleep  in  the  forest,  and  only  dreamed  a  wild
   dream of a witch-meeting?"
   ```

Documenting Primary Sources

Unless you are instructed otherwise, you should provide sufficient information for your reader to locate material you quote. Generally, literature papers follow the rules set forth by the Modern Language Association (MLA). These can be found in the *MLA Handbook for Writers of Research Papers* (sixth edition). You should be able to find this book in the reference section of your library. Additionally, its rules for citing both primary and secondary sources are widely available from reputable online sources. One of these is the Online Writing Lab (OWL) at Purdue University. OWL's guide to MLA style is available at http://owl.english.purdue. edu/owl/resource/557/01/. The Modern Language Association also offers answers to frequently asked questions about MLA style on this helpful Web page: http://www.mla.org/style_faq. Generally, when you are citing from literary works in papers, you should keep a few guidelines in mind.

Parenthetical Citations:

MLA asks for parenthetical references in your text after quotations. When you are working with prose (short stories, novels, or essays) include page numbers in the parentheses:

> Aylmer's conceit is clear: "Doubt not my power" (264).

When you are quoting poetry, include line numbers:

> Dickinson's speaker tells of the arrival of a fly: "There interposed a Fly— / With Blue—uncertain stumbling Buzz— / Between the light—and Me—" (12–14).

Works Cited Page:

These parenthetical citations are linked to a separate works cited page at the end of the paper. The works cited page lists works alphabetically by the authors' last name. An entry for the above reference to Hawthorne's "Birth-Mark" would read:

> Hawthorne, Nathaniel. "The Birth-mark." *Selected Tales and Sketches*. New York: Penguin, 1987. 259–78.

The *MLA Handbook* includes a full listing of sample entries, as do many of the online explanations of MLA style.

Documenting Secondary Sources

To ensure that your paper is built entirely upon your own ideas and analysis, instructors often ask that you write interpretative papers without any outside research. If, on the other hand, your paper requires research, you must document any secondary sources you use. You need to document direct quotations, summaries, or paraphrases of others' ideas and factual information that is not common knowledge. Follow the guidelines above for quoting primary sources when you use direct quotations from secondary sources. Keep in mind that MLA style also includes specific guidelines for citing electronic sources. OWL's Web site provides a good summary: http://owl.english.purdue.edu/owl/resource/557/09/.

Parenthetical Citations:

As with the documentation of primary sources described above, MLA guidelines require in-text parenthetical references to your secondary sources. Unlike the research papers you might write for a history class, literary research papers following MLA style do not use footnotes as a means of documenting sources. Instead, after a quotation, you should cite the author's last name and the page number:

> "Hester's revolutionary program is just the kind of misty-eyed vision that Hawthorne resentfully censures" (Wineapple 215).

If you include the name of the author in your prose, then you would include only the page number in your citation. For example:

> According to Brenda Wineapple, "Hester's revolutionary program is just the kind of misty-eyed vision that Hawthorne resentfully censures" (215).

If you are including more than one work by the same author, the parenthetical citation should include a shortened yet identifiable version of the title in order to indicate which of the author's works you cite. For example:

> According to Sacvan Bercovitch, "Hester errs, then, not in her sexual transgression but in her 'stern development' as an individualist of increasingly revolutionary commitment" (*Office* 6).

Similarly, and just as important, if you summarize or paraphrase the particular ideas of your source, you must provide documentation:

> In chapter 13 of *The Scarlet Letter,* Hawthorne criticizes Hester for her dreams of rebellion. Like the Puritans, he punishes her when he indicates that she has lost her feminine qualities (Wineapple 215).

Works Cited Page:

Like the primary sources discussed above, the parenthetical references to secondary sources are keyed to a separate works cited page at the end of your paper. Here is an example of a works cited page that uses the examples cited above. Note that when two or more works by the same author are listed, you should use three hyphens followed by a period in the subsequent entries. You can find a complete list of sample entries in the *MLA Handbook* or from a reputable online summary of MLA style.

WORKS CITED

Bercovitch, Sacvan. *The Office of the Scarlet Letter: Re-visions of Culture and Society.* Baltimore: Johns Hopkins UP, 1993.

———. *The Puritan Origins of the American Self.* New Haven: Yale UP, 1991.

Wineapple, Brenda. *Hawthorne: A Life.* New York: Knopf, 2003.

Plagiarism

Failure to document carefully and thoroughly can leave you open to charges of stealing the ideas of others, which is known as plagiarism, and this is a very serious matter. Remember that it is important to use quotation marks when you use language from your source, even if you use just one or two words. For example, if you wrote, Hester's dream of the future is a misty-eyed vision, you would be guilty of plagiarism, since you used Wineapple's distinct language without acknowledging her as the source. Instead, you should write: Hester's dream of the future is a "misty-eyed vision" (Wineapple 215). In this case, you have properly credited Wineapple.

Similarly, neither summarizing the ideas of an author nor changing or omitting just a few words means that you can omit a citation. Brenda Wineapple's biography of Nathaniel Hawthorne contains the following passage about the story "Rappaccini's Daughter":

> Like most of Hawthorne's fiction, "Rappaccini's Daughter" is a biographical palimpsest. Dr. Rappaccini is Sophia's father and Waldo Emerson. (Concord busybodies said Lidian Emerson was

poisoning herself with medicine extracted from several plants.) Rappaccini is also Fuller's father, whose stiff-backed education of Margaret was as destructive, if as well intentioned; he's Uncle Robert, another horticulturist of decided purpose; and he's Hawthorne, the father-gardener, who fusses over his wife's diet and her health.

Below are two examples of plagiarized passages:

Dr. Rappaccini of "Rappaccini's Daughter" represents Sophia Hawthorne's father, Emerson, Margaret Fuller's father, and Hawthorne himself, all rolled into one character.

Dr. Rappaccini is Sophia Hawthorne's father and Waldo Emerson. Rappaccini is also Margaret Fuller's father, whose education of Margaret was as destructive, if as well intentioned. He is also Hawthorne, the father-gardener, who fusses about his wife's diet and her health (Wineapple 181).

While the first passage does not use Wineapple's exact language, it does list the same people she proposes as models for Dr. Rappaccini without citing her work. Since this list is her distinct idea, this constitutes plagiarism. The second passage has shortened her passage, added some first names, changed some wording, and included a citation, but some of the phrasing is Wineapple's. The first passage could be fixed with a parenthetical citation. Because some of the wording in the second is the same as Wineapple's, though, it would require the use of quotation marks, in addition to a parenthetical citation. The passage below represents an honestly and adequately documented use of the original passage:

According to Brenda Wineapple, Dr. Rappaccini represents Sophia Hawthorne's father, Emerson, and Margaret Fuller's father, whose education of Margaret "was as destructive, if as well intentioned." Rappaccini is also

```
"Hawthorne, the father-gardener, who fusses over his
wife's diet and her health" (181).
```

This passage acknowledges that the list of people is derived from Wine-apple while appropriately using quotations to indicate her precise language.

While it is not necessary to document well-known facts, often referred to as "common knowledge," any ideas or language that you take from someone else must be properly documented. Common knowledge generally includes the birth and death dates of authors or other well-documented facts of their lives. An often-cited guideline is that if you can find the information in three sources, it is common knowledge. Despite this guideline, it is, admittedly, often difficult to know if the facts you uncover are common knowledge or not. When in doubt, document your source.

Sample Essay

```
Jodee Brown
Ms. Sterling
English 160
May 23, 2006


SCIENTIFIC OBSESSION IN HAWTHORNE'S "THE BIRTH-MARK"
In "The Birth-mark," Nathaniel Hawthorne first intro-
duces his main character as "a man of science" (259).
In the second paragraph, we learn the name of the man
of science: Aylmer. Scholars have noted that Aylmer's
name means "noble," and it does seem that there is much
that is noble about him (Reid 350). At first, the nar-
rator seems to admire Aylmer's scientific abilities.
But the story pits Aylmer's love of science against his
love for his wife, Georgiana. In the second paragraph,
the narrator tells us that this struggle has "a deeply
impressive moral" (260). This moral seems to be revealed
in Aylmer's determination to remove a birthmark from
Georgiana's face. Sadly, this experiment ends in Geor-
```

giana's death. This outcome seems to show that although Aylmer's name means "noble," he is not an entirely noble character. His science and his learning are admirable, but his obsession with his scientific experiments is a flaw in his character.

Since Aylmer's experiment ends in Georgiana's death, readers might not think of him as noble at all, but the story provides evidence suggesting that aspects of Aylmer's character are worthy of respect. Late in the story, the narrator calls Aylmer a "man of genius" (272). Clearly, there is something to admire in Aylmer's intelligence, and Georgiana sees this. Georgiana represents goodness in the story, and she falls in love with Aylmer. This alone must say something about his character. Later, when she reads his journal and learns of his failed experiments, Georgiana tells him, "It has made me worship you more than ever" (272). At the end of the story, as she is dying, Georgiana again professes her love for her husband and reinforces the idea that in some ways Aylmer is noble. She tells him, "You have aimed loftily!—you have done nobly! Do not repent that with so high and pure a feeling, you have rejected the best that earth could offer" (277). Even in the face of Aylmer's most awful failure, the word "nobly" is used to describe him. In spite of his obvious shortcomings, there is something noble about Aylmer.

This most significant failure shows the reader Aylmer's most significant flaws. His love of science becomes an obsession. The story's opening paragraph introduces the conflict that will drive the story's plot, Aylmer's love of science versus his love for his wife, and it asks whether his "love for his young wife might prove the stronger of the two" (259). It does not take long for the reader to see that Aylmer's love for science has become an obsession. Even the narrator's word choice in the first paragraph hints that Aylmer's love of science goes a bit too far: "He had devoted himself . . . too unreservedly to scientific studies, ever to be weaned from them by a second passion" (259). The phrase "too unreservedly" implies excess, as does labeling Aylmer's love for his wife a "second passion."

Similarly, it is helpful to chart Aylmer's changing attitude toward the birthmark. Although he did not think of the birthmark much before their marriage, afterward Aylmer wishes the mark away and tells Georgiana that it "shocks" him (260). Soon this shock grows into an obsession. The birthmark is all that Aylmer can think of. As Judith Fetterley says, "Of negligible importance to him before the marriage, the birthmark now assumes the proportions of an obsession" (23). It overshadows his love for Georgiana, and it consumes his thoughts:

> Aylmer's somber imagination was not long in rendering the birth-mark a frightful object, causing him more trouble and horror than ever Georgiana's beauty, whether of soul or sense, had given him delight.
>
> At all the seasons which should have been their happiest, he invariably, and without intending it—nay, in spite of a purpose to the contrary—reverted to this one disastrous topic. Trifling as it at first appeared, it so connected itself with innumerable trains of thought, and modes of feeling, that it became the central point of all. (262)

Finally, Aylmer even dreams about removing Georgiana's birthmark, and the narrator says, "Until now, he had not been aware of the tyrannizing influence acquired by one idea over his mind and the lengths which he might find in his heart to go, for the sake of giving himself peace" (263). By now, the reader should not have any doubts about Aylmer's obsession.

Closer examination of Aylmer's obsession with his science clearly displays his flawed character to the reader. The motivation behind his scientific experiments and the effects of his science clearly demonstrate his shortcomings. If we examine his motivations, we see how self-centered Aylmer really is. His conceit is clear when he assures Georgiana that he will be able to remove the birthmark: "Doubt not my power . . . what will be my triumph, when I shall have corrected what Nature left imperfect, in her fairest work! Even Pygmalion, when his sculptured woman assumed life, felt not greater ecstasy than mine will be" (264). He echoes this when he later says to Georgiana, "I even rejoice in this single imperfection, since it will be such rapture to remove it" (267). Both these comments show that Aylmer has forgotten about Georgiana and is only concerned with his own success and power. Fetterley even argues that the story's "subject is finally power" (31).

Not surprisingly, Aylmer's obsession with removing the birthmark in order to demonstrate his own power ends up affecting his marriage, even before he kills his wife. Georgiana's "self-image derives from internalizing the attitudes toward her of the man or men around her" (Fetterley 32). Although Georgiana at first thinks of the mark as a "charm" (260), she sees that Aylmer is obsessed with the mark. Soon she "learned to shudder at his gaze" (262) because he saw only the birthmark, not her. As a result, she urges him on in his experimentation. Eventually, Aylmer becomes so consumed with his work that he even accuses his wife of mistrusting him. When she enters his laboratory, he cries, "Have you no trust in your husband? . . . Would you throw the blight of that fatal birth-mark over my labors?" (273). But Aylmer's obsession with the birthmark, not the mark itself, is fatal. His refusal to see Georgiana instead of her birthmark ends in her death. Brenda Wineapple even claims that Aylmer is so self-centered that he kills Georgiana "so that in some way he can remain alone, untrammeled, asexual, and free from responsibility" (175). Georgiana's death is the clearest sign that Aylmer's love of science has gone too far.

To emphasize that Aylmer's relationship with science is fanatical, Hawthorne uses fire, smoke, and soot to characterize Aylmer's laboratory. When Georgiana first enters the laboratory, the scene reminds the reader of hell: "The first thing that struck her eye was the furnace, that hot and feverish worker, with the intense glow of its fire" (272). Aylmer is "pale as death, anxious, and absorbed" (273). In spite of this imagery, though, Georgiana's final words to her husband are positive, emphasizing what is good about him: "You have aimed loftily!—you have done nobly! Do not repent, that, with so high and pure a feeling, you have rejected the best that earth could offer" (277). Georgiana's words seem to convey the moral of the story, and the narrator echoes them at the end of the story. He says, "Yet, had Aylmer reached a profounder wisdom, he need not thus have flung away the happiness, which would have woven his mortal life of the self-same texture with the celestial" (278). "Profounder wisdom" would have told Aylmer that perfection does not exist on earth. Just as Georgiana loved him for his imperfections, Aylmer should have been content with Georgiana and her birthmark. Instead, Aylmer's obsession with science and obtaining perfection on earth led him to destroy "the best that earth could offer."

WORKS CITED

Fetterley, Judith. *The Resisting Reader: A Feminist Approach to American Fiction.* Bloomington: Indiana UP, 1978.

Hawthorne, Nathaniel. "The Birth-mark." *Selected Tales and Sketches.* New York: Penguin, 1987. 259–78.

Reid, Alfred. "Hawthorne's Humanism: 'The Birthmark' and Sir Kenelm Digby." *American Literature* 38.3 (1966): 337–51.

Wineapple, Brenda. *Hawthorne: A Life.* New York: Knopf: 2003.

HOW TO WRITE ABOUT NATHANIEL HAWTHORNE

WRITING ABOUT NATHANIEL HAWTHORNE: AN OVERVIEW

BECAUSE HAWTHORNE'S best-known works, *The Scarlet Letter* and "Young Goodman Brown," are set in Puritan New England and grapple with explicitly Puritan themes, students are often hard pressed to see his work as relevant and often find him puritanical himself. Even a broad familiarity with Hawthorne's biography, though, clearly shows how mistaken this kind of evaluation is. Born in Salem, Massachusetts, in 1804, Hawthorne was, indeed, descended from Puritan stock. His ancestors William and John Hathorne were both men of rank in Massachusetts Bay Colony. For Nathaniel Hawthorne, it seems that the most memorable aspect of his powerful forefathers was their sternness and their penchant for persecution. William was merciless in his legal prosecution of the Quakers, and John sat in judgment of several of the accused witches during Salem's witch trials of 1692. In an apparent act of shame or rebellion, Nathaniel changed the spelling of his last name from Hathorne to Hawthorne. Similarly, the semiautobiographical introduction to *The Scarlet Letter*, "The Custom-House," chronicles Hawthorne's problematic relationship with his forefathers and with Salem's Puritan legacy. By the end of the introduction, Hawthorne decides to disassociate himself from Salem: "Henceforth, it ceases to be a reality of my life. I am a citizen of somewhere else." In short, he seems to have reacted against his Puritan heritage more than he embraced it. The challenge for modern students of Hawthorne is to get beyond what we *think* we know about Hawthorne and recognize the nuances of his fiction and see his relevance.

Rather than associate Hawthorne and his values with his Puritan characters, then, modern readers might do better to link him with characters like Pearl and Hester Prynne from *The Scarlet Letter,* both of whom challenge the values and beliefs of the "dismal severity of the Puritanic code of law" (*The Scarlet Letter,* chapter 2). Certainly, Hawthorne shared more with his outcasts and progressive characters than he did with the Puritan leaders and statesmen that populate his fiction. For a brief time in 1841, Hawthorne even took up residence at Brook Farm, a utopian socialist community, hoping to find an arrangement that would allow him to write and to support his fiancée, Sophia Peabody. Hawthorne's fiction is filled with characters who are at odds with society and who challenge the status quo. While Hester must live on the fringes of her society, she envisions a new social order and believes that "at some brighter period, when the world should have grown ripe for it, in Heaven's own time, a new truth would be revealed, in order to establish the whole relations between man and woman on a surer ground of mutual happiness" (*The Scarlet Letter,* chapter 24). Similarly, *The Blithedale Romance,* set in Hawthorne's own time, focuses on a utopian community much like Brook Farm that aims at "a new arrangement of the world" (*The Blithedale Romance,* chapter 2). The residents at Blithedale include Zenobia, the ardent feminist, and Hollingsworth, whose life is centered upon a plan for the reform of prisoners. Even young Goodman Brown, who dies "a stern, a sad, a darkly meditative, a distrustful, if not a desperate man," defies the rules of Puritan society. After all, he chooses to go into the woods to meet the devil, ignoring the pleas of Faith, his wife.

If Hester Prynne embodies some of Hawthorne's discomfort with social norms, she is also, like her creator, an artist. Hester's art, her needlework, has the ability to transform and transfigure. When we first see Hester and her scarlet letter, the narrator tells us that the letter, "so fantastically embroidered and illuminated" by Hester's needlework, "transfigured the wearer,—so that both men and women, who had been familiarly acquainted with Hester Prynne, were now impressed as if they beheld her for the first time" (*The Scarlet Letter*, chapter 2). Pearl shares both her mother's rebelliousness and her creative ability. Pearl's imaginative play, which seems to transform the world around her, represents her best challenge to Puritan attitudes and seems to share a great deal with her creator's imaginative writing. In chapter 6, Hawthorne writes:

> The spell of life went forth from her ever creative spirit, and communicated itself to a thousand objects, as a torch kindles a flame wherever it may be applied. The unlikeliest materials, a stick, a bunch of rags, a flower, were the puppets of Pearl's witchcraft, and, without undergoing any outward change, became spiritually adapted to whatever drama occupied the stage of her inner world. Her one baby-voice served a multitude of imaginary personages, old and young, to talk withal. The pine-trees, aged, black, and solemn, and flinging groans and other melancholy utterances on the breeze, needed little transformation to figure as Puritan elders; the ugliest weeds of the garden were their children, whom Pearl smote down and uprooted, most unmercifully. It was wonderful, the vast variety of forms into which she threw her intellect. . . .

Hawthorne imagines that his Puritan ancestors would see his writing as little more than child's play: "'What is he?' murmurs one gray shadow of my forefathers to the other. 'A writer of story-books! What kind of a business in life, what mode of glorifying God, or being serviceable to mankind in his day and generation, may that be? Why, the degenerate fellow might as well have been a fiddler!'" ("The Custom-House"). By the end of *The Scarlet Letter*, Pearl leaves Massachusetts Bay Colony and, like Hawthorne, becomes "a citizen of somewhere else." Perhaps, then, you might think of Hawthorne and Pearl as creators whose play constructs alternate worlds, virtual realities not completely unlike those we create electronically today.

Hawthorne creates these alternate worlds through literary techniques like allegory and romance. Consider how clearly his descriptions of the genre of romance evoke the creation of a virtual reality, built of the elements of reality but existing as a world apart. In his preface to *The House of the Seven Gables*, he describes the work of the romance writer as "laying out a street that infringes upon nobody's private rights, and appropriating a lot of land which has no visible owner, and building a house, of materials long in use for constructing castles in the air." In "The Custom-House," he calls the world of romance a "neutral territory, somewhere between the real world and fairy-land, where the Actual and the Imaginary may meet, and each imbue itself with the nature of the other." Hawthorne's "neutral territor[ies]" include a house haunted by wizards and ancestral ghosts; a garden populated by poisonous man-made plants and a poisonous but beautiful woman; a town where a mechanical butterfly is endowed with life; and a forest where walking sticks seem to turn into serpents. Hawthorne builds these "neutral territor[ies]" from the elements of everyday life, and he invites us to become temporary residents of the worlds he creates. These worlds—and Hawthorne's invitation to the reader to inhabit them—provide us with ways to think about and to write about Hawthorne.

You might, for example, ask how and why Hawthorne invites the reader into these realms. And you might also enquire why Hawthorne builds these worlds in the first place. Reading and writing about Hawthorne requires careful attention to his narrative voice, and this voice provides us with answers to some of these questions. Scholars frequently speak of Hawthorne's ambiguity, the tendency for his works to raise more questions than they answer. Quite famously, at the end of "Young Goodman Brown," the narrator asks a question that many readers are no doubt already harboring: "Had Goodman Brown fallen asleep in the forest, and only dreamed a wild dream of a witch-meeting?" His next sentence resolutely refuses to answer the question: "Be it so, if you will." The narrator has thereby invited us into the world of "Young Goodman Brown." We must make sense of the nightmarish world of the nighttime forest, though the narrator has provided us little insight beyond what Brown himself sees and hears (or what he dreams). Hawthorne uses similar narrative techniques throughout his fiction. In the beginning of "Wakefield," for instance, he says, "Whenever any subject so forcibly affects the mind, time is well spent in thinking of it. If the reader choose, let him do his own meditation; or if he prefer to ramble with me. . . I bid him welcome." Be alert to these narrative techniques as you read his works and think about how he uses them to shape your experience and interpretation of the fiction.

Building virtual worlds from the elements of "the Actual," Hawthorne strives to do two things through his romances and allegories: to present "the truth of the human heart" and to "attempt to connect a by-gone time with the very Present that is flitting away from us" (*The House of the Seven Gables,* preface). Close examination of Hawthorne's characters should tell you about their hearts and their values, and your judgments of them should tell you something about yourself. Drawn into the world of Goodman Brown, Giovanni Guasconti ("Rappaccini's Daughter"), or Hester Prynne, consider if you would react to their experiences as they do. Would you, like Hester Prynne, have chosen to return to Boston and taken up the scarlet letter again? Why or why not? What do Hester's decisions tell us about her values? What do they tell us about her relationship to her society? Would you, like Giovanni, have suspected Beatrice's involvement in her father's plot? What does your response tell you about your own capacity for faith and love? What does Giovanni's response tell us about his capacities?

Thoughtful readers should have little difficulty connecting the worlds of Hawthorne's fiction to the present time. It hardly seems a stretch to see in Hawthorne's Puritans—his "men of iron" who extend their rigid interpretation of Scripture into the "iron framework" of their law—parallels to the modern world where strict religious doctrines have hardened regimes into ruling through repression and violence. Similarly, might a modern America preoccupied with physical beauty and plastic surgery find significance in "The Birth-Mark" and Aylmer's obsessive drive to remove his wife's "single imperfection"? In the poisonous plants of Dr. Rappaccini's creation might we see the forerunners of the genetically modified foods that find their way to our tables?

Finally, if Hawthorne creates these alternate worlds in order to comment on "the Actual," he seems to comment on this very enterprise through the artists, reformers, and scientists that populate his fiction. It seems that these characters' attempts to forge new worlds are rarely successful. Rather than helping to create a society founded on a "new truth," Hester returns to Boston while continuing to dream of a new world order. The "new arrangement of the world" attempted at Blithedale ends in conflict and tragedy. Beatrice and Giovanni, the Adam and Eve of Dr. Rappaccini's "Eden," are trapped in the garden against their will, and Rappaccini's "Eden" also ends in ruins. If you are familiar with

Hawthorne's work, you could easily add more ruined Edens to this list. Despite Hawthorne's sympathy for and his affinity with these creative visionaries, dreamers, and reformers, he rarely, if ever, affords them success. Their worlds are haunted by the past and ruined by the shortcomings of their creators. Why? What do these failures say? Does Hawthorne feel trapped in a world that refuses to see itself in the virtual worlds that he creates, thereby refusing to learn? Do these ruined Edens reflect his own despair at the state of his world? Or do they betray a more conservative philosophy? Does Hawthorne, finally, choose to side with the Puritans of Boston who seek to discipline and reform Hester and Pearl? Does he, along with Blithedale's neighbors, mock the "knot of dreamers" at Blithedale who seek a "new arrangement of the world" (*The Blithedale Romance,* chapter 3; chapter 2)? Hawthorne's narratives refuse to answer these questions definitively, and scholars have debated these very points for well over 100 years. "Be it so, if you will," Hawthorne answers, inviting you to become a resident of the worlds he creates, "a citizen of somewhere else."

TOPICS AND STRATEGIES

The paragraphs below should help you generate ideas for papers on Hawthorne's works. The topic suggestions provide broad ideas for essays about themes, characters, literary forms, language, and imagery. In addition, they should guide your thinking about the cultural context of both Hawthorne and his works, suggesting historical and philosophical topics for consideration. Remember that these topics are quite broad; they give you a general framework to guide you as you read, reread, and analyze the text or texts that you will write about. You will need to narrow the focus of your paper, constructing an analytical thesis, and bearing in mind its proposed length. An analysis of Pearl's role as a reflection of the scarlet *A* in *The Scarlet Letter,* for example, would be far too large to tackle in a four-page paper. While the chapters that follow consider topic ideas for individual Hawthorne texts, this chapter provides broad ideas for more general studies of Hawthorne's fiction. While these ideas may prove particularly helpful if you are planning a paper about more than one of his works, be sure that you choose the texts for your essay carefully. You should have a strong, thoughtful reason for selecting the texts you will analyze. A paper about father-daughter relationships in Hawthorne, for example, might focus on *The Scarlet Letter* and "Rappaccini's Daughter." Including "The Artist of the Beautiful" in your study, though, might prove a bit too difficult. Even though it contains a father-daughter pair of Peter and Annie Hovenden, Hawthorne does not seem to develop their relationship as an integral part of the text.

Themes

Often we begin our analysis of a work of literature by asking what the work is about; these questions lead us to the theme of the work. In order to write about the thematic concerns, you need not only to determine what the work is about, but also what it says about that particular theme. You might have observed that faith and doubt are important, if not central, themes of "Young Goodman Brown," "Rappaccini's Daughter," and "The Artist of the Beautiful." If you want to write about Hawthorne's treatment of faith in some of these works, you will need to determine what they say about faith and doubt. You might decide, for example, that both "Rappaccini's Daughter" and "Young Goodman Brown" explore the effects of the loss of faith, and you could forge a thesis for such an investigation by asserting what else you think Goodman Brown and Giovanni Guasconti lose when they lose faith. You may find that examining other elements of the texts—like character and imagery—will help to develop your understanding of Hawthorne's themes.

Sample Topics:

1. **Inheritance:** Examine the theme of inheritance in Hawthorne's fiction. What does he say about the values or the perils of inheritance?

   You might focus a response to this question in a number of different ways. One approach might be to evaluate parent-child relationships. Hawthorne sometimes addresses the idea of a monetary inheritance, as he does when he discusses the wealth that Pearl inherits at the end of *The Scarlet Letter* or when he discusses the "folly of tumbling down an avalanche of ill-gotten gold, or real estate, on the heads of an unfortunate posterity" in the preface to *The House of the Seven Gables.*

More often, though, he treats the notion of inheritance more abstractly, analyzing the legacy of parental values, beliefs, principles, or social institutions. You could easily consider many of Hawthorne's works in a paper about this more abstract notion of inheritance. "The Custom-House" sketch, the short stories "Rappaccini's Daughter" and "Roger Malvin's Burial," or the longer romances *The Scarlet Letter* and *The House of the Seven Gables* are just a few texts that you might consider. Additionally, Hawthorne's profound interest in American history should allow you to consider this question from the standpoint of national inheritance. What does Hawthorne say about the ideologies or the social systems that colonial America inherited from its ancestors? What has his own 19th-century society inherited from previous generations of Americans? You might think about *The House of the Seven Gables,* "My Kinsman, Major Molineux," *The Blithedale Romance, The Marble Faun,* or "The May-Pole of Merry Mount" in an essay that approaches the topic from this angle.

2. **Sin:** As a result of his interest in America's Puritan past, Hawthorne focuses a good deal on the idea of sin. How do his works comment on human sinfulness and its effects?

Once again, this theme is so broad and Hawthorne's treatment of it so complex, that you may shape a response to this question in many ways. Many of his texts, most notably "Young Goodman Brown," *The Scarlet Letter,* "The Minister's Black Veil," and *The Marble Faun,* explore the effect of sin on the individual. Hawthorne is also very interested in his characters' responses to the awareness of sin in others. In fact, any of the texts mentioned above would work quite well in a paper that considers this aspect of sin. As *The Scarlet Letter* shows, another of Hawthorne's interests was the very definition of sin. Hester's idea of sin seems quite different from that of the Puritan community that surrounds her. Other Hawthorne works, too, examine differing definitions of sin. You could easily work with "Rappaccini's Daughter," "The Birth-Mark," *The House of* the Seven Gables, or "The May-Pole of Merry Mount" in an exploration of this topic.

3. **Faith:** Analyze Hawthorne's treatment of faith in his fiction. Consider how he uses and explores this abstract quality. What does he say about the human capacity for faith?

While "Young Goodman Brown" is Hawthorne's best-known treatment of faith, he uses the language of faith and doubt repeatedly throughout his work. Sometimes, as in "Young Goodman Brown," his exploration is rooted in an explicitly theological context, yet at other times—as in "Rappaccini's Daughter" and "The Artist of the Beautiful"—his investigation is more secular. According to Hawthorne, is faith necessary? Is Hawthorne himself a skeptic? When, as in "Young Goodman Brown," "faith is gone," what else is lost?

4. **Art:** Hawthorne's fiction frequently examines the role of art in society. What commentary does he provide on the role and value of art in society?

You might begin by considering the role of art in some of Hawthorne's texts. In The Scarlet Letter, Hawthorne comments on the role and function of Hester's artistry in her society. The Marble Faun is set in a community of artists in Rome and spends a great deal of time discussing the value and function of art. In addition, the novel seems to grapple with the difficulty of artistic interpretation. In The House of the Seven Gables, the photographer Holgrave says that he "misuse[s] Heaven's blessed sunshine" with his photography (The House of the Seven Gables, chapter 3). And Owen Warland in "The Artist of the Beautiful" spends a lifetime achieving his artistic goal only to present it to individuals who misunderstand it and, ultimately, destroy it. In a paper, you might approach this theme by exploring Hawthorne's comments about the role of art in society or his fears about the use and misuse of art. Often, it seems that his commentary on art is a reflection on his own art. This, too, could provide the focus of a strong paper.

Character

Characters provide an attractive way to approach texts because we often react to them as we would to real people. As you develop a focus for a paper on Hawthorne's treatment of character, you might begin by considering your own reactions to the characters. Start with your initial reactions. Did you like or sympathize with them? Why or why not? From there, you should develop your analysis, examining the characters' language and behavior. Evaluate their relationships with other characters, as well as the language and imagery associated with individual characters. If you are planning a paper that analyzes characters in a few works, you should look for patterns. Are there, for example, characteristics that mark most of Hawthorne's women? What are they? What do they tell us about Hawthorne's attitudes toward women and their social roles? You might, instead, choose to explore patterns of relationships in Hawthorne's fiction. What might you conclude about male-female relationships in *The House of the Seven Gables, The Blithedale Romance,* and *The Marble Faun?*

Sample Topics:

1. **Hawthorne's women:** Evaluate Hawthorne's portrayal of his female characters. What models of femininity does he present in his fiction? What do the women of his fiction seem to say about his attitudes toward women and their social roles?

   Readers have long noted the diversity of female characters that populate Hawthorne's fiction. From your reading, what do you notice about Hawthorne's women? Do they all seem to possess the same characteristics and play the same roles in the social milieus that he creates? Some readers believe that his strong female characters demonstrate Hawthorne's feminist sensibilities. Others argue that he betrays these strong women, in essence arguing for traditional 19th-century gender roles. What do you think about these conflicting characterizations of Hawthorne's female characters? Yet another argument says that Hawthorne casts many of his women as victims. Do you think this assessment is accurate? Why or why not? If you agree that he does create a number of victimized women, do you believe that this reflects his beliefs about the position of women in society?

2. **Hawthorne's initiates:** Many of Hawthorne's stories feature young characters moving into the larger world for the first time. What does Hawthorne say about the movement from innocence to experience through these characters?

You could use any number of Hawthorne's works to address this question. A traditional approach would be to evaluate the young male characters of Hawthorne's shorter works: Goodman Brown, Robin Molineux, Reuben Bourne, and Giovanni Guasconti. Similarly, Donatello from *The Marble Faun* provides numerous parallels to these characters. What qualities do these characters share? What does the experience of these characters say about the movement from innocence to experience? Other characters could provide a fresher approach to this topic. Despite their advanced age, Clifford and Hepzibah from *The House of the Seven Gables,* cloistered from the world for years, venture out for the first time near the novel's end. Beatrice Rappaccini, too, has little experience beyond her father's garden. And while scholars often discuss Robin Molineux's position as a country boy entering the city for the first time, few note that Phoebe Pyncheon in *The House of the Seven Gables* is in a similar position, moving from country to town in search of a relative. Do questions of gender or age affect the movement from innocence to experience?

3. **Fathers:** Examine the fathers and father figures in Hawthorne's fiction. What arguments might you make about the relationships between fathers and children in his work?

An investigation into parent-child relationships might allow you to focus your paper on social and familial roles or on psychoanalytical character analysis. With the obvious exception of Hester Prynne in *The Scarlet Letter,* nearly all of the parental figures in Hawthorne's fiction are fathers. What about the absent mother in Hawthorne's fiction? What other patterns do you notice in the father-child relationships in Hawthorne's works? Are the father-daughter relationships different from the father-son relationships? How and why? What is the importance of the father's role in his child's life? "The Custom-House" charts Hawthorne's struggle with the ideas and beliefs of his forefathers. Do you see a similar struggle in any of his characters? What might Hawthorne be saying about the nature of father-son relationships?

4. **Hawthorne's artists:** Hawthorne populates his fiction with artist figures. What is their role in society? What is his attitude toward them? Does he condemn or praise them?

There are many characters to analyze in a paper on Hawthorne's artists: Hester Prynne, Pearl, Owen Warland, Holgrave, Miles Coverdale, even Dr. Rappaccini. And once again, there are a number of ways to focus and develop an essay on the artists in Hawthorne's work. You might begin by thinking about what qualities Hawthorne seems to value in his artists. Since he, himself, was an artist, you might expect Hawthorne's artists to be admirable characters. Is this always the case? Which of these figures are admirable? Which are not so admirable? What qualities leave some of his artists open to criticism? What conclusions can you draw from this analysis? Do Hawthorne's portraits of his artists reflect his conception of himself?

History and Context

Hawthorne was a product of his times, as well as a student of New England's history. His works reflect his interest in America's past and his attitudes toward his own culture and times. Background reading on antebellum America, New England's history, and Hawthorne's biography will provide a context for your analysis of his treatment of history and culture. Even some of Hawthorne's romances and allegories seemingly set in "neutral territory" outside of time provide commentary on his own culture. Hawthorne's America was moving toward civil war, and it was full of political, economic, and racial tensions. Do you see the effects of abolition or women's rights in Hawthorne's fiction? Does he address political or economic issues? You might focus an historical investigation quite specifically, examining the impact of a particular event or figure on Hawthorne's work. The Salem witch hysteria of 1692 and Anne Hutchinson, who challenged traditional Puritan theology, play significant roles in his writing. Similarly, 19th-century domestic ideology as well as the feminist writer Margaret Fuller figure prominently in some of his works. Keep in mind, though, that your historical research should inform your analysis of the text. Your paper should focus on the literature, exploring how the historical context can develop or inform your understanding of the text or texts you are studying.

Sample Topics:

1. **America's past:** A descendant of New England Puritans, Hawthorne was well read in the country's history, and he seemed particularly interested in the Puritan history of New England. Explore Hawthorne's treatment of American history in his works. What attitudes does he reveal about history and about the Puritans and their role in America's past? How does he use this history to make larger points in his fictions?

   Clearly Hawthorne's own ties to Salem and his ancestors' involvement with Salem's history, including the witch hysteria of 1692, play a particular role in his fiction. Biographies of Hawthorne should give you insight into his attitudes toward Puritan values and beliefs. You might focus on Hawthorne's use of history in a number of ways. You could focus on the witch hysteria and analyze its lasting effects in Hawthorne's fiction. *The Scarlet Letter, The House of the Seven Gables,* and "Young Goodman Brown" resonate with references to the witch hysteria. Puritan attitudes and values also figure strongly in "The Minister's Black Veil" and "The May-Pole of Merry Mount." Though *The Marble Faun* is set in the 19th century, the American expatriate artist Hilda repeatedly insists that she is "a daughter of the Puritans." So even here, the Puritan past plays an active role. Hawthorne moves beyond the Puritans to consider other elements of American history in "Roger Malvin's Burial," which considers the ideology of the frontier. Similarly, you might examine "My Kinsman, Major Molineux" as a commentary on the effects of revolution.

2. **America in the 19th century:** Despite his interest in American history and his frequent treatment of America's past, Hawthorne was keenly interested in his own time. How does Hawthorne's work comment on America in the decades prior to the Civil War?

You might do some background reading about 19th-century America to clarify your understanding of antebellum American culture and Hawthorne's cultural commentary. Many approaches to this topic could prove successful. You could note, for example, that even Hawthorne's historical fiction reflects on his own culture. In "The May-Pole of Merry Mount," Hawthorne indicates that in the struggle between the Puritans and the citizens of Merry Mount, "jollity and gloom were contending for an empire," adding, "[T]he future complexion of New England was involved in this important quarrel." With the exception of *The Scarlet Letter,* Hawthorne's romances are set in his own time and address American cultural concerns. You could evaluate his treatment of social class, gender roles, domestic ideology, transcendentalism, science and pseudoscience, race, and the tensions that were leading the country toward civil war. Both *The House of the Seven Gables* and *The Blithedale Romance* could easily find a place in a paper that focuses on domestic ideology and gender roles. *The Blithedale Romance,* Hawthorne's fictional treatment of his own experiences living at the socialist utopian community Brook Farm, includes commentary on other ideologies of his time—feminism, mesmerism, transcendentalism. Any of these could prove fruitful topics for papers. Clearly, feminism and gender roles figure in a number of other works that are much less overt in treating Hawthorne's own time. How might an exploration of "Rappaccini's Daughter" or "The Birth-Mark" help you to develop a paper on Hawthorne's attitudes toward gender roles in the 19th century? Still another topic for exploration is transcendentalism, which Hawthorne addresses in a number of his works, including *The House of the Seven Gables* and "The Artist of the Beautiful."

Philosophy and Ideas

You can also examine Hawthorne's engagement of philosophical, social, or cultural ideologies. While *The Blithedale Romance* clearly draws on Hawthorne's experiences at Brook Farm, does it also comment on the philosophical underpinnings of Brook Farm and similar socialist experiments of the 19th century? What does it say about the viability of communities built upon the tenets of socialism or Fourierism? Does Hawthorne address these same issues elsewhere in his fiction?

Hawthorne knew and lived among many of the transcendentalist writers and thinkers—Ralph Waldo Emerson, Henry David Thoreau, Margaret Fuller, and Bronson Alcott. You might consider Owen Warland from "The Artist of the Beautiful" as Hawthorne's portrait of the transcendental artist. Where else does he engage or comment on the philosophies of transcendentalism? As with historical investigation, be sure to focus any paper on Hawthorne and philosophy on the literature, using the philosophical and ideological issues to develop or support your reading of the text.

Sample Topics:

1. **The nature of symbolism and representation:** While *The Scarlet Letter* is Hawthorne's most famous and most sophisticated treatment of the nature of symbolism, he explores issues of representation throughout his works. What does an examination of signs and representation in Hawthorne's fiction tell us about the nature of signs and symbols?

   You cannot do this topic justice without examining *The Scarlet Letter,* and you must consider the shifting meaning of the scarlet *A* in that text. You should also consider just how often the letter *A* appears in other places in the novel. An examination of some of Hawthorne's other symbols and signs will allow you to extend this exploration. You might even want to consider some of his characters. Which signs, symbols, and characters are subject to interpretation and reinterpretation within the text? How are decisions about the meaning of these signs, symbols, and characters reached? What does Hawthorne seem to say through this multiplicity of interpretations? Quite a few texts might prove useful to such an investigation, including "The Birth-Mark," "Rappaccini's Daughter," "The Artist of the Beautiful," "The Minister's Black Veil," and "Young Goodman Brown."

2. **Humanity's fallen nature:** The fall of Adam and Eve, and the consequent mark of sin upon humanity, occupies much of Hawthorne's fiction. What kind of commentary does Hawthorne offer on the fall and humans' sinful nature?

Hawthorne's last completed romance, *The Marble Faun*, provides an extended examination of the fall and the idea of the fortunate fall through the character of Donatello. Questions of humanity's fallen nature are paramount in other Hawthorne texts as well. In "Young Goodman Brown," the devil proclaims, "Evil is the nature of mankind." Indeed, the story seems to focus on Brown's struggle to determine if humanity is good or evil. This same struggle occupies Giovanni Guasconti in "Rappaccini's Daughter" and is an issue in "The Birth-Mark" and "The Minister's Black Veil."

3. **Science and ethics:** What do Hawthorne's scientists say about the nature of science and the ethics of scientific advancement?

All of Hawthorne's scientists seem ethically flawed. You might consider Roger Chillingworth from *The Scarlet Letter*, Aylmer from "The Birth-Mark," Dr. Rappaccini and Dr. Baglioni from "Rappaccini's Daughter," and perhaps even Owen Warland from "The Artist of the Beautiful." What aspects of their work are ethically suspect? Through them, does Hawthorne cast doubt upon the efficacy of scientific advancement? Does he question the very notion that scientific investigation provides "advancement"? In considering this question, you would do well to examine the intersection between science and religion in Hawthorne's fiction. Consider, too, the relevance of such questions for modern science. Do the questions that Hawthorne asks still trouble us today? Why or why not?

Form and Genre

Examining the structure or form of a text can provide insight into its purposes and meanings, and you can build thoughtful papers from such an analysis. Hawthorne's complicated narrative voice often shapes his readers' responses to his texts and his characters, and casual readers often overlook the effects of the narrative voice. Examining the shifts of perspective in stories like "Young Goodman Brown" and "Rappaccini's Daughter" can provide a great deal of insight into their meanings. Does Hawthorne use similar narrative techniques elsewhere in his fiction? Why does he so often adopt his editorial pose, claiming that he is merely reshaping and presenting the works of others? Why is he so interested in "twice-told tales" (the name he gave to one of his collections of short stories)? What is the effect of his interest in allegory or his theory of romance?

Sample Topics:

1. **Romance:** Hawthorne called his novels "romances," and in the prefaces to all four he defined his theory of romance. How does Hawthorne's theory of romance and his distinction between romance and novel affect the shape and the style of his fiction?

Hawthorne's two most famous statements about the nature of romance, from "The Custom-House" and the preface to *The House of the Seven Gables*, are quoted in the early part of this chapter. In the preface to *The House of the Seven Gables*, Hawthorne seems to draw the distinction between novel and romance in terms of realism. He says, "[The novel] is presumed to aim at a very minute fidelity, not merely to the possible, but to the probable and ordinary course of man's experience. [The romance]—while, as a work of art, it must rigidly subject itself to laws, and while it sins unpardonably, so far as it may swerve aside from the truth of the human heart—has fairly a right to present that truth under circumstances, to a great extent, to the writer's own choosing or creation." Do you think that this distinction aptly accounts for Hawthorne's style and his treatment of his subject matter?

2. **Allegory:** In his preface to "Rappaccini's Daughter," Hawthorne claims that his stories "might have won him a greater reputation but for an inveterate love of allegory, which is apt to invest his plots and characters with the aspect of scenery and people in the clouds, and to steal away the warmth out of his conceptions." Allegory is a kind of extended metaphor in which characters, objects, and events represent abstract principles. Explore Hawthorne's use of allegory in his short stories. How might reading his works as allegories help to broaden your interpretation of the texts?

Hawthorne's best stories can rarely be limited to one allegorical interpretation, and they sometimes frustrate the reader who seeks to extend an allegorical interpretation across the entire text. In "Rappaccini's Daughter," for example, Hawthorne clearly gives allegorical weight to Rappaccini's garden through his many references to the Garden of Eden. Logically extending this allegory, though, will quickly frustrate a reader. Is Rappaccini Adam? God? Satan? What of Beatrice? Is she Eve? Is she Satan? Clearly the story can also be read as an allegory of faith and skepticism. Which of Hawthorne's other texts invite allegorical interpretation? Why? Do these tales, like "Rappaccini's Daughter," support multiple allegorical interpretations? What is the effect of these multiple possibilities on the reader?

3. **Narrative voice:** Examine the narrative voice in Hawthorne's works. How does narrative voice affect the reader's interpretation and understanding of the works?

Hawthorne's narrative voice is, in large part, responsible for his infamous ambiguity, and it is particularly important to remember that you should not assume that the narrator's voice is the author's. Therefore, consider the point of view of the texts you want to study. Is the story told in first or third person? When Hawthorne uses third person, how would you describe that third-person narration? Rarely does he provide the reader with an omniscient perspective, preferring instead a limited omniscient view. And often he chooses to tell the story largely through the perspective of a particular character. In such a case, whose point of view does the reader share? Why might Hawthorne have made this choice? Similarly, you should evaluate whether this perspective is consistent throughout the narrative. Are there places where the narrative point of view seems to shift? Where do these shifts occur? What effect do these shifts have upon your evaluation of the text?

Symbols, Imagery, and Language

Writers craft and build their art through the careful use of language, and careful attention to Hawthorne's language will provide you with a great deal of insight into his meanings. Students who are alert to the nuances of language and imagery have a much more vivid understanding and appreciation of a work, and their papers often provide penetrating analysis of the effects of an author's use of language and imagery. If you read widely in Hawthorne's fiction, you will begin to see familiar patterns of imagery. Language of light and dark and references to sunshine and moonlight are some of his favorites. You will also notice frequent references to dreams, to Eden, and to the wilderness. As you analyze the imagery of his texts, consider the common or traditional connotations of such language. Does Hawthorne rely on these traditional or common meanings, or does he develop or change these connotations? What are the effects of any changes that he makes? Hawthorne frequently centers his fiction on symbols that do not have traditional cultural connotations—the scarlet *A,* Georgiana's birthmark, Faith's pink ribbons. How do these symbols function within his texts? What is their effect? How does he develop meanings for them? Develop your analysis of imagery and symbolism by drawing connections to the themes or meaning of a work. How does an understanding of Hawthorne's figurative language enhance a reader's understanding of his meanings or purposes?

Sample Topics:

1. **Light and dark:** Herman Melville's 1850 review, "Hawthorne and His Mosses," describes the power of Hawthorne's prose in language that echoes the patterns of Hawthorne's own imagery. "For spite of all the Indian-summer sunlight on the hither side of Hawthorne's soul," says Melville, "the other side—like the dark half of the physical sphere—is shrouded in a blackness, ten times black." Examine Hawthorne's use of light and darkness and evaluate his use of this imagery in his fiction.

   The imagery of light and darkness pervades Hawthorne's works, and in order to do some justice to this topic, you should narrow your focus even more, selecting specific patterns of imagery to work with. You could conduct a broad investigation of the use of light and dark, though you should consider the nuances of Hawthorne's use of this traditional imagery. A cursory reading of "The May-Pole of Merry Mount," for example, will most likely simplify his use of light and dark within that work, overlooking the complexity of his argument about the "future complexion of New England." The same could be said for a number of other Hawthorne works. How does Hawthorne complicate the common connotations of this imagery? You could choose, instead, to focus your investigation more specifically on imagery of color. "Young Goodman Brown," *The Scarlet Letter,* and "Rappaccini's Daughter" provide obvious starting places for such an investigation, though nearly any Hawthorne text could play a role in your analysis. Another line of investigation might explore Hawthorne's use of sunshine and moonlight. These are some of his favorite invocations of light and darkness. What do sunshine and moonlight represent in Hawthorne's fiction? What patterns do you notice in his use of sunshine and moonlight? Who—or what—is associated with moonlight? With sunshine? Are the meanings of moonlight and shadow stable and consistent through his texts or do their meanings vary from text to text?

2. **The forest/wilderness:** How does Hawthorne use the imagery of the forest and the wilderness in his fiction? What is its role and how does it function?

The forest figures in many of Hawthorne's works, including *The Scarlet Letter*, "Roger Malvin's Burial," and "Young Goodman Brown." These would be good starting places for this topic. In addition, Hawthorne invokes the wilderness in "The May-Pole of Merry Mount" and *The Blithedale Romance*. What traditional associations does the imagery of the forest carry? Does Hawthorne depend on these traditional associations or does he complicate or change these associations? How and why? Further, you might consider if the forest and the wilderness have connotations that are particularly American. How and why does Hawthorne invoke particularly American myths of the forest or the wilderness? If you approach the topic from this angle, you may want to examine *The House of the Seven Gables*, paying particular attention to the relationship that the Pyncheons and the Maules have with the wilderness. What does Hawthorne's sketch of these families and their attitudes toward the wilderness tell us about them and about American values? How do these issues connect to the larger themes of the novel?

3. **Eden/Arcadia/paradise:** Hawthorne frequently evokes images of paradise—the Garden of Eden and Arcadia. How does this imagery function in his works? What point or points is he making through his references to paradise?

Hawthorne's references to paradise bear obvious connections to his thematic interests in sin and the movement from innocence to experience. "Rappaccini's Daughter," "The May-Pole of Merry Mount," *The Blithedale Romance,* and *The Marble Faun* would provide excellent starting places for an exploration of this topic. Other less obvious texts, too, could prove useful. The first chapter of *The Scarlet Letter* reminds the reader that "[t]he founders of a new colony, whatever Utopia of human virtue and happiness they might project, have invariably recognized it among their earliest practical necessities to allot a portion of the virgin soil as a cemetery, and another portion as the site of a prison." In *The House of the Seven Gables,* the narrator describes the Pyncheon garden as "the Eden of a thunder-smitten Adam" (*The House of the Seven Gables,* chapter 10). Like the question posed of Dr. Rappaccini's garden—"Was this garden, then, the Eden of the present world?"—these references seem to remind the reader that all of these Edens are worldly paradises. How might this fact be significant? What are the particularly American resonances of this imagery? How might the language of paradise be significant for the "new world"? You might also find it helpful to consider the imagery of Eden in light of Hawthorne's frequent infernal imagery. Where and how does his imagery evoke hell? Does he use this imagery in obvious contrast to that of paradise?

4. **Dreams:** Analyze Hawthorne's use of dreams. How do they function? What do they reveal about character?

While "Young Goodman Brown" might be an obvious starting place for this investigation, quite a few other texts should prove useful here, most notably "My Kinsman, Major Molineux," "The Birth-Mark," and "The May-Pole of Merry Mount." Do dreams seem to play similar roles in all these texts? You might choose to focus this even more by exploring the language of nightmare. Certainly, the experiences of Robin Molineux and Goodman Brown could be aptly described as nightmares. What other images in their stories help to develop these connotations? Why would Hawthorne cast their experiences as nightmares? Might you extend this nightmare analogy to any other Hawthorne texts?

Compare and Contrast Essays

Comparing and contrasting elements in or across works provides an effective strategy for developing an essay. Examining the author's language or techniques in one text often suggests important questions about another work. Why, for example, does Hawthorne use the language of faith and doubt to talk about love in "Rappaccini's Daughter" and to comment on science in "The Birth-Mark"? What insight does such a comparison provide into the stories' characters and meanings? Considering the whys behind comparisons and contrasts is extremely important. If you do not craft a thesis that proposes an answer to such questions, your paper is likely to become little more than a list of interesting—or not so interesting—similarities and differences. Teachers dread these papers because they have no apparent purpose or organizing principle. Whether you choose to compare and contrast elements within a work, across Hawthorne's fiction, or between Hawthorne's works and those of another author, be sure that you structure your paper around an analytical thesis that makes a point or an argument about the similarities and differences that you have observed.

Sample Topics:

1. **Examining elements across Hawthorne's work:** Compare and contrast Hawthorne's use or treatment of a particular element—theme, character type, philosophy, or pattern of imagery—in two or more of Hawthorne's works.

   You could begin by selecting an element of Hawthorne's work that you find particularly interesting or engaging and then examining that element across Hawthorne's work. Perhaps you found the portrayal of the father-daughter relationship intriguing in your reading of *The Scarlet Letter* and "Rappaccini's Daughter." You could begin to develop a focus for your paper by asking questions about the relationships in those two works, where the differences seem most striking. Pearl, after all, does not know her father, and when Bellingham questions her about her heavenly father, she replies, "I am mother's child" (*The Scarlet Letter,* chapter 8). Beatrice, on the other hand, seems to have no mother, and the story's title—"Rappaccini's Daughter"—seems to define her even more particularly as her father's daughter. Despite these differences, do Pearl and Beatrice share anything in common? Are there ways that you might compare the "parenting" styles of Rappaccini and Dimmesdale (or even Chillingworth, for that matter, who, after all, leaves his fortune to Pearl)? What does Hawthorne's portrait of these two women and their familial relationships say about the nature and the importance of fathering? Another element you could examine across Hawthorne's work is flower imagery. It is evident in these two texts and *The Blithedale Romance.* How might you develop a paper that analyzes Hawthorne's use of flower imagery in these three texts? What questions might you ask in order to evaluate this imagery and its function in the works?

2. **Analyzing elements within a work:** Much of Hawthorne's work allows for a comparative analysis of elements within a work. Choose one such element and develop an argument about Hawthorne's use of that element.

   The romances provide a particularly rich ground here. You could, for instance, compare Hester and Dimmesdale's definitions of sin in *The Scarlet Letter* or Kenyon and Miriam's art in *The Marble Faun.* What is Hawthorne saying through the similarities and differences between these characters and their philosophies? Or, you might compare the paired female characters in either *The Blithedale Romance* or *The Marble Faun.* What do you make of the differences among these women? What does Hawthorne seem to say about gender roles through the treatment of these women in the novels?

3. **Relating Hawthorne's work to that of another author:** Compare or contrast the work of another author with Hawthorne's work.

In order to construct a productive analysis, you should know why you have chosen an author. Why compare these two particular authors? What do you hope to show through your analysis? Keep in mind the projected length of your essay and focus your topic accordingly. You could write a great deal about the nature of symbolism in *The Scarlet Letter* and *Moby-Dick,* for instance, but the subject is far too broad to handle in a short paper. You might have more success comparing the treatment of gender issues in "The Birth-Mark" and Melville's "The Paradise of Bachelors and the Tartarus of Maids." Or, you might compare Melville's treatment of innocence in *Billy Budd* with "My Kinsman, Major Molineux." A comparison of Hawthorne's work and that of one of the women writers of his day might prove productive as well. For example, you could choose two short texts and compare Hawthorne and Stowe's treatment of gender roles. Another way to focus a paper comparing authors might center on Hawthorne's influence. How do Henry James or Rebecca Harding Davis show a debt to Hawthorne, for example?

Bibliography and Online Resources

Baym, Nina. *The Shape of Hawthorne's Career.* Ithaca, NY: Cornell UP, 1976.

Bell, Michael Davitt. *Hawthorne and the Historical Romance of New England.* Princeton, NJ: Princeton UP, 1971.

Bell, Millicent. *Hawthorne's View of the Artist.* Albany: SUNY P, 1962.

———, ed. *Hawthorne and the Real, Bicentennial Essays.* Columbus: Ohio State UP, 2005.

Carton, Evan. *The Rhetoric of the American Romance.* Baltimore: Johns Hopkins UP, 1985.

Chase, Richard. *The American Novel and Its Tradition.* Garden City, NY: Doubleday, 1957.

Colacurcio, Michael. *The Province of Piety: Moral History in Hawthorne's Early Tales.* Cambridge, MA: Harvard UP, 1984. (Reprint: Durham, NC: Duke UP, 1995.)

Crews, Frederick C. *The Sins of Fathers: Hawthorne's Psychological Themes.* New York: Oxford UP, 1966.

Crowley, J. Donald, ed. *Hawthorne: The Critical Heritage.* New York: Barnes, 1971.

Dauber, Kenneth. *Rediscovering Hawthorne.* Princeton, NJ: Princeton UP, 1977.

Doubleday, Frank Neal. *Hawthorne's Early Tales, A Critical Study.* Durham, NC: Duke UP, 1972.

Dryden, Edgar. *Nathaniel Hawthorne: The Poetics of Enchantment.* Ithaca, NY: Cornell UP, 1977.

Erlich, Gloria. *Family Themes and Hawthorne's Fiction: The Tenacious Web.* New Brunswick, NJ: Rutgers UP, 1984.

Fiedler, Leslie. *Love and Death in the American Novel.* Rev. ed. New York: Stein and Day, 1966.

Fogle, Richard Harter. *Hawthorne's Fiction: The Light and the Dark.* Norman: U of Oklahoma P, 1952.

Fossum, Robert H. *Hawthorne's Inviolable Circle: the Problem of Time.* Deland, FL: Everett/Edwards Inc., 1972.

Gollin, Rita K. *Nathaniel Hawthorne and the Truth of Dreams.* Baton Rouge: Louisiana State UP, 1979.

Hawthorne in Salem. Available online. URL: http://www.hawthorneinsalem. com. Downloaded November 8, 2006.

Herbert, T. Walter. *Dearest Beloved: The Hawthornes and the Making of the Middle Class Marriage.* Berkeley: U of California P, 1993.

Hoffman, Daniel G. *Form and Fable in American Fiction.* Oxford: Oxford UP, 1961.

Irwin, John. *American Hieroglyphics: The Symbol of the Egyptian Hieroglyphics in the American Renaissance.* New Haven, CT: Yale UP, 1980.

Levin, Harry. *The Power of Blackness.* New York: Knopf, 1958.

Male, Roy R. *Hawthorne's Tragic Vision.* New York: Norton, 1957.

Matthiessen, F. O. *American Renaissance: Art and Expression in the Age of Emerson and Whitman.* New York: Oxford UP, 1941.

Miller, Edwin H. *Salem Is My Dwelling Place: A Life of Nathaniel Hawthorne.* Iowa City: U of Iowa P, 1991.

Millington, Richard H., ed. *The Cambridge Companion to Nathaniel Hawthorne.* Cambridge: Cambridge UP, 2004.

Nathaniel Hawthorne (1804–1864) Home Page. Available online. URL: http://web.archive.org/web/20050124093523/www.eldritchpress.org/nh/ hawthorne.html. Downloaded November 15, 2006.

Pearce, Roy Harvey. *Hawthorne Centenary Essays*. Columbus: Ohio State UP, 1964.

Pease, Donald E. *Visionary Compacts: American Renaissance Writings in Cultural Context*. Madison: U of Wisconsin P, 1987.

Person, Leland S. *Aesthetic Headaches: Women and a Masculine Poetics in Poe, Melville, and Hawthorne*. Athens: U of Georgia P, 1988.

Reynolds, Larry J. *A Historical Guide to Nathaniel Hawthorne*. New York: Oxford UP, 2001.

Rueben, Paul P. "Nathaniel Hawthorne." PAL: Perspectives in American Literature—A Research and Reference Guide—An Ongoing Project. Available online. URL: http://www.csustan.edu/english/reuben/pal/chap3/hawthorne.html. Downloaded November 15, 2006.

Stoehr, Taylor. *Hawthorne's Mad Scientists*. Hamden, CT: Archon Books, 1978.

Turner, Arlin. *Nathaniel Hawthorne: A Biography*. Oxford: Oxford UP, 1980.

Waggoner, Hyatt H. *Hawthorne: A Critical Study*. Cambridge, MA: Belknap-Harvard UP, 1955.

Wineapple, Brenda. *Hawthorne: A Life*. New York: Knopf, 2003.

Wright, Sarah Bird. *A Critical Companion to Nathaniel Hawthorne: A Literary Reference to His Life and Work*. New York: Facts On File, 2006.

Von Frank, Albert J. *Critical Essays on Hawthorne's Short Stories*. Boston: G. K. Hall, 1991.

"MY KINSMAN, MAJOR MOLINEUX"

READING TO WRITE

THOUGH IT was not published until later in his career, Hawthorne wrote "My Kinsman, Major Molineux" when he was 25 years old. The story itself seems a clear chronicle of youth and immaturity—Robin, "a youth of barely 18 years," journeys to a New England city in search of his kinsman, hoping that Major Molineux will help him to establish himself and "begin the world." The story clearly shares elements with the classic coming of age story and with folktales that chronicle the country bumpkin's adventures in the city. Hawthorne begins the story, though, as if he were commencing one of his historical tales. The first paragraph provides a summary of the relationship that the colonial governors shared with the citizens of the colonies. The rest of the story tells little of history and focuses on Robin and his misadventures. Consequently, the opening paragraph feels like a false start, and as the narrator concludes the paragraph, he too seems to imply that the historical background is, in fact, extraneous. You may well ask whether the first paragraph is indeed a false start of a youthful writer or if the material that prefaces Robin's adventures plays a more integral role in the chronicle of the young man's experiences. Consider how a close investigation into this paragraph and its role in the story can prepare readers to see the multidimensionality of this early tale. Hawthorne begins:

After the kings of Great Britain had assumed the right of appointing the colonial governors, the measures of the latter seldom met with the ready and general approbation, which had been paid to those of their predecessors, under the original charters. The people looked with most jealous scrutiny to the exercise of power, which did not emanate from themselves, and they usually rewarded their rulers with slender gratitude, for the compliances, by which, in softening their instructions from beyond the sea, they had incurred the reprehension of those who gave them. The annals of Massachusetts Bay will inform us, that of six governors, in the space of about forty years from the surrender of the old charter, under James II., two were imprisoned by a popular insurrection; a third, as Hutchinson inclines to believe, was driven from the province by the whizzing of a musket ball; a fourth, in the opinion of the same historian, was hastened to his grave by continual bickerings with the House of Representatives; and the remaining two, as well as their successors, till the Revolution, were favored with few and brief intervals of peaceful sway. The inferior members of the court party, in times of high political excitement, led scarcely a more desirable life. These remarks may serve as preface to the following adventures, which chanced upon a summer night not far from a hundred years ago. The reader, in order to avoid a long and dry detail of colonial affairs, is requested to dispense with an account of the train of circumstance, that had caused much temporary inflammation of the popular mind.

Most of this paragraph chronicles the rapport that the governors had with the general population of the colonies about 100 years before Hawthorne wrote the tale. Astute readers should have two series of questions about this paragraph: What does it tell about the setting of the story, and why is this knowledge important? Some of the information provided about the setting is quite clear. This was a time of obvious political tension, and this tension represented a deterioration of the political situation—the colonial governors and the "inferior members" of their party "seldom met with the ready and general approbation, which had been paid to those of their predecessors." Beyond this, what does it show about those on either side of this political tension? Relying on the accounts of the last royal governor, Hutchinson, the narrator states that just two of six governors "in the space of forty years" were "favored with few and brief intervals of peaceful sway." The others were "imprisoned by popular insurrection," "driven from the province by the whizzing of a musket ball," and "hastened to [the] grave by continual bickerings with the House of Representatives." This list alone shows that the political tensions were pervasive. Beyond this, what does the description tell about the parties on either side of this tension? You might notice that the first two sentences tell a bit more about the position of the colonial governors. The narrator indicates that these governors often "soft[ened] their instructions from beyond the sea" and in so doing "incurred the reprehension of those who gave them." In return, though, the people "rewarded the rulers with slender gratitude" for their efforts. How does this initial description characterize the position and the character of the colonial governors? Does it seem to generate sympathy for them? Why or why not? Further, examine closely the language associated with "the people." Besides extending "slender gratitude" toward the governors, they "looked with most jealous scrutiny to the exercise of power that did not emanate from themselves." How does this description portray the citizenry of the colonies? Do you think that their resentment of the "exercise of power that did not emanate from themselves" is justified? What does the narrator's choice of the phrase "most jealous scrutiny" imply or connote about the people and their attitude toward those who govern them? Along this same line of questioning, you might look at the final sentence of the paragraph. Here, as the narrator demurs of telling of the more recent train of historical circumstances, he does say that these unnamed circumstances "had caused much temporary inflammation of the popular mind." How does this last phrase help to develop the portrait of the people that the narrator has drawn thus far? What implication does the word "inflammation" have in this context? Finally, you might note that this last sentence tells us one more thing about the setting of the story that is to follow. The action, he says, "chanced upon a summer night, not far from a hundred years ago." While this comment seems to have no immediate bearing on the politics just described, you might ask why the narrator gives this last detail about the setting. Is it significant that the events that are to follow take place on a summer night? How and why might those details be important?

Having drawn some conclusions about setting, politics, and the parties involved in the political tensions of the time, you might then inquire why it would be important to know this information before you begin to hear of Robin's adventures. What expectations do you have as a result of this information as you, along with Robin, enter the "little metropolis of New England" in the following paragraphs? What opinions do you have about the city, its citizens, and its leaders? In the second paragraph, you meet Robin, "a youth of barely eighteen years, evidently country bred, and now, as it should seem, upon his first visit to town." Does Robin seem to have the same expectations about the town and its inhabitants that you do? Why or why not? How might Robin's expectations and his mindset affect his first experience in town? How does the knowledge that you have gained in the first paragraph of the story affect your assessment of Robin and how might it affect your interpretation of his experiences in town? Armed with these questions and expectations, you are ready to follow Robin into the "little metropolis of a New England colony" on this midsummer eve and to assess both the young man's encounters and his growth.

TOPICS AND STRATEGIES

This section of the chapter builds upon the observations and questions above in order to help you develop essays on "My Kinsman, Major Molineux." The topic suggestions below should provide effective starting places as you develop and hone your own paper on the story.

Themes

Scholars often classify "My Kinsman, Major Molineux" along with "Young Goodman Brown" and "Rappaccini's Daughter" as Hawthorne's initiation stories. Each chronicles a young man's movement into the world and charts his growth from relative inexperience to experience. Certainly, initiation is the clearest theme of the story, and much of the story's humor comes at the expense of Robin and his naïveté. However, many readers see this theme as underlying another important theme in the story. Many interpret Robin's story, set against a popular uprising in prerevolutionary America, as a historical allegory about revolution. Given Hawthorne's fondness for both allegory and history, such an interpretation seems a likely, if complicated, thematic focus. Any thematic study of "My Kinsman, Major Molineux," though, must begin by assessing the course of Robin's initiation and evaluating his character and his growth.

Sample Topics:

1. **Initiation:** Robin, "a youth of barely eighteen years, evidently country bred . . . upon his first visit to town," travels to town in search of his kinsman because he thinks it "high time to begin the world." How might "My Kinsman, Major Molineux" be read as an initiation story that charts Robin's growth from naïve youth to adulthood?

   A paper that addresses this question needs to consider and address a number of different elements in the story. You will need to examine Robin and his journey very closely. How is Robin portrayed throughout the story? Do you think that Robin changes as a result of his experiences in the city? If so, how would you describe and evaluate his changes? As the section of this chapter on character suggests, you should consider the language and the images associated with Robin in your assessment of his character and his growth. Think, too, about his journey. Why does Robin decide to journey to the city and to search for his kinsman when he decides to "begin the world"? What do you think of Robin's motivations? If, as an initiation story, "My Kinsman, Major Molineux" should chart Robin's growth to maturity and adulthood, think about what qualities are necessary for adulthood. What does the story seem to imply is necessary for Robin to reach adulthood? Many readers see a psychological dimension in this initiation theme and believe that Robin must break from or overthrow his father in order to reach adulthood. You might, then, read Robin's journey from a psychoanalytic perspective. Does Robin encounter any father figures in his trip to the city? How would you evaluate his interactions and relationship with these figures? How do these interactions reflect upon the story's thematic concern with initiation?

2. **Revolution:** Do you agree that the story of Robin's initiation can be read as an allegory of the American Revolution? If so, what does the story say about revolution? If not, why do you believe that the story can not support such an allegorical interpretation?

Historical interpretations of the story are clearly rooted in its setting (prerevolutionary America) and its action (the popular uprising that comprises most of the activity in town). Begin by considering the validity of basing a historical allegory on these aspects of the story. You should also consider the story's first paragraph, which becomes a major component of any argument for the story's historical commentary. How might this paragraph provide the basis for seeing historical import in the story? How does it add dimension and background to the character of Major Molineux and to the actions of the citizens of the town? If you find that these elements provide a sufficient basis for a historical reading of the story, you will need to determine just what the story says about revolution. What commentary does it offer? In order to do this, you must evaluate a number of elements. Look closely at the imagery and the language that surround the insurrection as well as at the characters involved in it. What does the language imply about the nature of revolution?

Evaluate the characterization of Major Molineux in some detail. How is he characterized when we—and Robin—finally meet him? How and why is his characterization significant? Of course, you must also analyze Robin's actions at the story's end. What do you think of Robin's reaction when he encounters his kinsman? Why do you think that Robin reacts as he does? The kindly gentleman who waits with Robin says that he has "a singular curiosity to witness" Robin's meeting with his kinsman. What is his reaction to Robin's meeting with the major? What do you think of this kindly gentleman? What is his role in the story? Taken together, what do these elements say about America's revolution? Or, why do you think these elements make it unlikely that the story's subject is the American Revolution?

Character

While Robin is the most apparent candidate for a paper on character, you should quickly find that an analysis of his character could focus on a number of different questions. Astute readers quickly see that the word *shrewd* is repeatedly associated with young Robin, and assessing his shrewdness is a viable focus for a paper about him. Such a paper will need to closely examine the appearance of the word *shrewd* in the text. Who utters it? Why is this significant? How do these observations help you assess Robin's character? Another focus for your paper could be Robin's characterization as a country bumpkin. Clearly, he belongs to this tradition. Nor is Robin the only possibility for a paper on character in "My Kinsman, Major Molineux." Though he does not even have a speaking part in the story, the title character might prove a fruitful focus for an essay, as would the man with the "parti-colored" face who appears so many times throughout the course of the story. Even the crowd functions as a kind of character in this story, and you might write a thoughtful paper by analyzing its role.

Sample Topics:

1. **Robin as a character:** Consider Robin's characterization in the story. Repeatedly, the tale uses the word *shrewd* to characterize him. Do you agree that Robin is shrewd as his journey in town begins? Why or why not? At the story's end, after Robin asks to be directed to the ferry, the kindly gentleman echoes this language: "'No, my good friend Robin, not to-night, at least,' said the gentleman. 'Some few days hence, if you continue to wish it, I will speed you on your journey. Or, if you prefer to remain with us, perhaps, as you are a shrewd youth, you may rise in the world, without the help of your kinsman, Major Molineux.'" Do you think that Robin is shrewd at the story's end? Is Robin ready to rise in the world independently?

    This question asks you to consider Robin's growth. If this is a story of a successful initiation, Robin should have learned and matured as a result of his journey. Consider whether you believe that Robin has, in fact, grown by the story's end. In order to evaluate his growth, you will need to analyze quite a few elements in the story and evaluate how they reflect upon Robin's character. Evaluate Robin's assessments of his early encounters in town. Do you interpret the behavior of the people he meets in the same way that he does? Why or why not? What do his reactions tell us about Robin and his mindset? Evaluate Robin's reaction to his meeting with Major Molineux. What do you think of Robin's reaction? Why do you think Robin reacts as he does? The language that surrounds Robin's reaction is very important. Similarly, you must evaluate the setting in which this meeting occurs. Look closely at the language and the imagery surrounding the "mighty stream of people" containing the major. Look at the characterization of the "double-faced fellow" who is the leader of the activities. What does the language and the imagery say about the people and the process that surrounds Robin? How is Major Molineux characterized in this scene? What conclusions can you draw about Robin's behavior, his growth, his understanding, and his self-knowledge at the tale's end?

2. **The man with the "parti-colored features" as a character:** Robin encounters this character three times. What is his role in the story? What does he represent?

   Like *The Scarlet Letter*'s Roger Chillingworth, this "double-faced" fellow is largely a symbolic character. Look closely at his physical descriptions in each of his meetings with Robin. What do his appearance and the language that the narrator uses to describe him tell us about this character? In addition, link his appearance to his role in the story and in the uprising that Robin witnesses. Why does he watch Robin so intently during the final procession? While the narrator, the kindly gentleman, and Robin himself all use the word *shrewd* to describe Robin, this man calls Robin "fool." How might this encounter be important?

3. **Major Molineux as a character:** The reader does not meet Major Molineux until the end of the story, but the initial para-

graph of the story, as well as the brief personal history that Robin provides to the kindly gentleman near the story's end, also help to characterize the major. How is he characterized? What might he be said to represent?

This topic is clearly related to the thematic questions posed above, and your interpretation of Molineux will likely be dependent upon your assessment of the story's theme. If you believe that "My Kinsman, Major Molineux" is the story of Robin's growth to adulthood, you might choose to assess the major's role from a psychoanalytic perspective. Conversely, if you believe the story works better as a historical allegory, the major's role takes on added significance, since he is a member of the court party and a British representative in colonial America.

4. **The crowd as a character:** As Robin resigns himself to sit and wait for the promised appearance of his kinsman, the crowd that stages the insurrection begins to manifest itself in the story. As he wrestles with sleep, Robin passes the time "by listening to a murmur, which swept continually along the street," and which the narrator says was "altogether . . . a sleep-inspiring sound." Robin's intervals of drowsiness and dreaming are interrupted by the "uproar" from the crowd, and finally "A mighty stream of people now emptied into the street," ushering forth the final scene of Molineux's humiliation. What is the crowd's role in the story? What connections might you draw between Robin and the crowd?

You might treat the crowd in two very different ways. Many readers see the final scene of the story as Hawthorne's commentary on mob behavior, and they read the story as a comment on the dangers of "the mob." Do you think the story supports this type of interpretation? Why or why not? Alternately, there is support in the story for drawing a strong connection between Robin and the crowd. Examine the language that surrounds the crowd and its behavior closely. Compare it to the language that describes Robin's behavior at the end of the story. Similarly, examine the language of sleep and dreams in this section of the story. How does this help you draw connections between Robin and the mob that sweeps through the streets in the final scenes of the story?

Language, Symbols, and Imagery

"My Kinsman, Major Molineux" uses imagery familiar to readers of Hawthorne. Once again, as in many of the tales considered in early chapters, Hawthorne uses the language of darkness and light and his favorite symbol, moonlight. "Molineux" also relies heavily upon imagery that is somewhat less common in Hawthorne's works. The city and metaphors of illness prove important in this tale, as does his characterization of the mob in the final scene of insurrection. In his later work, Hawthorne would transform and adapt some of the images and symbols in this tale. This is especially so of his use of moonlight as a symbol and his treatment of the crowd (which is transformed late in his career into the celebration of Carnival in *The Marble Faun*). If you choose to focus your paper around Hawthorne's language or imagery, begin by tracing the imagery throughout the story. Then try to draw conclusions about how it functions in the work and how it helps to shape the story's meanings.

Sample Topics:

1. **Light and dark:** Like Young Goodman Brown's journey into the woods, Robin's trip to "the little metropolis of a New England colony" takes place at night. He journeys "near nine o'clock of a moonlight evening." Why does Hawthorne set Robin's journey at night? How does he use the evening's darkness to enhance the meaning and significance of Robin's encounters? Similarly, how does Hawthorne use light as a contrast to the darkness of the evening?

   It is obvious that Hawthorne depends on the metaphorical significance of nighttime. How is the story dependent on the darkness that surrounds Robin in the city? How does the darkness affect the course of Robin's misadventures? Consider the many types of light that make their appearance during the tale. Consider, too, how they are described and when they appear. A paper that evaluates Hawthorne's use of light and dark in this tale should draw conclusions about how and why Hawthorne uses the imagery as he does and it should consider how the imagery enhances or develops the meaning of the tale or interpretations of character.

2. **Moonlight:** In his introductory sketch to *The Scarlet Letter,* "The Custom-House," Hawthorne uses moonlight to provide his most famous definition of romance. Through the agency of moonlight, Hawthorne writes, "The floor of our familiar room has become a neutral territory, somewhere between the real world and fairy-land, where the Actual and the Imaginary may meet, and each imbue itself with the nature of the other." Moonlight was one of Hawthorne's favorite, and most used, symbols. In the second paragraph of "My Kinsman, Major Molineux," we learn that the events take place on a "moonlight evening," and Hawthorne makes references to the moon repeatedly throughout the story. Just beyond the story's midpoint, Hawthorne describes the effect of moonlight on Robin's journey: "and the moon, 'creating, like the imaginative power, a beautiful strangeness in familiar objects,' gave something of romance to a scene, that might not have possessed it in the light of day." Do you agree that the moon lends a degree of romance to Robin's experiences in town? Why or why not?

To address this question you will need not only to trace the references to the moon throughout "Molineux," you will also need to familiarize yourself with Hawthorne's definition of romance. (He discusses and refines this definition in his introductions to his novels.) You should consider that this story was written very early in Hawthorne's career, though he published it later in life. Do you see any evidence that Hawthorne's theory of romance was still evolving in this story? Why or why not? How do you think that moonlight functions in this story? What does it seem to represent?

3. **Laughter:** Laughter punctuates this tale, and it seems to reach its culmination as the crowd throngs the street toward the story's end. After Robin joins the laughter, the narrator remarks: "every man shook his sides, every man emptied his lungs, but Robin's shout was the loudest there. The cloud-spirits peeped from their silvery islands, as the congregated mirth went roaring up the sky! The Man in the Moon heard the far bellow; 'Oho,' quoth he, 'the old Earth is frolicsome to-night!'" How does laughter function in "My Kinsman, Major Molineux"? Do you agree with the Man in the Moon's assessment that it is the sign that the Earth is "frolicsome"? Why or why not?

To evaluate the role of laughter in the story, especially in this climactic scene, you will need to trace all the occurrences of laughter throughout the text. Pay careful attention to who is laughing and what motivates their laughter. As you assess this final burst of laughter, you must assess Robin's character, his experiences, and his growth. Similarly, you should closely examine all the language and imagery that surrounds the stream of people that throng the street at the story's end. How does the laughter fit as part of the characterization of this crowd of people? What does their laughter seem to represent?

4. **The language of illness/contagion:** After the narrator provides the broad historical background as a preface to Robin's story, he concludes the first paragraph by saying, "The reader, in order to avoid a long and dry detail of colonial affairs, is requested to dispense with an account of the train of circumstance, that had caused much temporary inflammation of the popular mind." Thus, long before readers are confronted with the insurrection that concludes the tale, the narrator has already characterized it through a metaphor of illness, a "temporary inflammation of the popular mind." How does "My Kinsman, Major Molineux" develop this metaphor of illness in its characterization of the insurrection that topples Major Molineux? How does this imagery of illness and contagion reflect upon or amplify the mean-

ing of the story? Why do you think that Hawthorne describes the crowd's behavior though this language?

The language of contagion is closely linked with much of the other imagery in the story. You might see what connections you can draw between this "inflammation of the mind" and the mentions of the moon and the references to laughter in the story. How might the connections between these patterns of imagery help to develop your understanding of the actions of the crowd at the tale's end? How might they help account for Robin's behavior at the end of the tale?

Compare and Contrast Essays

The theme of initiation provides the most common topic for comparison between "My Kinsman, Major Molineux" and Hawthorne's other works since it was a theme he frequently returned to, especially in his short stories. This story, though, provides other avenues of approach for compare and contrast papers. In fact, choosing a more unusual topic would allow you to develop a more interesting and original paper. As always, when you plan a compare and contrast essay, be sure that you forge a strong thesis that tells your reader the point of the comparisons and the contrasts you describe.

Sample Topics:

1. **Initiation stories:** Scholars frequently discuss "My Kinsman, Major Molineux" as an initiation story that charts a youth's journey from inexperience to maturity. Compare and contrast the theme of initiation in "My Kinsman, Major Molineux" and another of Hawthorne's works. How does each work treat the theme of initiation? What conclusions does each text reach?

   A paper on this topic must begin by addressing the questions posed in the discussion of the theme of initiation, and it must consider the characterization of the initiate. As the discussion of initiation indicated, a number of stories present clear grounds for comparison with "My Kinsman, Major Molineux," especially "Young Goodman Brown" and "Rappaccini's Daughter." A number of Hawthorne's other works also provide plenty of material for analysis, including "Roger Malvin's Burial" and *The Marble Faun*. Consider the characterization of the initiate in each of these tales. How is the character portrayed initially? In what way might he or she be considered inexperienced or naïve? What must the character learn or do in order to reach maturity, adulthood, or wisdom? While the characters in some of Hawthorne's initiation stories share a great many qualities, you might find that the individual works focus on different aspects of their characters. These characters, in turn, may learn very different lessons over the course of their journeys.

2. **Fathers and father figures:** As the discussion of the theme of initiation indicates, readers frequently see "My Kinsman, Major Molineux" as a kind of psychological story with an Oedipal dimension: Robin must overthrow his father in order to grow to adulthood. Many readers also see a host of father figures in Robin's adventures in the city. Compare Hawthorne's treatment of fathers and father figures in "My Kinsman, Major Molineux" and another of Hawthorne's works. What does each say about the relationship between father and child? Do you note a pattern in the relationships that Hawthorne describes between the children and their fathers?

This question provides a number of avenues for you to approach the topic. In "The Custom-House," Hawthorne seems to be haunted by his stern forefathers and their expectations, and in some ways, the same could be said of Robin. Tales such as "Roger Malvin's Burial" and "Rappaccini's Daughter" can easily be compared to "My Kinsman, Major Molineux" from an Oedipal perspective. Nor are father-son relationships the only complicated parent-child relationships in Hawthorne's fiction. There are a number of interesting and complex father-daughter relationships. Think of Pearl in *The Scarlet Letter*, Beatrice Rappaccini, or Beatrice Cenci in *The Marble Faun*. How might these works be fruitfully compared to "My Kinsman, Major Molineux"?

3. **Dreams:** As Robin sits on the steps of the church waiting for the arrival of his kinsman, "his mind kept vibrating between fancy and reality," and he dreams of his father's house. With a start he wakes, crying "Am I here, or there?" Later, after Robin's encounter with his kinsman, the kindly gentleman asks, "Well, Robin, are you dreaming?" Much in the tale seems to cast doubt on the substance and reality of Robin's experiences, and you might question the substantiality of Robin's experiences. Compare Hawthorne's use of dreams in this story and another of his works.

   You might frame a paper comparing the use of dreams in a few ways. Like "Young Goodman Brown," this story seems to cast doubt on the reality of the character's experience. Did Young Goodman Brown and Robin merely dream the events that their stories recount? Why might Hawthorne pose these kinds of questions? If Brown and Robin merely dreamed their adventures, what is the point of each of the stories? If they are not about a witch meeting in the woods and a political insurrection, what are their real subjects? On the other hand, in "The Birth-Mark," the narrator remarks that "Truth often finds its way to the mind close-muffled in robes of sleep and then speaks with uncompromising directness of matters in regard to which we practise an unconscious self-deception, during our waking moments." In "The Birth-Mark," Aylmer's dreams prove truthful and prophetic. Does Hawthorne use dreams in a similar way in "My Kinsman, Major Molineux"?

4. **The crowd:** Consider the behavior of the crowd in "My Kinsman, Major Molineux." How might you read it as a symbol? Conversely, how might you read it as a kind of political or sociological comment? Compare Hawthorne's treatment of the behavior of the crowd in "My Kinsman, Major Molineux" to that in another of his texts.

Celebratory or riotous crowds (sometimes the two are the same) appear in a number of Hawthorne's works, and you might find more than one viable interpretation of their function. You might compare the crowd in "My Kinsman, Major Molineux" with the scene of Carnival in *The Marble Faun,* the masquerade in *The Blithedale Romance,* or the May Day celebration in "The May-Pole of Merry Mount."

Bibliography and Online Resources for "My Kinsman, Major Molineux"

Baym, Nina. *The Shape of Hawthorne's Career.* Ithaca, NY: Cornell UP, 1976.

Bellis, Peter. *Writing Revolution.* Athens: U of Georgia P, 2003.

Colacurcio, Michael. *The Province of Piety: Moral History in Hawthorne's Early Tales.* Cambridge, MA: Harvard UP, 1984. (Reprint: Durham, NC: Duke UP, 1995.)

Crews, Frederick C. *The Sins of Fathers: Hawthorne's Psychological Themes.* New York: Oxford UP, 1966.

Fogle, Richard Harter. *Hawthorne's Fiction: The Light and the Dark.* Norman: U of Oklahoma P, 1952.

Fossum, Robert H. *Hawthorne's Inviolable Circle: the Problem of Time.* Deland, FL: Everett/Edwards Inc., 1972.

Friedman, Robert S. *Hawthorne's Historical Romances: Social Drama and the Metaphor of Geometry.* London: Harwood Academic Press, 2000.

Gollin, Rita K. *Nathaniel Hawthorne and the Truth of Dreams.* Baton Rouge: Louisiana State UP, 1979.

Gross, Seymour. "Hawthorne's 'My Kinsman, Major Molineux': History as Moral Adventure." *Nineteenth-Century Fiction* 12 (1975): 97–109.

Herbert, T. Walter. *Dearest Beloved: The Hawthornes and the Making of the Middle Class Marriage.* Berkeley: U of California P, 1993.

Herbert, T. Walter. "Doing Cultural Work: 'My Kinsman Major Molineux' and the Construction of the Self-Made Man." *Studies in the Novel* 23 (1991): 20–28.

Hoffman, Daniel G. *Form and Fable in American Fiction.* Oxford: Oxford UP, 1961.

Leavis, Q. D. "Hawthorne as Poet." *Sewanee Review* LIX (Spring and Summer 1951): 179–205; 426–85.

"Literature related to Hawthorne and Ideas of Good and Evil." Hawthorne in Salem. Available online. URL: http://www.hawthorneinsalem.com/ Literature/Faith&Religion/Hawthorne&TheSatanic/Literature.html. Downloaded June 7, 2006.

Male, Roy R. *Hawthorne's Tragic Vision.* New York: Norton, 1957.

McCall, Dan. *Citizens of Somewhere Else: Nathaniel Hawthorne and Henry James.* Ithaca, NY, and London: Cornell UP, 1999.

Millington, Richard H., ed. *The Cambridge Companion to Nathaniel Hawthorne.* Cambridge: Cambridge UP, 2004.

Shields, John C. *The American Aeneas: Classical Origins of the American Self.* Knoxville: U of Tennessee P, 2001.

Von Frank, Albert J. *Critical Essays on Hawthorne's Short Stories.* Boston: G. K. Hall, 1991.

Wineapple, Brenda. *Hawthorne: A Life.* New York: Knopf, 2003.

"ROGER MALVIN'S BURIAL"

READING TO WRITE

L IKE MUCH of Hawthorne's short fiction, "Roger Malvin's Burial" is rooted in history. In the first paragraph, the narrator remarks that "Some of the incidents contained in the following pages will be recognized, notwithstanding the substitution of fictitious names, by such as have heard, from old men's lips, the fate of the few combatants who were in a condition to retreat, after 'Lovell's Fight.'" The real Lovewell's Fight took place in 1725 in frontier territories that are now part of Maine. As he would do in "The May-Pole of Merry Mount," Hawthorne roots his story in a historical incident while claiming a good bit of artistic license. In the headnote to "The May-Pole of Merry Mount," he writes that the incidents at Mount Wollaston, or Merry Mount, contain "an admirable foundation for a philosophic romance." Similarly, the narrator in "Roger Malvin's Burial" claims Lovewell's Fight for the territory of romance; it is, he says, "One of the few incidents of Indian warfare, naturally susceptible of the moonlight of romance." In both tales, history provides the background against which to read the characters and the circumstances of Hawthorne's imagination. The main action of "Roger Malvin's Burial" centers on Reuben Bourne's physical and emotional journey from the wilderness to home and back to the wilderness after Lovewell's Fight, rather than on the historical incident itself. As with most of Hawthorne's uses of history, the historical grounding is important to an understanding of the story, and you should consider the plot and characters of Hawthorne's own creation as well as the historical context.

After the introductory paragraph that provides the historical context, Hawthorne introduces Reuben and his moral dilemma. Badly wounded in battle, he must decide whether to stay with his mortally wounded companion, Roger Malvin, or to travel on alone in the hope of saving his own life. The early discussion between Malvin and Bourne provides information pivotal to understanding and assessing Reuben's behavior later in the story, and if you are composing a paper on this text you will have to return to this section of the tale to develop an understanding of the story's meanings and purposes. Consider how much information the following passage provides about Reuben's complicated moral choice and his motivations in leaving Malvin. When Malvin declares "For me there is no hope and I will await death here," the debate ensues:

"If it must be so, I will remain and watch by you," said Reuben, resolutely.

"No, my son, no," rejoined his companion. "Let the wish of a dying man have weight with you; give me one grasp of your hand, and get you hence. Think you that my last moments will be eased by the thought, that I leave you to die a more lingering death? I have loved you like a father, Reuben, and, at a time like this, I should have something of a father's authority. I charge you to be gone, that I may die in peace."

"And because you have been a father to me, should I therefore leave you to perish, and to lie unburied in the wilderness?" exclaimed the youth. "No; if your end be in truth approaching, I will watch by you, and receive your parting words. I will dig a grave here by the rock, in which, if my weakness overcome me, we will rest together; or, if Heaven gives me strength, I will seek my way home."

"In the cities, and wherever men dwell," replied the other, "they bury their dead in the earth; they hide them from the sight of the living; but here, where no step may pass, perhaps for a hundred years, wherefore should I not rest beneath the open sky, covered only by the oak-leaves, when the autumn winds shall strew them? And for a monument, there is this grey rock, on which my dying hand shall carve the name of Roger Malvin; and the traveller in days to come will know, that here sleeps a hunter and a warrior. Tarry not, then, for a folly like this, but hasten away, if not for your own sake, for hers who will else be desolate." Malvin spoke the last few words in a faltering voice, and their effect upon his companion was strongly visible. They reminded him that there were other, and less questionable duties, than that of sharing the fate of a man whom his death could not benefit. Nor can it be affirmed that no selfish feeling strove to enter Reuben's heart, though the consciousness made him more earnestly resist his companion's entreaties.

"How terrible, to wait the slow approach of death, in this solitude!" exclaimed he. "A brave man does not shrink in the battle, and, when friends stand round the bed, even women may die composedly; but here—"

"I shall not shrink, even here, Reuben Bourne," interrupted Malvin. "I am a man of no weak heart; and, if I were, there is a surer support than that of earthly friends. You are young, and life is dear to you. Your last moments will need comfort far more than mine; and when you have laid me in the earth, and are alone, and night is settling on the forest, you will feel all the bitterness of the death that may now be escaped. But I will urge no selfish motive to your generous nature. Leave me for my sake; that, having said a prayer for your safety, I may have space to settle my account, undisturbed by worldly sorrows."

Clearly, one of the first tasks in analyzing the story is to assess Reuben's decision to leave Malvin, and this passage provides a good starting place. While the question of Reuben's culpability is complicated, this passage provides insight into his first moral choice within the story—his decision to leave the dying Roger Malvin. This passage shows that Reuben's initial intent is to stay with Malvin. As if to emphasize the point, the narrator says that Reuben assured Malvin of his intention "resolutely." What factors, then, affect Reuben's resolution and alter his decision, and what does the story seem to say about Reuben's decision? The dying man himself counsels Reuben to leave him behind. He begins his argument with an expectation that Reuben will defer to Malvin's age, position, and authority, calling Reuben "son," asking that "the wish of a dying man have weight," and claiming, "I have loved you like a father, Reuben, and at a time like this I should have something of a father's authority. I charge you to be gone, that I may die in peace." Still resolute, Reuben argues that he cannot leave Roger unburied. Malvin dismisses the need for burial and then changes the thrust of his argument altogether: "Tarry not, then, for a folly like this [burial] but hasten away, if not for your own sake, for hers who will else be desolate." Here we see the first crack in Reuben's resolve, for the narrator tells us as Malvin spoke "the last few words . . . their effect upon his companion was strongly visible." The narrator continues, "They reminded him that there were other, and less questionable duties, than that of sharing the fate of a man whom his death could not benefit. Nor can it be affirmed that no selfish feeling strove to enter Reuben's heart, though the consciousness made him more earnestly resist his companion's entreaties." This passage should raise a few questions. You might first examine the assertion that waiting with Roger was a "questionable" duty. Is this the assessment of the narrator, or does the narrator relay Roger's thoughts in this line? Further, how do you read the narrator's comment about the selfishness of Reuben's motives? His double negative—"Nor could it be affirmed that no selfish motive strove to enter Reuben's heart"—seems to assert that Reuben is moved by a selfish hope for his own future with Dorcas. The narrator's phrasing, though, is ambiguous, for he merely says, in essence, that he cannot confirm or deny the selfishness of Reuben's motivations. Careful readers might resolve this dilemma by referring to Roger's words at the end of the passage: "I urge no selfish motive to your generous nature. Leave me for my sake." But Hawthorne does not drop the issue of the selfishness or selflessness of Reuben's motivations in this passage. Where else does the initial portion of the story address the issue of Reuben's motivations in leaving Roger? What aspects of Malvin's argument finally convince Reuben to continue on alone? Examine the language of the narrator closely here. What does Roger's argument and the narrator's assessment of Reuben's reasoning tell us about Bourne's motivations? How does the story, finally, seem to assess these motivations?

Malvin's motivations seem a little easier to pin down in this opening section of the story. He appears intent on saving both Reuben Bourne and Dorcas, but elements of his argument might draw the attention of

a careful, curious reader. Why, for example, does Malvin almost immediately claim the authority of a "father"? How and why might this first
element in his argument be significant to the story's meaning? Further,
it is in this section of their debate that Reuben Bourne first brings up
the titular theme of burial: "And because you have been a father to me,
should I therefore leave you to perish, and to lie unburied in the wilderness?" Malvin addresses the issue of his own interment in the following
paragraph, arguing that because he will die in the wilderness, there is no
need for burial, and that it would be "folly" for Reuben to wait with him
in order to bury him. Why is the question of Malvin's burial so important to Reuben? Further, each of the men stresses their position in the
wilderness as he constructs his argument. What bearing does the wilderness setting have on the question of burial? How is this related to the
larger issues and themes of the story? Before moving beyond potentially
"selfish" motives for leaving him behind, Roger tells Reuben, "Your last
moments will need comfort far more than mine." Overtly, Malvin refers
here to the last moments that Reuben will experience should he choose to
stay in the wilderness with Malvin. But Malvin's words seem prophetic,
for it seems that, even having listened to Malvin's counsel, Reuben finds
that his life beyond the wilderness is nearly comfortless. How might this
comment of Malvin's provide an insight into the logic and the shape of
Hawthorne's story?

TOPICS AND STRATEGIES

The material below provides possible topics for papers on "Roger Malvin's Burial." Remember that the topics discussed are quite broad; they
give you a general framework to guide you as you read, reread, and analyze the story. Use these topics as springboards. You will need to narrow
the focus of your writing, constructing an analytical thesis and bearing
in mind the proposed length of your paper.

Themes

Most thematic studies of "Roger Malvin's Burial" will involve an analysis
of Reuben, his actions and his motivations. Reuben will play an integral
role in studies of secret sin or guilt. Other thematic investigations, like
an exploration of American identity, will focus on Reuben as part of the
story's treatment of that theme.

Sample Topics:

1. **Secret sin:** Much in the tale's beginning seems to absolve Reuben of culpability in his decision to leave Roger in order to save his own life. Once he returns home, Reuben's most overt sense of guilt seems to come from his inability to tell the truth of his experience to Dorcas and his fellow townspeople. Examine "Roger Malvin's Burial" as a study of secret sin and its effects.

   A paper that examines the theme of secret sin in "Roger Malvin's Burial" must be grounded in the initial moral debate between Roger and Reuben. What aspects of this first section would seem to absolve Reuben as he decides to leave Roger? You will also need to analyze the dialogue between Dorcas and Reuben when he regains consciousness after his rescue. How would you characterize Reuben's role in this conversation? How would you assess the accuracy of his version of the events in the woods? Why does Reuben not correct the community's understanding of his role in Malvin's death and burial? What do these elements tell us about Reuben? Taken together, how do these elements develop "Roger Malvin's Burial" as a story about secret sin and its effects on the individual?

2. **Guilt and redemption:** Though much in the tale's beginning seems to absolve Reuben of culpability in his decision to leave Roger, Reuben seems unable to come to terms with his decision, and he is plagued by guilt throughout his life. The story's concluding paragraph seems to indicate that Reuben is redeemed at the tale's end: "Then Reuben's heart was stricken, and the tears gushed out like water from a rock. The vow that the wounded youth had made, the blighted man had come to redeem. His sin was expiated, the curse was gone from him; and, in the hour, when he had shed blood dearer to him than his own, a prayer, the first for years, went up to Heaven from the lips of Reuben Bourne." Consider "Roger Malvin's Burial" as an examination of sin and redemption.

   As with the previous topic, you will need to ground an exploration of this theme in the debate between Reuben and Roger.

What explains Reuben Bourne's unresolved guilt throughout the story? Is he guilty merely because he has not been completely truthful with his wife and the townspeople? You might consider how you would feel if you were in Reuben's position. Is there, finally, a "right" way out of his dilemma? Why or why not? Similarly, you should closely analyze Reuben's motivations in leaving Malvin. In his portrait of Reuben, Hawthorne seems to have anticipated more modern understandings of the work of the unconscious. How conscious is Reuben of the factors that figure in his decision? In addition to analyzing Reuben's guilt, you will need to explore his apparent redemption at the story's end. Why or how has he been redeemed and his "sin . . . expiated"? You might want to think about this redemption on a psychological and a symbolic level. Clearly, Hawthorne makes sure that the symbolism comes together at the tale's end—the tree, the rock, Reuben, Roger, and Cyrus all come together with strong symbolic resonance. Additionally, you might think of Hawthorne's biblical allusions, especially the story of Abraham and Isaac. If you read the story psychologically instead of symbolically, do you think the sacrifice of Cyrus will bring redemption and relief to Reuben? Is there a way of reconciling a symbolic and a psychological reading of this story?

3. **Mythmaking, American history, and American identity:** While many readers of "Roger Malvin's Burial" regard the story's historical context as little more than a convenient setting for the story of Reuben Bourne and his guilt, others see Hawthorne's historical setting as integral to the story's meaning. Along with many of Hawthorne's historical tales, "Roger Malvin's Burial" might be considered a commentary on American history, specifically on the construction of a particular American identity. How might you read "Roger Malvin's Burial" as a commentary on American history and the construction of an American mythology?

   The richness of this story supplies numerous approaches to this topic. Scholars who have analyzed "Roger Malvin's Burial"

through a historical lens have commented upon the possible
significance of Lovewell's Fight to an understanding of Hawthorne's tale. In his introduction to the Penguin edition of
Hawthorne's short fiction, *Selected Tales and Sketches*, Michael
Colacurcio argues: ". . . though obscure to most modern readers, [Lovewell's Fight] was widely celebrated on its hundredth
anniversary [1825] as not only a triumph of advancing white
civilization but also as a signal instance of frontier virtue
and moral stamina. Well aware that the actual incident had
been altogether ragged and unlovely, Hawthorne's response is
clearly ironic and pointed." In other words, Colacurcio argues
that Hawthorne's first paragraph seeks to draw attention to
the fact that the mythology surrounding Lovewell's Fight
did not accurately reflect historical truth. Instead, the incident was used to construct and uphold a particular version of
American identity built upon the mythology of the frontier.
While further reading about Lovewell's Fight could provide
you with more historical grounding, you could easily pursue
this topic without much more historical exploration. Analyze
the images of the frontier in "Roger Malvin's Burial." How is
it characterized? Compare these characterizations with Reuben's lingering conceptions of the frontier toward the story's
end. At one point, the narrator tells us that "the world did
not go well with Reuben Bourne . . . he was finally a ruined
man, with but one remaining expedient against the evil fate
that had pursued him. He was to throw sunlight into some
deep recess of the forest, and seek subsistence from the virgin
bosom of the wilderness." How does the final section of the
story develop Reuben's particular version of the wilderness?
How does Reuben's understanding of the frontier compare to
the descriptions of the frontier and the wilderness at other
points in the story? What conclusions might you draw from
these comparisons? Finally, without recourse to the historical dimensions of the story, you could also pursue the issue
of mythmaking and the development of personal identity.
Compare the experience of Reuben and Roger to the town's
understanding of the incident. What has shaped the understanding of the townspeople? What conclusions might you

draw from this comparison about the roles of truth and myth in the development of personal identity?

Character

While all the thematic topics ask you to consider Reuben's role in the story, a psychological approach to the tale might allow you to analyze Reuben's characterization a bit more specifically. The other major characters—Roger Malvin, Dorcas, and Cyrus—can all provide productive subjects for papers on character.

Sample Topics:

1. **Reuben Bourne as a character:** Consider Reuben Bourne's name as a means of analyzing his character. Derived from Hebrew, the name Reuben means, "behold, a son." How does the story encourage a reading of Reuben as a son? Further, you might also analyze Reuben's last name, Bourne. While a bourne is a stream or a brook, it can also be the end point of a trip, a boundary. The word also evokes the homonyms *borne* and *born.* How might these homonyms help enhance our understanding of Reuben and his role in the story?

   Obviously, any paper that addresses the characterization of Reuben must grapple with the complex moral issues addressed in the discussion of guilt and redemption and secret sin. Analyzing Reuben through his name might provide you with a more character-centered, psychological approach to his role. Reuben's first name brings us back to the first part of this chapter where Roger's claim that he is "like a father" to Reuben and that he should have "a father's authority" is discussed. Coupled with the narrator's comment that Reuben "at times almost imagined himself a murderer," this clearly suggests an Oedipal dimension to the story.

   "Roger Malvin's Burial" can also be read as one of Hawthorne's "initiation" stories about a young man's growth to maturity and independence. How might you consider Reuben *born* of his relationship with Malvin? Consider also the relevance of *borne* as the past tense of the verb *to bear.* How might this word add resonance to your assessment of Reuben's character?

2. **Cyrus as a character:** Just before the final section of the story, the narrator says that Cyrus "was loved by his father, with a deep and silent strength, as if whatever was good and happy in his own nature had been transferred to his child." How might you read Cyrus as a reflection of Reuben? How does such a reading help to shed light on Reuben and on the direction and the purpose of the story?

While you might analyze Cyrus as a character in his own right, perhaps the most productive approach to Cyrus is to analyze his relationship to his father, especially in light of Reuben's reaction to the boy. How does the story develop this parallel between Cyrus and "whatever was good and happy in [Reuben's] own nature"? Analyze the characterization of Cyrus. What other characteristics does he share with his father? How might these similarities be significant? How does the fact that Reuben kills Cyrus at the very spot where Roger died help to develop this reading of the story?

3. **Dorcas as a character:** Dorcas has received less critical attention than the other characters in "Roger Malvin's Burial." Many critics see her as the embodiment of faithful and long-suffering love. She seems, though, to play a pivotal role in the shape of the story. How does Dorcas function in the development and the resolution of the plot?

A paper that focuses on Dorcas's role in the story will, no doubt, also explore Reuben's psychology and motivations. You should analyze Roger and Reuben's debate early in the story. Even though she is not physically present in this scene, both men invoke Dorcas, her well-being, and her imagined reaction to the events in the wilderness. Are the men fair to Dorcas in this discussion? Further, you will need to examine the dialogue between Dorcas and Reuben after his return. What is her role here? How does Reuben view Dorcas and her position? What do you think of his assessment of Dorcas? Finally, you will need to assess Dorcas's position in the family and in the family tragedy at the story's end. What is her role in the story? In the family tragedy?

4. **Roger Malvin as a character:** Many readers have observed that, while Roger Malvin's motivations in convincing Reuben to leave him seem altruistic, he steers Reuben away from his first, instinctive reaction, which is to stay with the dying man. Do you think that Malvin unintentionally plays the devil's role in the story by tempting Malvin to betray his initial ethical response to a difficult situation?

To write about this topic, you will need to evaluate the reasoning and the psychology that Roger uses as he convinces Reuben to leave. Examine how and why each of Malvin's arguments appeal to Reuben. Which of his tactics seem to sway Reuben or to cause his resolve to weaken? Why? How aware does Malvin seem to be of Reuben's motivations and desires? You could argue that Reuben is in a catch-22 situation, where neither option is a good one and neither will come without suffering. Do you think that Roger is justified in dissuading Reuben from staying with him? Why or why not?

Language, Symbols, and Imagery

Hawthorne uses two symbols, the rock and the tree, quite prominently in "Roger Malvin's Burial," and while it is quite clear that the author means them to function as symbols, their specific meaning is difficult to pin down. Readers have argued convincingly for varying interpretations of both. Other readers see symbolism in the story's setting, which moves from wilderness to town and back to wilderness. If you want to write on Hawthorne's use of symbol in the story, you would do well to focus on one symbol and to trace its use throughout the story. Closely examine the descriptions of the symbol to draw conclusions about its function.

Sample Topics:

1. **The forest/wilderness:** "Roger Malvin's Burial" begins and ends in the wilderness, far removed from human settlements. The middle of the story, by contrast, focuses on Reuben's life within a frontier settlement. In the beginning, Roger Malvin emphasizes that the spot where he will lie is far from human civilization, "where no step may pass, perhaps for a hundred years." As the story progresses and Reuben is "transformed into a sad and downcast, yet irritable man," the narrator says that his "one remaining expedient against the evil fate that had pursued him . . . was to throw sunlight into some deep recess of the forest, and seek subsistence from the virgin bosom of the wilderness." Reuben takes his family into the wilderness and it is there that the story ends. How does the forest/wilderness function symbolically in "Roger Malvin's Burial"? What might it be said to represent?

   This topic shares some territory with the question about frontier mythology. You might wish to explore the connection between the language of the frontier and references to the forest and the wilderness. What might the darkness and loneliness of the wilderness represent in this tale? How does the use of this symbolism help to develop the story's meanings?

2. **The rock:** Hawthorne makes very clear the rock's position as a gravestone. The story first introduces the rock in the second paragraph, saying, "The mass of granite rearing its smooth, flat surface, fifteen or twenty feet above their heads, was not unlike a gigantic grave-stone, upon which the veins seemed to form an inscription in forgotten characters." Toward the story's end it reiterates much of the same language when Reuben finds the stone. Similarly, as Malvin argues that Reuben should leave him without waiting for a "folly" like burial, he tells the young man, "And for a monument, here is this rock, on which my dying hand shall carve the name of Roger Malvin." Hawthorne draws so much attention to this large rock that he clearly intends it to have a more nuanced role in the

story. How might this rock function as a symbol in "Roger Malvin's Burial"? What does it represent?

As is the case with any good symbol, it is impossible to define an exact meaning of the rock. You must be sure to forge a strong, logical argument about your interpretation of the rock's function and purpose. You might begin by finding other references in the story to the rock (or to a rock) and examining them closely. Notice, for example, that when Reuben comes across the rock near the story's end the narrator says, "As if reflected in a mirror, its likeness was in Reuben's memory. He even recognized the veins which seemed to form an inscription in forgotten characters." Why does the story use the same language to describe the rock the second time? Further, what is the significance of "the veins which seemed to form an inscription in forgotten characters"? What might those characters be? Why are they "forgotten"? As you focus on a particular interpretation of the rock you would do well to consider the associations that rocks carry in Western culture. Think of the modern advertising slogan for Chevrolet pickup trucks: "Like a rock." What does that slogan suggest about the trucks? Since Hawthorne's story is set in the historical past and depends on biblical imagery, you should also think of historical and biblical references to rocks. Do any of these help to develop a reading of the large mass of granite in "Roger Malvin's Burial"?

3. **The tree:** "A young and vigorous sapling" stands near the large rock in the story's second paragraph. By the story's end, that sapling has "strengthened into an oak, far indeed from its maturity but with no mean spread of shadowy branches." However, the mature tree is blighted and almost seems to play an active role in the final scenes of the story. Explain the symbolic importance of the tree in "Roger Malvin's Burial."

Clearly, the tree is linked to the rock. It stands nearby and is mentioned in the same passages. You could consider the similarities and differences between these two major symbols in the story. You will need to closely examine the passages that describe the oak tree in order to analyze its meaning.

Compare and Contrast Essays

Since "Roger Malvin's Burial" addresses concerns that Hawthorne frequently visited, it lends itself to a wide variety of compare and contrast topics. Be careful that your compare and contrast paper does not become a mere laundry list of similarities and differences. Remember that your job in these papers is to argue an analytical point.

Sample Topics:

1. **Secret Sin:** "Roger Malvin's Burial" implies that at least some of Reuben's discontent stems from his inability to share his misgivings and his guilt with Dorcas. Compare Hawthorne's treatment of the theme of secret guilt or secret sin in this story and another of his works.

   While this theme is a common one in Hawthorne's fiction, "Roger Malvin's Burial" allows you to address some interesting nuances in this familiar theme. The paragraph above mentions both secret guilt and secret sin. The two are not necessarily the same. Does guilt or sin affect Reuben, or do both affect him? How would you compare Reuben to Arthur Dimmesdale in *The Scarlet Letter* or to Reverend Hooper in "The Minister's Black Veil"?

2. **Initiation:** Perhaps the character in Hawthorne's work who bears the greatest resemblance to Reuben Bourne is Young Goodman Brown. Both Bourne and Brown go into the forest and come back changed men. Both seem embittered by their experiences, and yet their experiences are quite different. Readers often see both tales as stories of initiation, where young men encounter evil, sin, or moral ambiguity for the first time. Compare "Roger Malvin's Burial" and "Young Goodman Brown" as initiation stories.

   These two stories share many similarities in theme, character, and symbolism, so you will have to focus this topic a great deal. Remember, too, that your goal is not to argue that both are initiation stories, but to construct an argument about how or why they treat the theme as they do.

3. **Dreams:** While "Roger Malvin's Burial" does not incorporate a dream like those experienced by Georgiana in "The Birth-Mark" and Robin in "My Kinsman, Major Molineux," the narrator speaks of a "day-dream" as the Bourne family ventures into the wilderness toward the story's end: "Oh! Who, in the enthusiasm of a day-dream, has not wished that he were a wanderer in a world of summer wilderness, with one fair and gentle being hanging lightly on his arm." Compare the story's treatment of dreams and daydreams with that of another Hawthorne work.

   In some of Hawthorne's texts, dreams are prophetic; in others they reveal something of their characters' psychology; in still others, they emphasize the insubstantiality or falseness of characters and/or their beliefs. How does the daydream of "Roger Malvin's Burial" function? You might want to narrow further the focus of your paper and examine the language of daydreams. "Roger Malvin's Burial," "The May-Pole of Merry Mount," and *The Blithedale Romance* all use the language of daydream and fantasy.

4. **Father figures:** As the discussion of Reuben as a character indicates, you could easily evaluate this story from a psychological perspective, reading an Oedipal dynamic between Reuben and Roger. Compare and contrast Hawthorne's treatment of father figures in this tale and another of his works.

   This, too, is a common theme in Hawthorne, and you have a number of works that could prove worthwhile subjects for a paper on Oedipal tensions. "My Kinsman, Major Molineux" provides the most obvious example, although Hawthorne clearly deals with Oedipal anxieties in "The Custom-House."

Bibliography for "Roger Malvin's Burial"

Colacurcio, Michael. *The Province of Piety: Moral History in Hawthorne's Early Tales.* Cambridge, MA: Harvard UP, 1984. (Reprint: Durham, NC: Duke UP, 1995.)

Crews, Frederick C. *The Sins of Fathers: Hawthorne's Psychological Themes.* New York: Oxford UP, 1966.

Daly, Robert. "History and and Chivalric Myth in 'Roger Malvin's Burial.'" *Essex Institute Historical Collections* 109 (1978): 99–115.

Doubleday, Neal F. *Hawthorne's Early Tales: A Critical Study.* Durham, NC: Duke UP, 1972.

Erlich, Gloria Chasson. "Guilt and Expiation in "Roger Malvin's Burial.'" *Nineteenth-Century Fiction* 26 (1972): 377–389.

Fogle, Richard Harter. *Hawthorne's Fiction: The Light and the Dark.* Norman: U of Oklahoma P, 1952.

Fossum, Robert H. *Hawthorne's Inviolable Circle: the Problem of Time.* Deland, FL: Everett/Edwards Inc., 1972.

Male, Roy R. *Hawthorne's Tragic Vision.* New York: Norton, 1957.

Millington, Richard H., ed. *The Cambridge Companion to Nathaniel Hawthorne.* Cambridge: Cambridge UP, 2004.

Ortolano, Guy. "The Role of Dorcas in 'Roger Malvin's Burial.'" *Nathaniel Hawthorne Review* 25 (1999): 8–16.

Schulz, Dieter. "Imagination and Self-Imprisonment: The Ending of 'Roger Malvin's Burial.'" *Studies in Short Fiction* 10 (1973): 183–186.

Stock, Ely. "History and Bible in Hawthorne's 'Roger Malvin's Burial.'" *Essex Institute Historical Collections* 100 (1964): 279–296.

Turner, Arlin. *Nathaniel Hawthorne.* New York: Holt, Rinehart, and Winston, 1962.

Waggoner, Hyatt H. *Hawthorne: A Critical Study.* Cambridge, MA: Belknap Press of Harvard University, 1955.

"YOUNG GOODMAN BROWN"

READING TO WRITE

WRITING ABOUT "Young Goodman Brown" more than 30 years ago, literary critic Neal Doubleday quoted the 17th-century essayist Montaigne, saying, "When do we agree and say: 'There has been enough about this book; henceforth there is nothing more to say concerning it?'" Nevertheless, literary scholars continue to write about "Young Goodman Brown," and so do countless students. It remains Hawthorne's most well-known and widely analyzed tale. Nearly every American student knows the story: Brown takes leave of his allegorically named wife, Faith, journeys into the woods, meets the devil, and sees his Puritan neighbors at a witch meeting. And we also know the doubt that Hawthorne plants in his readers' minds at the tale's end: "Had Goodman Brown fallen asleep in the forest, and only dreamed a wild dream of a witch meeting?" While it may be challenging and a little intimidating to write a paper on a story that innumerable scholars and students have already analyzed, "Young Goodman Brown" allows for a great breadth of response. While questions of faith and doubt underlie most analyses of the tale, you should find that "Young Goodman Brown" easily supports papers on topics as diverse as dreams, sexuality, and witchcraft.

Student papers often spend a great deal of time analyzing the ambiguity of Brown's experiences in the forest, but the beginning of the tale, Brown's leave-taking from Faith, introduces the story's themes, tensions, and imagery and reveals a great deal about both Brown and Faith. Consider how a close reading of the following paragraphs lays the groundwork for an examination of Brown's experiences in the forest while at the same time suggesting other topics for analysis:

> Young Goodman Brown came forth, at sunset, into the street of Salem village, but put his head back, after crossing the threshold, to exchange a parting kiss with his young wife. And Faith, as the wife was aptly named, thrust her own pretty head into the street, letting the wind play with the pink ribbons of her cap, while she called to Goodman Brown.
>
> "Dearest heart," whispered she, softly and rather sadly, when her lips were close to his ear, "pr'y thee, put off your journey until sunrise, and sleep in your own bed to-night. A lone woman is troubled with such dreams and such thoughts, that she's afeard of herself, sometimes. Pray, tarry with me this night, dear husband, of all nights in the year!"
>
> "My love and my Faith," replied young Goodman Brown, "of all nights in the year, this one night must I tarry away from thee. My journey, as thou callest it, forth and back again, must needs be done 'twixt now and sunrise. What, my sweet, pretty wife, dost thou doubt me already, and we but three months married!"
>
> "Then, God bless you!" said Faith, with the pink ribbons, "and may you find all well, when you come back."
>
> "Amen!" cried Goodman Brown. "Say thy prayers, dear Faith, and go to bed at dusk, and no harm will come to thee."
>
> So they parted; and the young man pursued his way, until, being about to turn the corner by the meeting-house, he looked back, and saw the head of Faith still peeping after him, with a melancholy air, in spite of her pink ribbons.
>
> "Poor little Faith!" thought he, for his heart smote him. "What a wretch am I, to leave her on such an errand! She talks of dreams, too. Methought, as she spoke, there was trouble in her face, as if a dream had warned her what work is to be done to-night. But, no no! 'twould kill her to think it. Well; she's a blessed angel on earth; and after this one night, I'll cling to her skirts and follow her to Heaven."

With this excellent resolve for the future, Goodman Brown felt himself justified in making more haste on his present evil purpose.

The story's initial paragraph sets the scene and introduces both Brown and Faith. In fact, the very first sentence introduces all three elements. Brown and his story start out at "sunset" in "Salem village," and careful readers should find aspects of the setting suggestive. Why would Goodman Brown leave his home at sunset, when most people would be settling into their homes for the night? Why does Hawthorne name Salem village—famous as the site of the Salem witch trials—as Brown's home? Does the story of Brown's journey have anything to do with witchcraft?

You might also question the significance of the phrase "crossing the threshold." While Brown must, quite literally, cross the threshold of his home as he crosses into the street, you might wonder about the metaphorical significance of the phrase. Is the story about "crossing thresholds"? If so, what kinds of thresholds does Brown cross? Conversely, Brown's "young wife," Faith, stays inside the home. Immediately, the narrator says that Faith is "aptly named," clearly preparing readers for an allegorical reading of the tale. Already, it is clear that we may interpret Faith as a character in her own right and as an embodiment of the abstract quality of faith. (Hawthorne emphasizes this point again just two paragraphs later when Brown refers to her as "My love and my Faith.") Before the paragraph ends, Hawthorne adds to the story's symbolism, drawing the reader's attention to the pink ribbons on the cap of the "aptly named" Faith. The image is striking, and Hawthorne mentions Faith's pink ribbons two more times before the end of this passage. We do not typically associate the color pink with the Puritan palette of colors. Instead, popular consciousness links the Puritans with dark colors, the "sad-colored garments and gray, steeple-crowned hats" of the first line of *The Scarlet Letter*. Nor does pink have a particular symbolic resonance. It does not fit neatly into our codes of color symbolism, where white represents purity and goodness, black represents evil, and red represents passion. Why would Hawthorne link Faith so overtly to pink ribbons? What does this symbol imply about her?

The rest of the passage develops the initial impressions of Faith, Brown, and his movement across the threshold. He is, indeed, embarking on a journey that he insists "must needs be done 'twixt [sunset] and sunrise." What kind of errand or journey must be done at night? What implications might there be to such a nighttime journey? Whatever the journey, clearly Faith seeks to discourage it when she asks Brown to delay the journey until after sunrise, and to "sleep in your own bed to-night." Both Brown and the narrator have misgivings about his errand into the forest. Brown calls himself a "wretch . . . to leave her on such an errand," and he fears that Faith's dreams have "warned her what work is to be done to-night." In the final line of the passage the narrator bluntly describes that work as Brown's "evil purpose." While you do not yet know the specifics of Goodman Brown's journey, you can be assured by the characters' misgivings and the narrator's overt assertion that Brown's "errand" is for no good purpose.

Once again, you might find yourself wondering what threshold Brown is about to cross, and you might explore the motivations behind his nighttime expedition. Despite his own misgivings, the young man clearly believes that he can embark on his "evil purpose" without harming his goodness, his faith, or his reward in heaven, telling himself that "after this one night, I'll cling to [Faith's] skirts and follow her to Heaven." The narrator then remarks that "[w]ith this excellent resolve . . . Goodman Brown felt himself justified" in hurrying on his journey. What do you think of Brown's reasoning here? Do you think that he is being honest with himself? What do you think of his theology? How likely is he to "follow [Faith] to Heaven" after "[leaving] her on such an errand"? His plan might be especially problematic after he has questioned her faith in him, asking "dost thou doubt me already, and we but three months married!" In this line, you can see reflections on Faith both as a character and as an allegorical representation. If she represents "[his] love and [his] Faith," what does this question say about the quality of Brown's love and his faith? Does he doubt his faith? Is it significant that he calls her "Poor little Faith"? What does this say about the quality of Brown's love and his faith? You might also consider Brown's comment that "'twould kill her to think" of "what work is to be done" on his journey. Will the work of his journey "kill" Brown's "[p]oor little Faith," or do we believe, along with Brown, that "no harm will come to [Faith]"?

You might want to consider Faith's role as a character in her own right in addition to analyzing her position as an allegorical representation of

Brown's faith. This passage asks you to consider how much Faith knows or suspects about her husband's errand. Brown fears that "a dream had warned her what work is to be done" in the forest, but he concludes, instead, that she is ignorant of his purpose: "But, no, no! 'twould kill her to think it. Well; she's a blessed angel on earth." How realistic is Brown's assessment of his wife? You would do well to consider Puritan beliefs about human nature (as well as your own experiences with others) as you examine his assertion that she is an "angel on earth." Similarly, consider Faith's request that her husband delay his journey until after sunrise; the "trouble in her face"; and her parting comment, "Then, God bless you . . . and may you find all well, when you come back." Are these reflections of her knowledge of and her uneasiness with her husband's purpose? Similarly, consider her comment that "A lone woman is troubled with such dreams and such thoughts, that she's afeard of herself, sometimes." What might this comment tell us about Faith and her character? Is Brown's "sweet, pretty wife" more worldly and knowledgeable than her husband realizes? Have her own dreams told her something about what Brown might experience on his nighttime journey?

A careful reader gains particular insight into Faith, Goodman Brown, and his expedition into the forest through a close examination of the story's opening paragraphs. As a result, you are well prepared as you take the "dreary road" into the forest with young Goodman Brown. Most likely, you are more prepared than Brown himself, and your preparation should provide you with quite a few effective paper topics as you plan an essay on "Young Goodman Brown."

TOPICS AND STRATEGIES

The topics below provide possible approaches for papers about "Young Goodman Brown." Remember that these topic suggestions are broad ideas. Use these as springboards, and narrow the focus of your own analysis.

Themes

The narrator's emphasis that Faith is "aptly named" clearly indicates that faith is the central theme of "young Goodman Brown," and nearly every paper on this story must at least touch on this issue. Other thematic concerns emerge from the text, though, including Brown's status as a naïve initiate at the tale's opening. Does Brown learn anything in his journey away from Faith? As you read and reread the story, identify thematic concerns that attract your attention and chart the story's treatment of those themes. Assess what Hawthorne seems to be saying about these topics and analyze how the story communicates them. This process should prepare you to develop and focus an essay on Hawthorne's treatment of a specific theme in "Young Goodman Brown."

Sample Topics:

1. **Faith and doubt:** Clearly, you can read "Young Goodman Brown" as an allegory of faith. In the midst of his forest experience, young Goodman Brown declares, "With Heaven above, and Faith below, I will yet stand firm against the devil!" Just after his declaration, a cloud sweeps overhead, he hears voices, including "one voice, of a young woman, uttering lamentations." As Brown shouts, "Faith," he sees pink ribbons "fluttering lightly through the air," and he cries, "My Faith is gone!" Does young Goodman Brown lose his faith? If so, why do you think he looses faith? What, according to Hawthorne, are the consequences of losing faith?

You will need to focus this question a great deal to work with it effectively in a paper. You might begin by deciding if you want to approach faith as a theological issue in the context of the Puritan religion or if you want to approach it as a more secular issue. (Brown, after all, loses faith in his wife.) Clearly, you will need to examine Brown's character in detail and consider some of the questions about his character and motivations addressed in the "Reading to Write" section of this chapter. Consider his beliefs about faith, and interpret his wife's role allegorically. What is faith? Why is it necessary or important? Be sure to examine the other qualities to which Faith is linked in the story. When faith is lost, what else is lost? What are Goodman Brown's attitudes and his beliefs about the importance and the necessity of faith? Analyze Brown's conversations with the devil closely in order to address these questions. Finally, examine the passage where Brown tells Faith, "Look up to Heaven, and resist the Wicked One!" during the witch meeting. The narrator tells us, "Whether Faith obeyed, he knew not." Explain the significance of this passage in particular.

2. **Initiation:** Young Goodman Brown is one of Hawthorne's young male initiates, traveling beyond the safe boundaries of the world he knows. How might you read "Young Goodman Brown" as an initiation story about the movement from innocence to experience?

This question requires you to analyze Brown's journey into the woods as well as his character. You might begin by questioning Brown innocence. Is he innocent? Is he naïve? Are the two one and the same? What, exactly, does Brown's journey seem to represent? Does Brown learn anything as a result of his journey? If so, what does he learn? In order to narrow this topic even further, you might choose to focus your response on either a theological or a psychological interpretation. A theological reading would chart Brown's encounter with evil and sin and would explore Brown's response to the devil and his invitations. In the woods, the young man strives to resist and apparently thinks that he has resisted "the Wicked One." He has no assurance, though, that Faith obeyed his command to resist. He does clearly believe that he sees his neighbors in the forest. Explore and analyze Brown's response to his new awareness of the sin in others. In the final passages we see his return home and his encounters with his fellow townspeople. Examine the narrator's language here; what does it seem to imply about Brown and his beliefs? What do you think of Brown's theological understanding and his worldview after his encounter in the forest?

A psychological approach to the theme of initiation would take a slightly different tack. Taking its cue from the narrator's question, "Had Goodman Brown fallen asleep in the forest, and only dreamed a wild dream of a witch meeting," this approach sees Brown's journey into the woods as a dreams-cape from the young man's psyche. You might begin such an approach by considering the elements in the story that support the theory that the tale records the events of a dream. Then, consider dreams as projections of the dreamer's unconscious. What does the dream tell us about Brown? If you agree that the reader learns about Brown's psyche through his dream, do you think that Brown, too, learns about himself through the dream? Why or why not? Some readers focus their psychological interpretation of the story even further. Noting that Brown is but "three months married" and that his discovery of Faith's presence in the woods is far more disturbing than that of the other citizens, they see in Brown's dream a link between sexuality and sin. Can you develop a reading of the story that argues that it charts a Puritan youth's reactions to sexuality and original sin?

3. **Ambiguity as a theme:** Toward the story's end, the narrator poses a question to the reader—"Had Goodman Brown fallen asleep in the forest, and only dreamed a wild dream of a witch-meeting?" Refusing to answer the question, the narrator continues: "Be it so, if you will." Throughout the story, the narrative voice often—but not always—seems to limit our perceptions to those of Goodman Brown. In the forest, we see what he sees. And yet, the narrator peppers the story with language and comments that question the evidence of Brown's senses. In other words, the narrator directly asks the reader to question and evaluate Brown's experiences and to make a determinations about the veracity of the events. Why does the narrator refuse to provide answers for the readers? How might you read this refusal as a way of making ambiguity itself a theme of the story?

You might tie this question to issues of faith and doubt. Without commenting definitively on the events, the narrator causes us to doubt the evidence of Brown's senses. Examine the language of doubt in the story. How does it work? What is its effect? Similarly, you might draw parallels between the reader's situation and Brown's. Like him, we must interpret his experiences. Like Brown, we are unsure "[w]hether Faith obeyed" his command or not. You might also consider the color imagery in the text. How might it support an assertion that ambiguity is one of the story's themes?

Character

Both Goodman Brown and Faith can prove engaging subjects for a study of character. Hawthorne clearly encourages readers to observe and assess Brown. You may find that separating Faith from her allegorical associations and assessing her as a character, as the woman wed to Goodman Brown, provides a fresh way to analyze her. Begin any exploration of character by noting the characters' language and actions. Chart their interactions with and assessments of other characters. Examine what the narrator has to say about them. This should allow you to ask appropriate questions about Hawthorne's portrayal of character and focus an analytical thesis about his use of a particular character.

Sample Topics:

1. **Goodman Brown as a character:** Readers routinely mention the allegorical significance of Brown's name. He is "young"— innocent and naïve. While "Goodman" is an honorific term of address, meaning husband, the term bears obvious allegorical weight in the story—Brown, it implies, is a good man. Finally, the last name Brown seems to mark Hawthorne's character as a kind of representative everyman. Does the story provide us with any evidence that Brown is not so innocent, even before his encounter with the devil? How might the shortcomings in his character explain his reaction to his experiences in the woods?

   In order to answer these questions, you must analyze the initial scenes as well as Brown's encounters in the forest. Think about his reasons for journeying into the woods in the first place and analyze his initial attitudes toward Faith (both the woman and the abstract principle). Consider his reactions and his interpretations in the woods. What do Brown's responses to the devil's assurance that he has "a very general acquaintance here in New-England" and to the appearances of his fellow townspeople tell us about Brown and his faith? What does the "communion" of the witch meeting promise for Brown? Is that promise fulfilled? Examine the narrator's assessment of Brown's behavior in the woods and his life after "the night of that fearful dream."

2. **Faith as a character:** Most readings of the story consider Faith's allegorical role in the story. Consider her as a character, as young Goodman Brown's wife. Brown calls her "a blessed angel on earth." Do you agree with his assessment of his wife? Why or why not?

   An examination of Faith's qualities as a character will depend largely on the beginning of the tale. Does the story's opening provide you with any evidence to suggest that Faith knows and understands the nature of her husband's errand into the woods? Does she, as Brown suggests, "doubt" her husband? If you believe that Faith does understand the nature of Brown's experiences in the forest, you might wish to compare her response to human sinfulness to Brown's response.

History and Context

Having some familiarity with Puritan New England and with Hawthorne's attitudes toward Puritanism will clearly help you analyze "Young Goodman Brown." Biographies of Hawthorne should provide sufficient insight into Hawthorne's relationship with Puritan attitudes and values. Similarly, Hawthorne's decision to set the story in Salem, Massachusetts, has resonance for a story about a young Puritan's encounter with the devil and a witch meeting in the forest, so some research about the Salem witch trials of 1692 would be another good place to focus your historical investigation. Remember, though, to focus your paper on the text, using the historical context as a lens through which to view the story.

Sample Topics:

1. **The Salem witch trials:** Hawthorne sets "Young Goodman Brown" in and around Salem village, and he uses the names of historical residents of Salem who were accused in the hyste-

ria. How might an understanding of the Salem witch trials of 1692 help to enhance your understanding of "Young Goodman Brown"?

Much of the evidence used to convict the accused in Salem was spectral evidence, evidence that the image or specter of the accused had appeared to the accuser in a dream or vision. Might you accuse young Goodman Brown of "convicting" people based on spectral evidence? What does this say about the quality of Brown's judgments of his neighbors? Examine the language of Hawthorne's story carefully, perhaps even comparing it to the language of the witch trials in 1692. How do the language and the imagery of the tale help you to draw comparisons between the witch trials and Brown's experiences in the forest?

Language, Symbols, and Imagery

Like Hester's scarlet *A*, Faith's pink ribbons are another of Hawthorne's elusive symbols. Hawthorne uses other evocative language in "Young Goodman Brown" as well. If you plan to analyze Hawthorne's use of a particular symbol or image, read closely, taking note of its role in the story. Where does the image appear? What language is used to describe it? Is the image common, carrying traditional connotations, as the wilderness of "Young Goodman Brown," or is it unique to the author or the text? If the image is traditional, evaluate whether Hawthorne changes or develops these common connotations. If the image is unique, ask why Hawthorne may have shaped that particular image. Why, for instance, is Faith associated with pink ribbons? Do ribbons have particular uses or connotations that Hawthorne hopes to evoke? Why would he choose *pink* ribbons specifically? Remember that a strong paper on imagery or symbolism will propose some conclusions about their function or meaning.

Sample Topics:

1. **The forest and Salem village:** Goodman Brown's journey takes him from Salem village to forest and back to the village. What is the significance of each of these settings? Why does the major-

ity of the story take place in the forest? What does the forest represent?

Many scholars have described Brown's journey as archetypal. Indeed, the structure, setting, and imagery of his journey share a great deal with archetypal fairy tales like "Little Red Riding Hood." You might begin by considering the similarities between Brown's experiences and those of Little Red Riding Hood. Both characters take trips from home to the woods and back again. (Depending on the version, Little Red Riding Hood does not always make it home.) Do the woods represent the same thing in "Little Red Riding Hood" and "Young Goodman Brown"? How might you compare the wolf and the devil that Brown encounters? Think, too, about how the Puritans might have viewed the forest. Consider what their actual relationship with the forest might have been like. What symbolic resonances might they, in turn, have seen in the woods? Analyze Hawthorne's language carefully. How does his language and imagery help to characterize the forest? Does it partake of Puritan attitudes about the wilderness? Pay particular attention to the passage after Brown sees Faith's pink ribbons fluttering down from the cloud. How does that description of the forest compare to earlier descriptions? How might the differences in these descriptions help you to assign a metaphorical significance to the woods? During this scene, the narrator says that "Goodman Brown cried out; and his cry was lost to his own ear, by its unison with the cry of the desert." Can you explain this reference to "the cry of the desert"? How does it add resonance to the metaphorical implications of the forest in this passage? Finally, you could develop a response to this question by considering other aspects of the setting, particularly Hawthorne's use of day and night, darkness and sunshine. How might you connect the forest, the nighttime setting, and the language of dream?

2. **Dreams:** It is quite possible to read all of Brown's experiences in the woods as a dream, and there is a great deal of evidence

in the story to support such a reading. Nor is Brown the only dreamer in the story; Faith, too, speaks of her dreams. What is the function of dreams in "Young Goodman Brown"? Are they, as they are in "The Birth-Mark," prophetic, or do they serve another function?

You might want to approach this question by first compiling evidence that suggests that Brown's experiences in the woods can be convincingly interpreted as a dream. There is, of course, no way to definitively prove that Brown only dreamed the witch meeting, so this evidence should serve to substantiate the credibility of your interpretation. It should serve as background to your argument about the function or the role of dreams in the story. Your analysis of the significance of Brown's dream will probably share much with this chapter's earlier discussion of Brown's character and his psyche. Do dreams reveal the subconscious or inner worlds of Brown and Faith?

3. **Color imagery:** From the name of his title character to Faith's pink ribbons to the hues of the forest and the witch meeting, Hawthorne fills "Young Goodman Brown" with color imagery. How does Hawthorne's use of color in "Young Goodman Brown" support his purpose or his themes?

Pink is not a color laden with obvious symbolism like black, red, or white. Why, then, do you think Faith's ribbons are pink? What do you associate with the color pink? What connotations does it carry? What do you think the ribbons imply about Faith's character or about the nature of faith? Brown, while a common name that certainly works to support a characterization of the title character as an "everyman," is also without strong symbolic associations. Why might Hawthorne associate his title character with the color brown? What colors are associated with the forest and the witch meeting? Do they carry strong symbolic meanings? How and why are the colors of the forest different from those associated with Faith and with Goodman Brown?

Compare and Contrast Essays

Most of Hawthorne's historical fiction considers issues of faith, doubt, and human sin, so "Young Goodman Brown" provides ample opportunity for comparison with other Hawthorne works. *The Scarlet Letter* and "The Minister's Black Veil" examine sin in the context of Puritan beliefs. "Rappaccini's Daughter" and "The Artist of the Beautiful" treat faith from a more secular perspective, and these, too, could form the grounds of an effective compare and contrast paper. Brown's youth and naïveté also supply a connection to a number of the author's short works. Whatever topic you choose, be sure to structure your argument around significant similarities and/or differences in order to make an analytical point about the texts.

Sample Topics:

1. **Sympathy and the discovery of sin:** When the devil welcomes Brown and the veiled image of Faith to the "communion of your race," he promises, "By the sympathy of your human hearts for sin, ye shall scent out all the places—whether in church, bedchamber, street, field, or forest—where crime has been committed." Later, the narrator says that "the Shape of Evil . . . [prepared] to lay the mark of baptism upon their foreheads, that they might be partakers of the mystery of sin, more conscious of the secret guilt of others, both in deed and thought, than they could now be of their own." Examine Brown's experience of sin and his apparent ability to "scent out" the sin of others and compare it with the similar experiences of other Hawthorne characters. How does Brown's experience with and knowledge of sin affect his interaction with others? Does he, as the devil suggests, have a "sympathy" for sin?

   In chapter 5 of *The Scarlet Letter,* Hester Prynne feels that her sin has given her a second sense about others' sin. Indeed, by the novel's end, others seek her out for her counsel. How might you compare Hester and Brown in their experience and understanding of sin and transgression? You could also compare Goodman Brown's experiences in the forest with those of Arthur Dimmesdale in *The Scarlet Letter;* both emerge from the forest as changed men. Similarly, Reverend Hooper of "The

Minister's Black Veil" could provide an interesting topic for comparison.

2. **Laughter:** After Brown sees Faith's pink ribbons fluttering from the cloud above and cries, "My Faith is gone!" he runs through the forest. The narrator's description of his flight through the woods is striking: "And maddened with despair, so that he laughed loud and long, did Goodman Brown grasp his staff and set forth again." Compare the use of laughter in this tale with that in "My Kinsman, Major Molineux."

Laughter seems a strange response to despair, and yet Robin Molineux also laughs loudly at what seems the lowest moment of his journey. After he sees the major in his "tar-and-feathery dignity" Robin "sent forth a shout of laughter that echoed through the street; every man shook his sides, every man emptied his lungs, but Robin's shout was the loudest." What conclusions can you draw about the laughter of Robin Molineux and Goodman Brown? You might develop your response to this question by examining the other parallels between the experiences of Brown and Robin. Both are on a nighttime journey described through the language of dream. While Robin moves from countryside to town, Brown travels from town to forest. Compare the imagery of the city in "My Kinsman, Major Molineux" with that of the forest in "Young Goodman Brown." How do they compare? What does your comparison suggest about the nature and the effects of their journeys?

3. **Initiation stories:** Compare Hawthorne's treatment of the theme of initiation and the journey from innocence to experience in "Young Goodman Brown" with that in another of his works.

A response to this question must consider some of the issues presented in the discussions of theme and of Brown's character. "My Kinsman, Major Molineux," "Rappaccini's Daughter," and "Roger Malvin's Burial" all focus around naïve young men and their experiences in the larger world. You could also examine Hawthorne's treatment of innocence and experience in *The Marble Faun*, especially as it is manifested in Donatello's story line.

4. **Faith and doubt:** Compare Hawthorne's treatment of faith and doubt in "Young Goodman Brown" with his treatment of the same theme in another work.

As the introduction to this section indicates, *The Scarlet Letter* and "The Minister's Black Veil" both examine sin in the context of Puritan beliefs. Both would provide solid grounds for comparison. Two of Hawthorne's later tales, "Rappaccini's Daughter" and "The Artist of the Beautiful" also treat faith and skepticism quite overtly. The former story provides a particularly interesting comparison with "Young Goodman Brown," since both examine the issue of faith within love relationships.

5. **Dreams:** Compare Hawthorne's use of dream and dreamscapes in "Young Goodman Brown" and another Hawthorne work.

As mentioned above, both Brown's journey and that of Robin Molineux share similar qualities, and the narrator of each tale remarks on the dreams of the main characters. Both stories could be aptly described as nightmare journeys. You could also examine Hawthorne's treatment of dreams in "The Birth-Mark," "Roger Malvin's Burial," or "The May-Pole of Merry Mount."

Bibliography and Online Resources for "Young Goodman Brown"

Baym, Nina. *The Shape of Hawthorne's Career*. Ithaca, NY: Cornell UP, 1976.

Bell, Michael Davitt. *Hawthorne and the Historical Romance of New England*. Princeton, NJ: Princeton UP, 1971.

Bell, Millicent, ed. *Hawthorne and the Real, Bicentennial Essays*. Columbus: Ohio State UP, 2005.

Boyer, Paul, and Stephen Nissenbaum. *Salem Possessed: The Social Origins of Witchcraft*. Cambridge, MA: Harvard UP, 1974.

Colacurcio, Michael. *The Province of Piety: Moral History in Hawthorne's Early Tales.* Cambridge, MA: Harvard UP, 1984. (Reprint: Durham, NC: Duke UP, 1995.)

Connolly, Thomas Edmund. *Nathaniel Hawthorne: Young Goodman Brown.* Columbus, OH: Merrill Publishing Company, 1968.

Crews, Frederick C. *The Sins of Fathers: Hawthorne's Psychological Themes.* New York: Oxford UP, 1966.

Doubleday, Frank Neal. *Hawthorne's Early Tales, A Critical Study.* Durham, NC: Duke UP, 1972.

Fogle, Richard Harter. *Hawthorne's Fiction: The Light and the Dark.* Norman: U of Oklahoma P, 1952.

Fossum, Robert H. *Hawthorne's Inviolable Circle: the Problem of Time.* Deland, FL: Everett/Edwards Inc., 1972.

Gollin, Rita K. "Figurations of Salem in 'Young Goodman Brown' and 'The Custom-House.'" Hawthorne in Salem. Available online. URL: http://www. hawthorneinsalem.com/Literature/Faith&Religion/FrameworkOfFaith/ Scholars.html. Downloaded November 8, 2006.

———. *Nathaniel Hawthorne and the Truth of Dreams.* Baton Rouge: Louisiana State UP, 1979.

Herbert, T. Walter. *Dearest Beloved: The Hawthornes and the Making of the Middle Class Marriage.* Berkeley: U of California P, 1993.

Hoffman, Daniel G. *Form and Fable in American Fiction.* Oxford: Oxford UP, 1961.

Levin, David. *In Defense of Historical Literature.* New York: Hill and Wang, 1967.

Male, Roy R. *Hawthorne's Tragic Vision.* New York: Norton, 1957.

Matthiessen, F. O. *American Renaissance: Art and Expression in the Age of Emerson and Whitman.* New York: Oxford UP, 1941.

Miller, Edwin H. *Salem Is My Dwelling Place: A Life of Nathaniel Hawthorne.* Iowa City: U of Iowa P, 1991.

Millington, Richard H., ed. *The Cambridge Companion to Nathaniel Hawthorne.* Cambridge: Cambridge UP, 2004.

Modugno, Joseph R. "The Salem Witchcraft Hysteria of 1692 and 'Young Goodman Brown.'" Hawthorne in Salem. Available online. URL: http://www. hawthorneinsalem.com/Literature/Quakers&Witches/YoungGoodman Brown/Introduction.html. Downloaded November 8, 2006.

Moore, Margaret. "Salem and Hawthorne." Hawthorne in Salem. Available online. URL: http://www.hawthorneinsalem.com/ScholarsForum/SalemAnd Hawthorne.html. Downloaded November 8, 2006.

Pearce, Roy Harvey. *Hawthorne Centenary Essays.* Columbus: Ohio State UP, 1964.

Pease, Donald E. *Visionary Compacts: American Renaissance Writings in Cultural Context.* Madison: U of Wisconsin P, 1987.

"Salem Witchcraft Hysteria." National Geographic.com. Available online. URL: http://www.salemweb.com/memorial/. Downloaded June 26, 2006.

"The Salem Witch Trials 1692: A Chronology of Events." Salem Web. Available online. URL: http://www.salemweb.com/memorial/. Downloaded November 15, 2006.

"Salem Witch Trials Home Page." Famous American Trials. Available online. URL: http://www.law.umkc.edu/faculty/projects/ftrials/salem/SALEM.HTM. Downloaded November 15, 2006.

Walker, Pierre A. "Why We Still Read Hawthorne 150 Years Later." Hawthorne in Salem. Available Online. URL: http://www.hawthorneinsalem.com/ScholarsForum/MMD2004.html. Downloaded November 8, 2006.

Waggoner, Hyatt H. *Hawthorne: A Critical Study.* Cambridge, MA: Belknap Press of Harvard University, 1955.

Wineapple, Brenda. *Hawthorne: A Life.* New York: Knopf, 2003.

Von Frank, Albert J. *Critical Essays on Hawthorne's Short Stories.* Boston: G.K. Hall, 1991.

"WAKEFIELD"

READING TO WRITE

"WAKEFIELD" HAS long perplexed readers. Its structure and style of narration are among its most perplexing qualities. The narrator lays out the plot of the entire story in the first paragraph. "In some old magazine or newspaper," he begins, "I recollect a story, told as truth, of a man—let us call him Wakefield—who absented himself for a long time, from his wife." The narrator continues the paragraph, contemplating this "strangest instance of marital delinquency," and then informs the reader that "after so great a gap in his matrimonial felicity . . . he entered the door one evening, quietly, as from a day's absence, and became a loving spouse till death." The plot, then, can hardly be Hawthorne's main interest or his method of maintaining his reader's interest, for the ending is already known. Or is it? Despite saying that the man we will call Wakefield returned home and became "a loving spouse till death," the rest of Hawthorne's story never again returns to that homecoming, and at the end the narrator demurs from showing us Wakefield's return: "We will not follow our friend across the threshold," he says in the final paragraph. The final line of the sketch furnishes a moral that seems at odds with the newspaper account "told as truth." Wakefield, the narrator says, became "the Outcast of the Universe." What, finally, seems to be Hawthorne's purpose in telling and retelling this anecdote? A careful reading of the first paragraph may provide some clues about Hawthorne's method and purpose. Consider how the first paragraph directs the reader's attention:

In some old magazine or newspaper, I recollect a story, told as truth, of a man—let us call him Wakefield—who absented himself for a long time, from his wife. The fact, thus abstractly stated, is not very uncommon, not—without a proper distinction of circumstances—to be condemned either as naughty or nonsensical. Howbeit, this, though far from the most aggravated, is perhaps the strangest instance, on record, of marital delinquency; and, moreover as remarkable a freak as may be found in the whole list of human oddities. The wedded couple lived in London. The man, under pretense of going a journey, took lodgings in the next street to his own house, and there, unheard of by his wife or friends, and without the shadow of a reason for such self-banishment, dwelt upwards of twenty years. During that period, he beheld his home every day, and frequently the forlorn Mrs. Wakefield. And after so great a gap in his matrimonial felicity—when his death was reckoned certain, his estate settled, his name dismissed from memory, and his wife, long, long ago, resigned to her autumnal widowhood—he entered the door one evening, quietly, as from a day's absence, and became a loving spouse till death.

The very first sentence of the story alerts the reader to three particular aspects of the tale. First, it announces that Hawthorne's tale is a retelling of a magazine or newspaper story "told as truth." It also introduces the central character and his behavior. Finally, it briefly introduces his wife. Perhaps the most arresting of these three elements is Hawthorne's indication that the tale is a retelling of a magazine story, for Hawthorne is drawing attention to his story's status as a twice-told tale. As a reader, you might have two questions already. First of all, why does Hawthorne emphasize that the "story" was "told as truth"? Is he casting doubt on the veracity of the original tale by saying that it was "told as truth" and by labeling it as a "story"? Astute readers will also notice how pointedly Hawthorne draws our attention to his own version's status as a retelling and an embellishment when he introduces the main character. The story is "of a man—let us call him Wakefield." Here he emphasizes that the name is his own addition. Throughout the paragraph, Hawthorne continues to draw attention to his own storytelling and to the differences between his story and its predecessor, perhaps giving us insight into his motivations for retelling the tale. The original story line, "thus abstractly stated," carries no particular meaning or significance. It is "not very uncommon, nor—without a proper distinction of circumstances—to be condemned either as naughty or nonsensical." Is Hawthorne's purpose in telling the story, then, to move it from the abstract by providing "a proper distinction of circumstances"? Should his reader, finally, be able to determine whether Wakefield's actions are "naughty or nonsensical"? We might wonder, finally, if the very process of storytelling is one of Hawthorne's subjects in "Wakefield" since he so overtly draws attention to his processes and his purposes.

Hawthorne's comment that Wakefield's behavior cannot be "condemned as either naughty or nonsensical" without "a proper distinction of circumstances" should encourage us to question whether Hawthorne's retelling provides that "proper distinction of circumstances," thereby allowing us to evaluate both Wakefield and his behavior. Does the initial paragraph provide any indication of Hawthorne's assessment of Wakefield and his behavior? Hawthorne's word choice here might also give you pause. Think about the connotations of "naughty." Synonyms of "naughty" include "bad," "wicked," and "disobedient." If Hawthorne had chosen one of those words to describe Wakefield's behavior might we think about it differently? With whom is naughty behavior most associated? How does Hawthorne's word choice affect both the tone of his work and the attitude toward its protagonist? Continue to evaluate the words Hawthorne chooses to describe both Wakefield and his behavior. He says that Wakefield's 20-year absence is "as remarkable a freak as may be found in the whole list of human oddities." How do the words "freak" and "oddity" characterize Wakefield's behavior? What does Hawthorne's word choice tell us about his attitudes toward Wakefield's behavior and his reasons for examining it? Similarly, you might seek clues about Wakefield's character through the author's choice of name, especially since the first sentence emphasizes the choice of that name—"let us call him Wakefield." Why might Hawthorne have chosen this name for a character who "without a shadow of a reason" left his wife and home for more than 20 years, only to return "when his death was reckoned certain, his estate settled, his name dismissed from memory, and his wife, long, long ago, resigned to her autumnal widowhood"? What potential resonance might the name "Wakefield" have for such a man? Further, why might

Hawthorne describe his actions as a "self-banishment"? What are the effects of such "self-banishment"? Is it significant that Wakefield returns only after he is assumed dead? The paragraph also provides insight into Wakefield's activities during his "marital delinquency," indicating that he "took lodgings in the next street to his house," and that "he beheld his home every day." How does this description help to build the portrait of Wakefield? The paragraph concludes by telling the reader that "he entered the door one evening . . . and became a loving spouse till death." Most readers will probably question the likelihood of such a return. How likely is it that a man who left his wife for 20 years, "without the shadow of a reason," will return and be a "loving husband"?

This last question might also lead you to inquire about Mrs. Wakefield. How might you imagine her response to her husband's return? What do we learn of Mrs. Wakefield? She is scarcely mentioned in this first paragraph. We learn that Wakefield "absented himself for a long time, from his wife." We learn that Wakefield observes his home daily, "and frequently the forlorn Mrs. Wakefield." We learn that she "resigned herself to her autumnal widowhood." The narrator remarks that Wakefield's disappearance was "far from the most aggravated" in history. Does this comment characterize Mrs. Wakefield at all, albeit vaguely? Is the reader free to flesh out her character just as Hawthorne feels justified in naming Wakefield and developing the narrative of his self-banishment?

Developing such questions in response to the first paragraph of "Wakefield" should facilitate your evaluation of the rest of this brief tale, providing you with specific aspects of the tale to analyze.

TOPICS AND STRATEGIES

The topic selections below should provide you with ideas for papers on "Wakefield" or on its connections with other Hawthorne texts. These sample topics are relatively broad, so you will need to shape and focus them as you develop the purpose and direction of your paper.

Themes

As the previous section indicates, two themes of "Wakefield" that become apparent are identity and storytelling. Additionally, you might find that an investigation into identity in "Wakefield" could lead you into an exploration of the significance of human community, especially given Hawthorne's final comment that Wakefield became "the Outcast of the Universe." As you consider questions of identity, then, consider the relationship between human identity and human community. As you sort out the story's statements about any of the themes listed below, be sure that you examine how other elements in the story, like character and imagery, help to develop the story's treatment of the theme.

Sample Topics:

1. **Identity:** Hawthorne's tale begins by labeling his protagonist— "let us call him Wakefield." In the two following paragraphs, he speculates about his hero's character and asks, "What sort of a man was Wakefield? We are free to shape our own idea, and call it by his name." At other points in the story Hawthorne seems to comment on Wakefield's identity; he sketches Mrs. Wakefield's assessment of her husband's character, and he considers Wakefield's own self-assessments. What does Hawthorne seem to say about the nature of human identity in "Wakefield"? What factors construct and shape an individual's identity?

   This question asks you to consider individual assessments of Wakefield's character, in essence asking, "Who is Wakefield?" You would also do well to examine the language and imagery of the tale. Consider the story's treatment of disguise, as well as the language of death and ghostliness. Is Wakefield still the same man once he leaves his home for an extended period of time? After he alters his appearance? After others consider him dead? Why or why not? Where and how does the story comment on Wakefield's identity? You could also consider the story's treatment of Mrs. Wakefield in response to this question. How does Wakefield's disappearance affect her identity? How do the language and the imagery that surround Mrs. Wakefield help to develop your response to this question?

2. **Storytelling:** How might you consider "Wakefield" as a story about storytelling? What does Hawthorne say about the nature and the function of storytelling?

An examination of this issue should start with the questions that the "Reading to Write" section posed about the story's status as a twice-told tale. These overt comments on the construction of the tale continue throughout "Wakefield." Hawthorne invites the reader to "ramble with me through the twenty years of Wakefield's vagary," and he questions his hero's character, asking, "What sort of man was Wakefield?" and immediately answering, "We are free to shape our own idea and call it by his name." Where else do you see Hawthorne drawing attention to the construction and the shape of his story? Taken together, what do these aspects of the tale say about the nature of storytelling and about its relationship to truth? You might also want to take into consideration the fact that Hawthorne's version of the tale ends differently than the version he tells us of in the first paragraph. Why?

3. **Voyeurism:** Wakefield seems to pass most of his time during his 20-year absence observing his home and his wife. Consider Wakefield's penchant for observation and spying. What does Hawthorne say about this interest of Wakefield's and about its effect upon his character?

While you will need to analyze Wakefield's voyeurism and his assessments of the things he sees, you should also consider the tale's other uses of the language of watching, seeing, and being seen. How does such an analysis help to develop your understanding of Hawthorne's commentary on the ethics and the effects of watching? Consider whether Wakefield is astute in his observations and his assessments. Consider his own fear of being seen. Are Hawthorne and his readers in any way guilty of some of Wakefield's sins? Do we, too, become watchers who draw conclusions about those we watch?

Character

While the story clearly asks readers to evaluate Wakefield's character, you might find it interesting to analyze Mrs. Wakefield's position in the story as well. Although she seems to play a minor role, consider how her position reflects upon some of Hawthorne's larger themes. As you study either of these characters, be sure to note their own words and actions as well as the narrator's assessments of them. You might also find that the language and patterns of imagery associated with them are helpful to your analysis.

Sample Topics:

1. **Wakefield as a character:** Evaluate Wakefield as a character. Does he grow as a result of his "self-banishment"? What elements of his character are responsible for his growth or the lack thereof?

You might begin a response to this question by considering Wakefield's name. Does he in any way "wake" as a result of his experiences? Is this a story about awakenings? Closely examine his return home at the end of the tale. What motivates his return? Consider this passage's treatment of "the dwelling which he still calls his own" in the final paragraphs. What does this treatment tell us about Wakefield's homecoming and his attitudes toward and understanding of the notion of home? Examine Mrs. Wakefield's appearance in these final paragraphs. We see her as "a grotesque shadow of good Mrs. Wakefield . . . an admirable caricature." How and why might this image be significant? Might it tell us anything about Wakefield? You could also consider alternate connotations of the word *wake,* which constitutes the first part of Wakefield's name. A wake can also be a watch kept over the body of a deceased person or the track or course left behind something that has passed. How might these meanings have resonance for Wakefield's character and his development over the course of the story? Consider, too, the language and the imagery associated with Wakefield, especially the language of death and of ghostliness. What do these imply about him? Finally, the narrator sometimes makes fairly overt comments about Wakefield's character, the changes that he undergoes, and his awareness of these changes. Consider these comments in light of the other issues discussed in this section.

2. **Mrs. Wakefield as a character:** Examine Mrs. Wakefield as a character in the story. What does her role in the story tell us about her, about her husband, or about the focus of Hawthorne's tale?

Throughout the tale, Mrs. Wakefield appears mainly through the eyes of Wakefield. Early in the tale, Hawthorne describes her through her assessment of her husband and his character. After this passage, though, Hawthorne tells us, "But, our business is with the husband," and he follows Wakefield down the street. Can you develop a character for Mrs. Wakefield, as Hawthorne does for Wakefield? Why or why not? What insight does Hawthorne provide into Mrs. Wakefield's response to her husband's disappearance? What do you make of his commentary or his lack thereof? His last characterization of her is as a shadowy reflection on the ceiling: "On the ceiling, appears a grotesque shadow of good Mrs. Wakefield. The cap, the nose and chin, and broad waist, form an admirable caricature, which dances, more-over, with the up-flickering and down-sinking blaze, almost too merrily for the shade of an elderly widow." How might this last image be significant? What does it say about Mrs. Wakefield and her role in the story? Does Mrs. Wakefield have an identity apart from Wakefield? Why or why not?

Symbolism, Imagery, and Language

A close examination of the language of "Wakefield" can deepen your understanding of the story's themes and purposes. If you would like to write about Hawthorne's use of imagery, identify patterns of imagery that seem significant in the story, and then reread the text analyzing the function of the imagery within the story.

Sample Topics:

1. **Images of the city:** In the first paragraph Hawthorne tells us that the story is set in London. Examine the language and the imagery of the city and its citizens in "Wakefield." What does it say about the nature of urban living? How does the story's

urban setting and the imagery that surrounds it relate to the larger thematic issues of the story?

Had the story not been set in a large city it seems impossible that Wakefield could live "in the next street to his own house" and remain "unheard of by his wife or friends," and this might provide a way to connect the setting and the imagery to the larger themes of the story. Examine the description of Wakefield after he bids adieu to his wife and hurries down the city street. Consider his fears of being seen and discovered and the near misses that he has with such discovery. Where else does Hawthorne use imagery to describe the city or its citizens? How can you connect this imagery to questions of theme or character?

2. **Imagery of death:** In the opening paragraph, Hawthorne says that Wakefield does not return home until "his death was reckoned certain, his estate settled, his name dismissed from memory, and his wife, long, long ago, resigned to her autumnal widowhood." Examine the language and imagery of death and of ghostliness in the story and consider how they reflect upon or develop issues of theme or character.

   You might approach this question in a number of ways. Some might consider Wakefield's "vagary" a kind of death wish, and his return a return from the dead. How and why might this be so? What insight does such a reading of the story provide about Wakefield's character? Quite a few times, the story describes Wakefield through the language of ghostliness. What is the effect of these descriptions? What do they say about Wakefield's character and his relationships with others? You might want to focus on Mrs. Wakefield's illness during her husband's absence. At one point, Wakefield decides that "[h]e will not go back until she be frightened half to death." When he sees the physician and the apothecary visiting he asks, "Dear woman! Will she die?" How does Mrs. Wakefield's near-death experience function within the text?

Compare and Contrast Essays

Although "Wakefield" is an early Hawthorne work and many scholars consider it a sketch rather than a fully developed story, Hawthorne treats a number of themes and character types here that he will develop in later works. Consequently, "Wakefield" provides useful material for compare and contrast essays. As you develop your focus, be sure that you shape a thesis that discusses the significance of the similarities and differences that you observe.

Sample Topics:

1. **Wakefield as a precursor of other men in Hawthorne's fiction:** Consider Wakefield as a precursor of some of Hawthorne's other male characters. What elements does he share with them? What is Hawthorne saying through their character traits?

   Hawthorne's language often seems to ask that we not take Wakefield too seriously. And yet, for all the mockery that Hawthorne levels at Wakefield, the "crafty nincompoop" shares traits with some of Hawthorne's more well-developed characters. Perhaps the best subjects for comparison are Roger Chillingworth of *The Scarlet Letter* and Miles Coverdale who narrates *The Blithedale Romance*. Both Chillingworth and Coverdale share Wakefield's propensity for voyeurism, as well as other personality traits. Chillingworth, like Wakefield, has severed his relationship with his former life. A paper that considers Wakefield as a precursor to either of these men should have plenty of material for consideration.

2. **Masking of identity:** Consider the theme of the masking of identity in "Wakefield" and another of Hawthorne's works. What is Hawthorne saying about the nature of identity and the use of masks?

   You might consider the imagery of masks, disguises, and veils in response to this question. Roger Chillingworth, like Wakefield, masks his true identity just as Wakefield dons a disguise to separate himself from his former life. Both *The Blithedale*

Romance and "The Minister's Black Veil" are filled with the imagery of veils and veiling, and in both this imagery seems to comment on and connect with issues of identity.

Bibliography for "Wakefield"

Bell, Millicent. *Hawthorne's View of the Artist.* Albany: SUNY P, 1962.

Colacurcio, Michael. *The Province of Piety: Moral History in Hawthorne's Early Tales.* Cambridge, MA: Harvard UP, 1984. (Reprint: Durham, NC: Duke UP, 1995.)

Doubleday, Neal Frank. *Hawthorne's Early Tales: A Critical Study.* Durham, NC: Duke UP, 1972.

Easton, Alison. "Hawthorne and the question of women." *The Cambridge Companion to Nathaniel Hawthorne.* Ed. Richard H. Millington. Cambridge: Cambridge UP, 2004. 79–98.

Fogle, Richard Harter. *Hawthorne's Fiction: The Light and the Dark.* Norman: U of Oklahoma P, 1952.

Gatta, John. "'Busy and Selfish London': The Urban Figure in Hawthorne's 'Wakefield.'" *ESQ* 23 (1977): 164–72.

Harris, Kenneth Marc. *Hypocrisy and Self-Deception in Hawthorne's Fiction.* Charlottesville: U of Virginia P, 1988.

McCall, Dan. *Citizens of Somewhere Else: Nathaniel Hawthorne and Henry James.* Ithaca, NY: Cornell UP, 1990.

Morsberger, Robert. "Wakefield in the Twilight Zone." *American Transcendentalist Quarterly* 14 (1972): 6–8.

Newman, Lea. *A Reader's Guide to the Short Stories of Nathaniel Hawthorne.* Boston: G. K. Hall, 1979.

Perry, Ruth. "The Solitude of Hawthorne's 'Wakefield.'" *American Literature* 49 (1978): 613–619.

Schiller, Andrew. "The Moment and the Endless Voyage: A Study of Hawthorne's 'Wakefield.'" *Diameter* 1 (1951): 7–12.

Waggoner, Hyatt H. *Hawthorne: A Critical Study.* Cambridge, MA: Belknap Press of Harvard University, 1955.

"THE MAY-POLE OF MERRY MOUNT"

READING TO WRITE

HAWTHORNE'S CLEAR reliance on colonial history and personages in "The May-Pole of Merry Mount" may discourage modern-day readers who fear that, without a thorough knowledge of Puritan history, they will find the story impenetrable or irrelevant. However, Hawthorne's headnote to the story provides some insight into his use of history in the text; it addresses both his subject matter and his method. His subject, "the curious history of the early settlement of Mount Wollaston, or Merry Mount," he tells us, provides "admirable foundation for a philosophic romance." Further, he says that in his romance, the facts of history "have wrought themselves, almost spontaneously, into a sort of allegory." In other words, Hawthorne is using that "curious history" as a literary vehicle to discuss something else. A romance writer rather than a historian, Hawthorne seems to claim Mount Wollaston for the realm of romance. It is "a neutral territory, somewhere between the real world and fairy-land, where the Actual and the Imaginary may meet, and each imbue itself with the nature of the other" ("The Custom-House"). That the history of Mount Wollaston is a vehicle rather than the subject matter is implied even in Hawthorne's decision to forgo that name and use Merry Mount instead. The latter serves his purposes better because it begins to build a characterization of the colony and its people. To the reader just beginning the story, though, that purpose has not been clearly laid out.

Careful readers should find clues to Hawthorne's allegorical purpose in the story's first paragraph. The tale begins:

> Bright were the days at Merry Mount, when the May-Pole was the banner-staff of that gay colony! They who reared it, should their banner be triumphant, were to pour sunshine over New England's rugged hills, and scatter flower-seeds throughout the soil. Jollity and gloom were contending for an empire. Midsummer eve had come, bringing deep verdure to the forest, and roses in her lap, of a more vivid hue than the tender buds of Spring. But May, or her mirthful spirit, dwelt all the year round at Merry Mount, sporting with the Summer months, and reveling with Autumn, and basking in the glow of Winter's fireside. Through a world of toil and care, she flitted with a dreamlike smile, and came hither to find a home among the lightsome hearts of Merry Mount.

The first sentence clearly works to characterize Merry Mount and its inhabitants. Indeed, the first word alone might be sufficient to describe Merry Mount and the worldview of its inhabitants: "Bright." Notice that this first sentence—an exclamation—uses two more words that might serve as synonyms for "bright": "Merry" and "gay." The second sentence continues to describe the citizens of Merry Mount in language brimming with positive connotations: their intent was to "pour sunshine over" New England and to "scatter flower-seeds throughout the soil." Alert readers will note that the second sentence, though, without significantly darkening the language or the tone of the tale, introduces the hint of conflict: the citizens of Merry Mount would "pour sunshine" and "scatter flowers" "should their banner be triumphant." Over what, or whom, do these bright people need to triumph in order to spread their philosophy of good cheer? As you read the rest of the paragraph you should examine both the further characterization of Merry Mount and further hints about the conflict that may be facing the colony.

You need not read far to glean more about the conflict, for the next sentence announces, "Jollity and gloom were contending for an empire." The citizens of Merry Mount, clearly, represent jollity. Gloom stands in opposition, and yet the paragraph gives little insight into the nature of the conflict between jollity and gloom, nor does it indicate who or what represents this opposing gloom. Instead, the fourth sentence reverts to the setting, telling us "Midsummer eve had come." Why might Hawthorne set this story on Midsummer Eve? Is there any way in which Midsummer Eve—the day before the longest day of the year—might hint at or embody a conflict for these people whose goal is to "pour sunshine over" New England?

Further, after he says that Midsummer brought "deep verdure to the forest, and roses in her lap, of a more vivid hue than the tender buds of Spring," Hawthorne begins the next sentence with the word "But," signaling a turn or a change in direction: "But May, or her mirthful spirit, dwelt all the year round at Merry Mount." What does that contrast imply about the inhabitants of Merry Mount? This sentence continues to describe the perpetual May of Merry Mount. May was "sporting with the Summer months, and revelling with Autumn, and basking in the glow of Winter's fireside." What connotations do the words "sporting," "revelling," and "basking" carry? How does the description of May's activities help to characterize the citizens of Merry Mount? Further, even the verb tense that Hawthorne chooses here seems to reflect on the citizens of the colony. Why might he have used present participles ("ing" verbs) rather than past tense ("sported," "reveled," and "basked")? The next sentence extends this personification of May: "Through a world of toil and care, she flitted with a dreamlike smile, and came hither to find a home among the lightsome hearts of Merry Mount." Once again, consider the connotations of the language. How do "flitted," "dreamlike," and "lightsome" work to characterize both May and the colonists?

While such an analysis of this light and positive language works to characterize the inhabitants of Merry Mount, this analysis has done little to explain the conflict described in the second and third sentences. The paragraph seems to spend little time describing the forces of gloom. You might ask yourself if the paragraph provides any contrast to the light, positive language that surrounds the colonists of Mount Wollaston. As noted above, the narrator introduces the perpetual May of Merry Mount by contrasting it with Midsummer Eve and the inevitable change of seasons. Similarly, the final sentence says that the mirthful spirit of May "flitted with a dreamlike smile" "through a world of toil and care." How does this sentence present a contrast between Merry Mount and the world around it? What does this contrast tell us about Merry Mount's relationship with the world around it? Attentive readers might also notice that the second sentence briefly presents a similar contrast between the "sunshine" and "flowers" of the colonists' plans and "New England's rugged hills."

Taken together, all these details should work to undermine the reader's initial positive impression of Merry Mount. Though the narrator describes these people with language loaded with positive impressions, close reading shows them to be at odds with the realities of the world around them. Through these contrasts, Hawthorne prepares the reader for the confrontation that is to come between the jolly inhabitants of Merry Mount and the forces of gloom, John Endicott and his Puritan followers. The careful reader can see the shortcomings in further descriptions of both the inhabitants of Merry Mount and the Puritans.

TOPICS AND STRATEGIES

The paragraphs that follow provide some topic ideas for papers about "The May-Pole of Merry Mount." Remember that the topics discussed are quite broad. They offer you a framework to guide you as you read, reread, and analyze the story. Use these topics as springboards. You will need to narrow the focus of your writing, constructing an analytical thesis, and bearing in mind the proposed length of your paper.

Themes

To write about themes in "The May-Pole of Merry Mount," you will need to determine the subject of Hawthorne's "spontaneous sort of allegory." In other words, what do you think "The May-Pole of Merry Mount" is about? What can the confrontation between Merry Mount and Endicott's Puritans be said to represent? Not surprisingly, readers over the years have read Hawthorne's allegory in different ways. Many see in the tale a psychological allegory that chronicles warring impulses within the individual psyche. Others claim that the story is an historical allegory that presents the tensions in America's early history as the country began to shape its identity. You must decide what you think is the subject of Hawthorne's allegory and then proceed to determine the function of the story's various elements in that allegory. For instance, if you believe that the story is most productively read as a psychological allegory, what does Merry Mount represent? Whatever your belief about the story's import, a close analysis of the language and imagery should help you develop your analysis of the allegory.

Sample Topics:

1. **Psychological allegory:** Many critics believe that "The May-Pole of Merry Mount" is an allegory of the human psyche. If this is so, what elements in the human psyche are in conflict, and what conclusions does the story reach about this collision?

Even after you have decided to examine the story as a psychological allegory, you still have a good bit of narrowing to do to focus your paper. There are quite a few ways to interpret this story as a psychological allegory. First, you must decide what Merry Mount and the Puritans each represent; what two warring elements of an individual consciousness do they seem to embody? Analyzing the language and imagery should help you to draw conclusions here. You might begin by focusing on Merry Mount's obsession with May and the May-Pole, their "banner staff." What does May seem to represent? Why are the citizens of Merry Mount associated with flowers throughout the text? What might the May-Pole symbolize? How do the Puritans present a contrast to these elements of Merry Mount? At one point the narrator says that the whipping post "might be termed the Puritan May-Pole." What language does the story continually associate with the Puritans? How does this language contrast with that which describes the inhabitants of Merry Mount? What elements of the human personality does this language seem to suggest? Why? In addition you should examine the interaction between the Puritans and the "votaries of the May-Pole." How does the story describe their confrontation? What language does Hawthorne use? How is this language significant? In addition, you must examine the role of Edgar and Edith, the King and Queen of the May. What do they seem to represent, and why are they, unlike the other citizens of Merry Mount, taken into the Puritan community? What does their interaction with Endicott at the story's end suggest about the conclusions that Hawthorne is drawing?

2. **Historical allegory:** In the first paragraph Hawthorne writes, "Jollity and gloom were contending for an empire." Later the story seems to develop this assertion saying, "The future complexion of New England was involved in this important quarrel. Should the grisly saints establish their jurisdiction over the gay sinners, then would their spirits darken all the clime, and make it a land of clouded visages, of hard toil, of sermon and psalm, forever. But should the banner-staff of Merry Mount be fortunate, sunshine would break upon the hills, and flowers would beautify the forest, and late posterity do homage to the May-Pole." How might you read this story as a statement on American history and the establishment of American identity? What conclusions does Hawthorne seem to reach?

While there are clear historical grounds for the Puritan triumph at the end of the tale, in order to settle upon the allegorical significance of the story you must determine the allegorical grounds for the Puritan triumph at the story's end. Does it seem to make allegorical sense that the dark, stern, unyielding Puritans emerge triumphant at the end of this tale? What is Hawthorne saying about the "complexion" of America? What shortcomings does Hawthorne cast in the jollity of Merry Mount? Why would Merry Mount not make a suitable foundation for American identity? Again, you will need to analyze the language and imagery of the story quite closely, especially the language and imagery associated with Merry Mount. What shortcomings does the community at Merry Mount have? How does the imagery communicate these shortcomings? Once again, you must also consider the significance and role of Edgar and Edith. Why are they integrated into the Puritan community at the end? What does this integration imply about the "future complexion of New England"?

Character

Hawthorne's use of character is essential to the story's meaning. However, unlike stories such as "Young Goodman Brown" and "Rappaccini's Daughter," "The May-Pole of Merry Mount" seems to offer few characters for close analysis. The only individually drawn characters are Edgar, Edith, and John Endicott, and Endicott himself seems little more than a representation of the Puritans as a people. He is, the story says, "the Puritan of Puritans." Despite this, Edgar and Edith do provide room for character analysis. In addition, they allow the reader a window into the settlement of Merry Mount. You could easily consider the colony of Merry Mount a character in this story. Similarly, Endicott, as "the Puritan of Puritans" provides a starting place for an analysis of the Puritan community as a character within the story.

Sample Topics:

1. **Edgar and Edith as characters:** The festivities around the May-Pole on this Midsummer Eve celebrate the marriage of Edgar and Edith, the Lord and Lady of the May. The story tells us that "This wedlock was more serious than most affairs of Merry Mount. . . . The Lord and Lady of the May, though their titles must be laid down at sunset, were really and truly to be partners for the dance of life. . . ." Edgar and Edith are the most fully drawn of all the characters in this story. Why does Hawthorne develop them more fully? How does their characterization reflect upon both Merry Mount and Endicott's Puritans? What role do Edgar and Edith play in Hawthorne's allegory?

   Any discussion of Edgar and Edith's role must focus not only on the characters themselves, but also on their relationship. While you might choose to begin with the initial physical descriptions of the characters, this does little to develop or shed light upon their personalities or their roles within the story. They are young, beautiful, "gaily decorated" in rainbow colors and roses. They seem, in their roles as Lord and Lady of the May, like pure embodiments of Merry Mount itself. When do they begin to develop as more fully formed characters? In what ways do they present a contrast to the characters and attitudes of Merry Mount? You will need to examine their dialogue closely as you address these questions. What do their own words tell us about Edgar and Edith?

Similarly, you will need to analyze their interactions with Endicott and the Puritans at the tale's end. What qualities do Edgar and Edith have that allow them to be integrated into the Puritan community? How does Endicott, "the Puritan of Puritans," react to them? Why? Finally, examine the discussion of Edgar and Edith in the final paragraph of the story. How does that discussion, especially the final image of Edgar and Edith, help you develop your understanding of them and their role in the story?

2. **John Endicott as a character:** While Governor John Endicott was a historical character, Hawthorne clearly draws and shapes him to his own purposes in his allegory. What is Endicott's role in the story? Why is he the only Puritan in the tale who is given much of an individual personality? What is his effect on the tale's conclusion, and how does his role affect the apparent meaning of Hawthorne's story?

In order to explore Endicott's role in the story, you might start by analyzing the language and imagery associated with him. Clearly his characterizations as "the Puritan of Puritans" and "the man of iron" tell us a good deal about him and his relationship with his community. You might want to explore some of the less obvious statements about his personality and his role. As the Puritan band descends upon the revelers at Merry Mount, the narrator says that Endicott stood at "at the center of the circle, while the rout of monsters cowered around him, like a dread magician." What is surprising about this analogy? What is significant about it? Does this analogy develop or affect the characterization of Endicott?

3. **The Puritans, collectively, as a character:** How does Hawthorne portray the Puritans in "The May-Pole of Merry Mount"? Why, despite their apparently negative portrayal, does Hawthorne cast them as the victors in this struggle? Do you find any redeeming qualities in these "men of iron"?

Examining Endicott's characterization in this story could easily lead you into an investigation of the story's sketch of the Puritans as people. Clearly, Hawthorne uses much of the same language to describe both the Puritans and their leader. Besides the rather obvious images of hardness, darkness, and gloom, what other language characterizes the band of Puritans that makes its appearance in the tale? Does this language help to strengthen your first impression or does it add nuance to the portrayal of the Puritans?

4. **The colony of Merry Mount as a character:** You might consider Merry Mount and its citizens, collectively, as a character. On an initial reading of the tale, the characterization of the revelers at Merry Mount seems quite obvious—the story repeatedly associates them with light in contrast to the darkness of the Puritans. Upon closer inspection, though, Hawthorne complicates their portrait, deepening and darkening his portrait of Merry Mount. In what ways is the characterization of Merry Mount not so positive as it might first appear? What drawbacks does Hawthorne see in these perpetually merry people? How might their portrait affect the final outcome of the story?

This question asks you first to consider the nuances of the language of light that the story continually associates with the Merry Mounters. The word *light* has more than one meaning, and Hawthorne develops upon this multiplicity of meanings. What effect do these multiple meanings have upon the characterization of Merry Mount? How do the other patterns of imagery associated with these colonists help to develop this characterization? Taken together, what does this language say about the qualities of Merry Mount? Further, this question asks you to examine other language used to describe the citizens of Mount Wollaston. The first seven paragraphs of the story should prove useful here. What other descriptors does Hawthorne use in his portrayal of the revelers? What connotations do these descriptors carry? In what ways might these

142 Bloom's How to Write about Nathaniel Hawthorne

connotations aptly describe the attitudes and the activities of Merry Mount?

History and Context

As Hawthorne's headnote makes quite clear, historical incidents underlie "The May-Pole of Merry Mount." Examining the actual confrontation between Mount Wollaston and Plymouth Plantation might provide you with some insight into Hawthorne's purpose and methods in this story.

Sample Topics:

1. **The historical conflict between Plymouth Colony and Ma-re Mount/ "Merry Mount":** Hawthorne's tale provides a fictionalized account of an actual struggle between a settlement originally called Mount Wollaston (renamed Ma-re Mount by the adventurer Thomas Morton who established himself as its leader in 1626) and Plymouth Colony. The events that Hawthorne fictionalizes took place largely between 1627 and 1628; Hawthorne compressed a good bit of strife into a single event. Research the conflict between Plymouth and Merry Mount and compare it to Hawthorne's version. How do Hawthorne's changes help him to craft a specific message out of the historical conflict?

   While you can certainly find historians' summaries of the conflict between Plymouth and Merry Mount, your research should also quickly inform you that there were various accounts of this conflict written by those involved in it. William Bradford, a governor of Plymouth Colony, wrote a lengthy history of the colony between 1630 and 1650, *Of Plymouth Plantation.* In it, he recounts the events that took place at Merry Mount. ("Merry Mount" is Bradford's spelling.) Thomas Morton wrote his own version of the events. Not surprisingly, Bradford and Morton's accounts differ significantly. It is not clear that Hawthorne had access to either of these texts, but he read widely in New England history, and his headnote to the tale tells us that one of his sources for the story was Joseph Strutt's *The Sports and Pastimes of the People of England* (1801). Examining these texts in addition to reading historical analysis of the conflict between Merry Mount and Plymouth should provide helpful information in shaping a paper on Hawthorne's reshaping of history.

Language, Symbols, and Imagery

Hawthorne's allegory and his heavy reliance on imagery in this story make it nearly impossible to write a paper on this tale without considering the imagery, as the previous discussions of theme and character make clear. While some of Hawthorne's patterns of imagery—like his use of light and dark—are apparent in even the most cursory reading, others are discovered through closer analysis. Even his more apparent imagery, though, takes on deeper resonance through close analysis. This tale is not quite as straightforward as it often appears to first-time readers

Sample Topics:

1. **Light and darkness:** A favorite of Hawthorne's patterns of imagery, light and darkness, provides the primary imagery in "The May-Pole of Merry Mount." Its connotations are almost immediately apparent: Merry Mount is continually associated with light, while the Puritans are associated with darkness. The latter appear in the story like "a momentary cloud [that] had overcast the sunshine." How does Hawthorne complicate the ready contrast between light and dark in this story? What other connotations or meanings does "light" carry, and how does this duality of meaning affect our interpretation of Merry Mount? How does the other imagery associated with Merry Mount partake of and amplify this portrait of Merry Mount?

   A close reading soon reveals that the imagery of light and dark is much more complicated than it first appears. In addition to considering the other resonances of light, you might consider how Hawthorne alleviates some of the negativity associated with darkness. You might consider that the story takes place on Midsummer Eve and also the final paragraph of the story where the narrator makes a rather philosophical comment about the role of "moral gloom" in the world.

2. **Dreams:** Dreams and the language of dreaming play a pivotal role in "The May-Pole of Merry Mount." When the Puritans invade the revels at Merry Mount the narrator says, "Their darksome figures were intermixed with the wild shapes of their foes, and made the scene a picture of the moment, when waking thoughts start up amid the scattered fantasies of a dream." How does Hawthorne use dreams and dreaming in the story to underline his moral point? How does this language connect with some of the other imagery that the story depends upon?

Connecting the language of dreams with the other language used to characterize the revelers is perhaps one of the most fruitful ways to pursue this topic. What other language does Hawthorne use to describe the revelers and their merriment? Taken together, how do these descriptions paint a more thorough description of Merry Mount? What do they say about the viability of Merry Mount and its philosophy of pleasure?

3. **Order and disorder:** Examine the language of order and disorder in "The May-Pole of Merry Mount." How does this language work to characterize Merry Mount? The Puritans? How does it help to establish a moral framework for the story and explain the ending?

Like the examination of light and dark, an investigation of images of order and disorder will prove more complicated than it might first appear. You will discover that it is relatively easy to find language that comments on the disorder at Merry Mount. When Endicott and his followers appear, these men from New England's "well-ordered settlements" seem, strangely, to bring disorder. The narrator says that "The ring of gay masquers was disordered and broken." And Endicott is like a "dread magician" who stands "in the center of the circle while the rout of monsters cowered around him." What do you make of this apparent overturning of the patterns of order and disorder in the story? Further, you might want to explore the kinds of disorder that seem to be present at Merry Mount. How might this exploration help you to refine your analysis of order and disorder in "The May-Pole of Merry Mount"?

Compare and Contrast Essays

"The May-Pole of Merry Mount" provides opportunity for constructing compare and contrast essays about theme, character, and language. Because it, like much of Hawthorne's work, concerns itself with New England's history, his treatment of the Puritans and of American identity can be fruitfully compared with Hawthorne's other works. The story's imagery also allows you to draw connections with his other works. As always, be sure that you explore the reasons that underlie the similarities and differences that you note in your paper. Why are these similarities and/or differences important? What do they tell us about Hawthorne's points or his purposes?

Sample Topics:

1. **The Puritans:** Compare Hawthorne's characterization and treatment of the Puritans in "The May-Pole of Merry Mount" with that in some of his other works. What does this portrait share with his other Puritan portraits? What do these portraits tell us about his beliefs about the Puritans?

   If you choose to address this question, you must be careful to move beyond the obvious. In general, Hawthorne does not portray the Puritans in a sympathetic light. They are stern, unyielding "men of iron" who he frequently associates with darkness. As indicated earlier, though, Hawthorne's lack of sympathy does not always translate into completely negative treatment. Clearly, the Puritans in this story share qualities of the Puritan leaders in *The Scarlet Letter*, and in neither text do they seem to get very sympathetic treatment from the author. Both works, though, emphasize that the Puritans are not without their place, and both texts show that the forces they oppose are not without their own shortcomings. There are many other Hawthorne texts that could provide you with material for a paper such as this.

2. **The imagery of light and dark:** Compare the use of the language of light and darkness in "The May-Pole of Merry Mount" with that of another Hawthorne work.

As with his treatment of the Puritans, you will find some commonality among Hawthorne's texts in his use of light and dark. Once again, though, you would do well to be aware of the nuances in Hawthorne's language. This chapter has indicated that light and darkness function in a more complicated manner in this story than you might first expect. In the same way, "My Kinsman, Major Molineux" uses light and moonlight in a complex manner. In *The Scarlet Letter* sunshine, shadow, and moonlight receive still different treatment. Be careful to avoid oversimplification and generalizations, and be sure to draw conclusions about the way that Hawthorne uses imagery of light and darkness in individual texts.

3. **Dreams:** While "The May-Pole of Merry Mount" does not feature the dreams—or apparent dreams—of one particular character, the story is filled with the language of dreams and daydreams. How is Hawthorne's treatment of dreams similar or different in this text from some of his other uses of dreams? What conclusions can you draw about the author's use of dreams in the texts that you examine?

Dreams abound in Hawthorne's fiction. You might choose to examine dreams and dreaming in "My Kinsman, Major Molineux" or "Young Goodman Brown." While these two stories seem to incorporate the dreams of specific characters, how would you compare their treatment of dreams with the dreamlike quality of life at Merry Mount. Similarly, you might compare the dreamlike quality of Robin's journey through town in "My Kinsman, Major Molineux" with the perpetual "day-dream" of Merry Mount. How does the use of dreams in the two tales allow for a more metaphorical or allegorical consideration of the two tales?

4. **American identity:** If you choose to read "The May-Pole of Merry Mount" as a comment on American identity, how does it compare to Hawthorne's other statements about the American identity in his fiction?

Once again, you might choose to read "My Kinsman, Major Molineux" as a historical allegory about the American Revolution and compare it productively to "The May-Pole of Merry Mount." The opening chapters of *The Scarlet Letter*, discussing the utopian dreams of the Puritans, also provide plenty of room for comparison. Any of Hawthorne's historical fiction could provide you with a suitable topic for a paper such as this.

Bibliography and Online Resources for "The May-pole of Merry Mount"

Baym, Nina. *The Shape of Hawthorne's Career.* Ithaca, NY: Cornell UP, 1976.

Bradford, William. *Of Plymouth Plantation.* Excerpts available online. URL: http://www.swarthmore.edu/SocSci/bdorsey1/41docs/14-bra.html. Downloaded September 17, 2006.

Bush, Harold K. *American Declarations: Rebellion and Repentance in American Cultural History.* Urbana: U of Illinois P, 1999.

Colacurcio, Michael. *The Province of Piety: Moral History in Hawthorne's Early Tales.* Cambridge, MA: Harvard UP, 1984. (Reprint: Durham, NC: Duke UP, 1995.)

Crews, Frederick C. *The Sins of Fathers: Hawthorne's Psychological Themes.* New York: Oxford UP, 1966.

Dawson, Edward. *Hawthorne's Knowledge and Use of New England History: Study of Sources.* Nashville, TN: Joint University Libraries, Vanderbilt University, 1939.

Doubleday, Neal F. *Hawthorne's Early Tales; A Critical Study.* Durham, NC: Duke UP, 1972.

Flanigan, Tom. "Trumping the 'Annalists' with the Higher Truth of Fiction: Systematic Ambiguity in Hawthorne's 'The May-Pole of Merry Mount.'" *Nathaniel Hawthorne Review* 29 (2003): 50–75.

Fogle, Richard Harter. *Hawthorne's Fiction: The Light and the Dark.* Norman: U of Oklahoma P, 1952.

Fossum, Robert H. *Hawthorne's Inviolable Circle: the Problem of Time.* Deland, FL: Everett/Edwards Inc., 1972.

Heath, William R. "Thomas Morton and 'The May-Pole of Merry Mount.'" Hawthorne in Salem. Available online. URL: http://www.hawthorneinsalem. com/ScholarsForum/MMD1308.html. Downloaded June 7, 2006.

Hoffman, Daniel. *Form and Fable in American Fiction.* New York: Oxford UP, 1961.

Joplin, David D. "'The May-Pole of Merry Mount': Hawthorne's 'L'Allegro' and 'IlPenseroso.'" *Studies in Short Fiction* 30 (1993): 185–93.

Martin, Terence. *Nathaniel Hawthorne.* New York: Twayne, 1983.

Morton, Thomas. *New English Canaan.* Excerpts available online. URL: http:// www.swarthmore.edu/SocSci/bdorsey1/41docs/19-mor.html. Downloaded September 17, 2006.

Waggoner, Hyatt H. *Hawthorne: A Critical Study.* Cambridge, MA: Belknap Press of Harvard University, 1955.

"THE MINISTER'S BLACK VEIL"

READING TO WRITE

CRITIC ROBERT FOSSUM says that Hawthorne is "exasperatingly vague" in his description of Hooper's worldview in "The Minister's Black Veil." Indeed, many students—and literary critics as well—have found "The Minister's Black Veil" "exasperatingly vague." But its richness and its potential for spawning thoughtful papers derive from this vagueness, from this celebrated ambiguity. Not surprisingly, most of the critical attention focuses on Hooper's veil, since the story's title clearly points to it as a central figure for interpretation. As Fossum's words suggest, both the minister and the story remain closemouthed about the precise meaning of the veil until the final page. Even then, there is reason to doubt this final explanation given by Hooper on his deathbed. And while Hooper's veil is the most apparent avenue through which to approach this story, you will soon see that this avenue intersects with nearly all the story's themes and characters. It can, therefore, lead to a number of promising paper topics. Your first introduction to the veil quickly demonstrates how numerous these possibilities are. After first providing a glimpse of the Sunday morning activities of the town of Milford and telling of the general astonishment of the collected townspeople at the appearance of their minister, Hawthorne writes:

> The cause of so much amazement may appear sufficiently slight. Mr. Hooper, a gentlemanly person of about thirty, though still a

bachelor, was dressed with due clerical neatness, as if a careful wife had starched his band, and brushed the weekly dust from his Sunday's garb. There was but one thing remarkable in his appearance. Swathed about his forehead, and hanging down over his face, so low as to be shaken by his breath, Mr. Hooper had on a black veil. On a nearer view, it seemed to consist of two folds of crape, which entirely concealed his features, except the mouth and chin, but probably did not intercept his sight, farther than to give a darkened aspect to all living and inanimate things. With this gloomy shade before him, good Mr. Hooper walked onward, at a slow and quiet pace, stooping somewhat and looking on the ground, as is customary with abstracted men, yet nodding kindly to those of his parishioners who still waited on the meeting-house steps. But so wonder-stuck were they, that his greeting hardly met with a return.

Hawthorne continues to recount the response of the bewildered congregation, a few paragraphs later remarking:

That mysterious emblem was never once withdrawn. It shook with his measured breath as he gave out the psalm; it threw its obscurity between him and the holy page, as he read the Scriptures; and while he prayed, the veil lay heavily on his uplifted countenance. Did he seek to hide it from the dread Being whom he was addressing?

Such was the effect of this simple piece of crape, that more than one woman of delicate nerves was forced to leave the meeting-house. Yet perhaps the pale-faced congregation was almost as fearful a sight to the minister, as his black veil was to them.

Most readers will share the response of Mr. Hooper's congregation and wonder about the black veil. Why does Hooper choose to wear it, and what does this "mysterious emblem," this "gloomy shade," represent? These two questions alone have kept scholars and students busy for over a century. Careful attention to this passage quickly demonstrates, though, how thoroughly this symbol is woven into the texture of the tale. This is the first meeting with Hooper, and beyond the veil, it tells a great deal about him and his character. Already you should have questions about the "gentlemanly person" that precede questions about his veil. Is it significant that he is "a person of about thirty, though still a bachelor"? Further, what does the "due clerical neatness" of his dress, "as if a careful wife had starched his band, and brushed the weekly dust from his Sunday's garb," tell us about him? Does it hint at a certain fastidiousness or, as some critics have implied, evidence an effeminacy? If so, is this impression amplified by his decision to adopt a piece of women's clothing, "a simple black veil, such as any woman might wear"? Further, what do the minister's "quiet pace," his "kindly" nods, and his "abstracted" demeanor tell about his character and personality?

While Hooper's congregation is at first too bewildered to wonder explicitly about the import or purpose of the veil, the narrator soon begins this line of questioning. Asking, "Did he seek to hide [his face] from the dread Being he was addressing?" he questions the state of Hooper's soul and his relationship with God. Clearly such inquiries into the meaning and intent of Hooper's decision to wear the veil should continue to occupy you as you read the story.

Note that in addition to introducing the veil, introducing Hooper, and questioning the minister's motivation, the passage draws attention to the "*effect* of this simple piece of crape." Right away, Hawthorne says that the effects are numerous and varied. At the end of the passage above, the narrator states that the "women of delicate nerves" need to leave the meetinghouse. In the passage that links the quotes cited above, the sexton asserts that he cannot "really feel as if good Mr. Hooper's face was behind that piece of crape," and an old woman remarks that "He has changed himself into something awful, only by hiding his face." How do you feel about the initial reactions of Hooper's congregation? Do they seem justified or do they seem inappropriate? Notice that the narrator speculates about how their responses might appear to Hooper: "Yet perhaps the pale-faced congregation was almost as fearful a sight to the minister, as his black veil was to them." What do you make of this comment? Why might the frightened white faces of his congregation be "fearful" to Hooper? Is this a comment on the congregation? On Hooper? On the nature of human sympathy and tolerance? Nor is this comment the only insight on the effect of the veil on Hooper himself. As he first describes the crape, the narrator speculates that it "probably did not intercept his sight, farther than to give a darkened aspect to all living and inanimate things." What do you make of this observation? Clearly, this "gloomy shade" must in some way affect Hooper's sight, and it seems logical that it would, quite literally, "give a darkened aspect" to everything he sees. Does Hawthorne imply a metaphorical meaning in this sentence? What does he seem to be saying about the minister's worldview? Are there other spots in this passage where you might question the efficacy and effectiveness of Hooper's vision? If so, how and why are these passages significant?

You could even pursue this question further. All of these responses happen before Hooper speaks a word, and all are dependent on the sense of sight. Even the reference to the veil as a "gloomy shade" and the question about its effect on the minister's perception emphasize vision and the act of seeing. Indeed the veil itself, as a "mysterious emblem," draws attention to vision and sight. An emblem is a visual sign, and its interpretation depends on perception. Additionally, a veil's very purpose highlights the importance of seeing, for it is used to obscure something from sight. You might wish to think more about the efficacy of veils and veiling. What is the natural human response to something that is veiled—purposely and obviously concealed? Why might Hooper—and Hawthorne—have chosen this particular symbol? Do they both seem to be using the symbol in the same way? Why or why not?

These are the kinds of questions to bring to the rest of the text as you continue to read. Any one of these avenues might provide a strong paper on this complex and exasperatingly ambiguous story.

TOPICS AND STRATEGIES

This section provides more material to help you develop paper topics on "The Minister's Black Veil" by providing broad ideas. Remember that these topics are quite broad—they give you a general framework to guide you as you read, reread, and analyze the work. Use these topics as springboards. You will need to narrow the focus of your writing, constructing an analytical thesis, and bearing in mind the proposed length of your paper.

Themes

As previously noted, the major themes of this story grow from its focus on Reverend Hooper's black veil. As you consider the veil and its relation to Hooper and to Hawthorne, you can begin to bring thematic issues into clearer development.

Sample Topics:

1. **Sin:** The first and most obvious thematic concern of the story is the nature and effect of human sin. Hooper calls his veil a "type and a symbol," and it seems clear that in donning the veil, he is intent on turning himself into a kind of walking text or sermon on sin. Yet the meaning of this sermon is never quite clear. Some interpret the veil as a sign of secret sin. Hooper, in his conversation with Elizabeth, calls it "a sign of mourning" or sorrow. And on his deathbed, Hooper claims that the veil is representative of the human tendency to hide our inmost hearts—and our inmost guilt or sin. What, finally, seems to be the meaning of Hooper's "sermon" on sin? What does he want to say about human sinfulness? How successful is his attempt to turn himself into a walking sermon? Do you think that Hawthorne's point in the story is the same as Hooper's? Why or why not? If you think Hawthorne's point is different, what, finally, is his point about human sinfulness and how does he express it?

   The question of human sinfulness is a common theme in much of Hawthorne's work, though his approach and the conclusions that he reaches often vary. You must read the story closely and make some determinations about the meaning of the veil before you begin to shape a paper on this topic. You will need to examine Hooper carefully and try to evaluate his purpose as well as the success of his endeavor. This should lead you to evaluate the community response to Hooper. Be sure, too, to read the narrator's perceptions closely. Pay close attention to the language he uses to describe Hooper, Elizabeth, and the citizens of Milford. This should allow you to assess Hawthorne's position on sin and on Hooper.

2. **Human community:** If the veil is the "type" of human isolation as Hooper finally claims, how successful is Hooper at making his point about sin's propensity of isolating people from one

another? What are the effects of Hooper's veil on the community relations in Milford? How do Hooper's veil and his actions affect his relationships with others? What, finally, seems to be Hawthorne's point about human community and humans' ability to know one another in our fallen, sinful state?

Clearly this topic is related to the issue of human sinfulness, but it asks you to consider the issue from a specific perspective. Hawthorne begins the story by showing the community members going about their daily Sunday business, and he spends a good deal of time chronicling their response to the veil and to Hooper. While the minister's actions are the story's central mystery, Hawthorne also invites readers to evaluate the community response to Hooper and his behavior. Elizabeth and her interaction with Hooper provide a particular bit of insight into both the nature of human community and the effects of sinfulness on humans' abilities to relate to one another.

Character

Once again, consideration of character in this story necessarily grows from the characters' relation to Hooper and his black veil. As you consider questions of character you might begin with your own personal response. How do you feel about the characters? What do you think of Hooper's behavior? How do you think you would respond to him and to his veil? Once you've thought about the characters and their behavior, you should return to the text to look for elements that support your reading or assessments. What elements of the story help to support or develop your interpretation of the characters? Which elements challenge your reading? Why and how? As you consider these questions, do you find yourself modifying or developing your interpretation of character? How? Why?

Sample Topics:

1. **Reverend Hooper:** Well into the story, the narrator tells us of Milford's response to Hooper: "But with the multitude, good Mr. Hooper was irreparably a bugbear." What do you think of Hooper and his decision to turn himself into a walking symbol

by wearing, and refusing to quit wearing, his black veil? How does Hawthorne seem to be using Hooper in this text?

This question shares territory with the thematic questions. To assess Hooper in a paper you will need to consider quite a few aspects of his character. Clearly, in donning the veil, which he views as a symbol, he has turned himself into a sort of symbol too, since the veil seems both to obscure and to represent the minister. You should look closely at the language the narrator and the other characters use to describe Hooper the man. What kind of character, what kind of man, is he? Is he likeable? Is he arrogant? Pushy? Mean-spirited? Shy? Is he, as some of the characters conclude, mad? What leads you to draw these conclusions? As you study the story, try to draw conclusions about why Hooper decides to wear the veil. He suggests that he wears it to make a point about sin and human isolation. Does he seem well intentioned in this purpose? Is there any logic to his choice?

On the other hand, some characters and critics believe, as Elizabeth suggests, that the veil represents a "secret sin" of the minister's. And some critics have suggested that Hooper, rather than making a point about human isolation, instead desires to isolate himself from others, and his veil is a vehicle to achieve this isolation. What do you think about this assessment of his character? Think, too, about the effectiveness of the veil. Does it seem to fulfill his intentions? Why or why not? Are there any effects of wearing the veil that Hooper did not seem to intend? What are they? How might they affect any assessment of his character? Do you think that Hooper changes throughout the story? Why or why not?

2. **Elizabeth:** Hooper's fiancée, Elizabeth, reacts very differently to the veil than the other members of the community. The narrator tells us "there was one person in the village, unappalled by the awe with which the black veil had impressed all beside herself." She directly questions Hooper about his behavior, and she

says of the black crape: "there is nothing terrible in this piece of crape, except that it hides a face which I am always glad to look upon. Come, good sir, let the sun shine from behind the cloud." More that one critic has suggested the story presents Elizabeth as an ideal character. Do you agree with this assessment? Why or why not? If so, what separates Elizabeth from Hooper and from the rest of the community?

A paper that assesses Elizabeth's character and her role in the story must analyze the interview between Elizabeth and Hooper very thoroughly. The language that the narrator uses in his description of her is important, as is her complex reaction to the veil. You should think about her tears after Hooper refuses to acquiesce to her request and her subsequent "trembling." Is Elizabeth's final response to the veil, her "terror," the same as that of the other villagers? Why or why not? Read Hooper's role in this discussion carefully too. What does it tell us about him, and how does this further develop your assessment of Elizabeth? How else does Hawthorne develop Elizabeth's character in the story?

3. **The community of Milford:** As Hooper looks out over his congregation on the first day that he wears the veil, the narrator observes, "Yet perhaps the pale-faced congregation was almost as fearful a sight to the minister, as his black veil was to them." How do you assess the reaction of the townspeople to Hooper and his veil? Do they respond to their pastor as a Christian community or do they become an illustration of the kind of sin that Hooper means the veil to represent?

Hawthorne spends a good deal of time cataloguing the responses of the people of Milford to Hooper's veil. These responses are varied and span the length of the story. You will also need to think a bit about your assessment of Hooper's decision to wear the veil. Your assessment of the community reaction could vary depending on your interpretation of the minister's motivations.

Language, Symbols, and Imagery

As with much of Hawthorne's work, symbols play an important role in "The Minister's Black Veil." Like the *A* in *The Scarlet Letter*, Hooper's veil becomes the story's title and its central symbol. Almost any paper on "The Minister's Black Veil" must grapple in some way with its central figure, Hooper's "gloomy shade."

Sample Topics:

1. **The veil:** Reverend Hooper explains the veil as "a type and a symbol" of "mourning," and the story seems to amplify the veil's representation of the "secret sin" that isolates individuals from one another. The meaning of Hooper's veil, though, remains elusive throughout the story. The narrator refers to it as a "mysterious emblem," and so it remains throughout the course of the story. What does the minister's black veil represent?

   There are quite a few ways to approach this question, and a paper that assesses the symbol of the veil needs to be carefully focused. In general, interpretations of the veil have divided into three camps. The first sees the veil as representing some secret crime of Hooper. (Many, beginning with Edgar Allan Poe, suspect him of sexual involvement with the young woman over whose funeral he presides early in the story.) The second reads the veil as a symbol of the more abstract notion of secret sin, which causes individuals to veil their hearts or inner selves from others. The third sees Hawthorne using the veil to point out the minister's shortcomings, arguing that he is wrong to wear the veil and refuse to relinquish it. Does one of these readings seem more valid to you? Why?

   Any response must tackle both Hooper's apparent intent in donning the veil and the ambiguity of the symbol throughout the story, and this might suggest another, more philosophical, way to approach the veil. Since the narrator describes it as a "mysterious emblem" early in the story, and since its precise meaning remains elusive, it is worth exploring the veil's association with mystery throughout the story. How often is the veil, or that which it represents, described as a "mystery" or as "mysterious" in the story? Why might this be significant? While good literary symbols, by definition, defy precise explanation or categorization, Hooper's veil, like Hester Prynne's scarlet A, seems particularly elusive. Given that the story and the narrator seem to insist on this elusiveness, you might consider that this is the point of the story. Is "The Minister's Black Veil" a tale about symbols? Is the veil, as W. B. Carnochan's article "The Minister's Black Veil" suggests, a "symbol of symbols"? If so, what does the story say about the nature of literary symbols or about the power of art?

2. **Reverend Hooper's smile:** In addition to his black veil, Hooper is associated with his smile. Examine the story carefully, and find all the references to Hooper's smile. How is it described? When does it appear? What does it say about the character of Hooper? Like the black veil, it seems to represent Hooper himself. How do you balance these two symbols—veil and smile? Are they complementary or do they contradict each other? Explain.

   This question clearly asks you to consider issues discussed in the section on Hooper's character and to consider the meaning and use of the omnipresent veil. Hooper's smile, though, is nearly as omnipresent as his black crape veil.

3. **Mirrors:** Early in the story, the narrator says that Hooper chances to see himself in a mirror and recoils: "the black veil involved his own spirit in the horror with which it overwhelmed all others. His frame shuddered—his lips grew white." Later the narrator emphasizes that "his own antipathy to the veil was known to be so great, that he never willingly passed before a mirror, nor stooped to drink at a still fountain, lest, in its peaceful bosom, he should be affrighted by himself." Much like Hester Prynne's scarlet *A*, Hooper's veil is mirrored and replicated throughout the story. Examine the story carefully for such reflections of the veil and of Hooper. What does Hawthorne seem to be saying through this repeated mirroring and replication of Hooper's black veil?

To address this question, you need to read the story closely to find reflections of the veil. This question is tied to the issues you were asked to consider in the discussion of Hooper's character. Why, for example, is Hooper scared of his own reflection? What does this suggest about him? Similarly, this question also asks you to consider Hooper's perception or vision. Apparently, his reflection is something Hooper chooses not to look at, not to see. Why? What else does Hooper choose not to see? Are there other places where Hooper sees his own countenance reflected back at him? What do these passages tell us about Hooper and his vision/perception?

Compare and Contrast Essays

Because this story examines themes found throughout Hawthorne's fiction, you should find a wealth of material from which to develop compare and contrast papers. The story's focus on sin and on the nature of symbolism clearly links it to *The Scarlet Letter* and to "Young Goodman Brown." Similarly, the symbol of the veil and the theme of veiling present strong links to *The Blithedale Romance,* which also revolves around veils and their metaphors. The questions below present a few subjects from which to develop compare and contrast papers.

Sample Topics:

1. **Hooper and Dimmesdale:** Hooper and Dimmesdale are both ministers who wear signs that they insist are "types" or "symbols" of sin, and these symbols can be linked through their association with "secret sin." Further, both figures are regarded as effective ministers. Dimmesdale is renowned for his abilities, and the narrator tells us that "Among all its bad influences, the black veil had the one desirable effect, of making its wearer [Hooper] a very efficient clergyman." How would you compare Dimmesdale and Hooper? How are they alike? How are they different? How does each deal with his own sin?

   This question depends on analyzing the characters of both men. Remember that both characters in the story and critics have argued that Hooper was involved sexually with the young woman whose funeral comes early in the story. This could deepen the association between Dimmesdale and Hooper, as each carried a secret sexual sin. If you concur with this assessment of Hooper, how does his handling of his secret sin compare with Dimmesdale's? What conclusions can you draw about Hawthorne's points through this comparison? Does it matter that Hooper bears the symbol of his sin in public, while Dimmesdale, at least until the novel's end, bears his in private? Similarly, you might think about the issue of confessing secret sin. Dimmesdale discusses his sinful nature in his sermons, but seems to know that the congregation will misinterpret his meaning. If Hooper's veil does, indeed, represent his own personal sin, how effectively does it act as a mechanism of "confession" or penance?

You could also approach a comparison of these two men through their ministerial positions. How effective are each of these men in their vocations? How do their sinful natures affect their abilities to do their jobs? What does Hawthorne seem to be saying about their effectiveness as ministers?

2. **Hooper and Hester Prynne:** Though they might, at first, seem unlikely characters for comparison, Hooper and Hester Prynne share some striking commonalities. Like Hester, Hooper wears a public symbol of sin. Each becomes, in the words of *The Scarlet Letter*, "a living sermon against sin." Similarly, both become known for ministering to the sick. In "The Custom-House," Hawthorne writes that it was Hester's habit "to go about the country as a kind of voluntary nurse, and doing whatever miscellaneous good she might; taking upon herself, likewise, to give advice in all matters, especially those of the heart; by which means ... she gained from many people the reverence due to an angel." And Hooper's veil made him "a very efficient clergyman." The veil's "gloom, indeed, enabled him to sympathize with all dark affections." Why might these apparently dissimilar characters share these qualities?

A paper that explores the connections between Hester and Hooper should consider both their characters and their social positions. You should keep in mind, too, that Hooper's veil is self-imposed and Hester's is not (until the final chapter of the story). What does Hawthorne seem to be saying about the nature of sin and of human sympathy through these characters? Who, finally, is the more sympathetic and powerful character? Why?

3. **Hooper and the "sanctity of the human heart":** In "Ethan Brand," Hawthorne writes of a character who seeks the "Unpardonable Sin," "the sin of an intellect that triumphed over the sense of brotherhood with man, and reverence for God." In *The Scarlet Letter*, Dimmesdale describes this sin when he says that Chillingworth has "violated . . . the sanctity of a human heart." After he first dons the veil, Hooper delivers a particularly powerful sermon. The narrator tells us that "Each member of the congregation, the most innocent girl, and the man of hardened breast, felt as if the preacher had crept upon them, behind his awful veil, and discovered their hoarded iniquity of deed and thought. Many spread their clasped hands on their bosoms." Is Hooper guilty of the same kind of violation that Chillingworth and Brand are guilty of? Why or why not?

Clearly this question involves an investigation into Hooper. While his motivations seem vastly different from Chillingworth's, his veil is, tantalizingly, linked to the issue of secret sin, and the language that describes his sermon is certainly provocative. Could Hooper be linked to characters who violate the souls and hearts of others? Remember, too, that Hawthorne's artist figures are often dangerously close to such violation. They often appear as observers who lack sympathetic engagement.

4. **Hooper and Young Goodman Brown:** Both Reverend Hooper and Young Goodman Brown share an awareness of the universality of human sinfulness. Compare their responses to the discovery of sin. Do you see them as fundamentally alike or different? Why?

To effectively compare these two characters and their awareness of sin, you will need to look at both their responses to sin
and the effects of these responses. Remember, too, that you
need to draw some conclusions in a paper like this. You might
want to think about why Hawthorne focuses on the human
response to sin in these two characters. What is his larger
point?

5. **The theme of veiling:** Hawthorne commonly uses veils as symbols and metaphors in his fiction. Choose another instance of
Hawthorne's use of the theme or symbol of the veil and evaluate
his purpose.

Two works come to mind immediately. Early in "The Custom-
House," Hawthorne speaks of the "autobiographical impulse"
that sparked that sketch. He concludes that it is possible to
write of oneself and "still keep the inmost Me behind its veil."
How does Hawthorne's metaphorical veil here compare with
Hooper's black crape?

Similarly, *The Blithedale Romance* repeatedly uses the
image of the veil: Priscilla has played the role of "the veiled
lady," Zenobia tells the legend of "The Silvery Veil," and Coverdale, engaging in a kind of autobiographical impulse, tells
the story of his experiences at Blithedale, but never seems to
fully reveal himself though his narrative. Consider how and
why Hawthorne uses the metaphor of the veil in both of these
texts. What conclusions can you draw?

Bibliography and Online Resources for "The Minister's Black Veil"

Barry, Elaine. "Beyond the Veil: A Reading of Hawthorne's 'The Minister's Black
Veil.'" *Studies in Short Fiction* 17 (Winter 1980): 15–21.

Bell, Michael Davitt. *Hawthorne and the Historical Romance of New England.*
Princeton, NJ: Princeton UP, 1971.

Carnochan, W. B. "The Minister's Black Veil." *Nineteenth-Century Fiction* 24
(1969): 182–92.

Crews, Frederick C. *The Sins of Fathers: Hawthorne's Psychological Themes.* New
York: Oxford UP, 1966.

Crowley, J. Donald, ed. *Hawthorne: the Critical Heritage.* New York: Barnes and Noble, 1970.

Doubleday, Neal Frank. *Hawthorne's Early Tales: A Critical Study.* Durham, NC: Duke UP, 1972.

Fogle, Richard Harter. *Hawthorne's Fiction: The Light and the Dark.* Norman: U of Oklahoma P, 1952.

Fossum, Robert H. *Hawthorne's Inviolable Circle: the Problem of Time.* Deland, FL: Everett/Edwards Inc., 1972.

Garino, R. M. "The Hoarded Iniquity of Deed or Thought: Secret Sin in Hawthorne's 'The Minister's Black Veil.'" American Writers.com. Available online. URL: http://www.americanwriters.com/archivecriticism2.htm. Downloaded July 19, 2006.

Levin, Harry. *The Power of Blackness: Hawthorne, Poe, Melville.* New York: Alfred A. Knopf, 1958.

McCarthy, Judy. "'The Minister's Black Veil': Concealing Moses and the Holies of the Holy." *Studies in Short Fiction* 24 (Spring 1987): 131–39.

Millington, Richard H., ed. *The Cambridge Companion to Nathaniel Hawthorne.* Cambridge: Cambridge UP, 2004.

Newman, Lea Bertani Vozar. "One-Hundred-and-Fifty Years of Looking At, Into, Through, Behind, Beyond, and Around the Minister's Black Veil." *Nathaniel Hawthorne Review* 13 (1987): 5–12.

Stibitz, E. Earle. "Ironic Unity in Hawthorne's 'The Minister's Black Veil.'" *American Literature* 34 (1962): 182–91.

Tharpe, Jac. *Nathaniel Hawthorne: Identity and Knowledge.* Carbondale and Edwardsville: Southern Illinois UP, 1967.

Wineapple, Brenda. *Hawthorne: A Life.* New York: Alfred A. Knopf, 2003.

"THE BIRTH-MARK"

READING TO WRITE

BECAUSE "THE Birth-Mark," like "Rappaccini's Daughter," does not require knowledge of New England's history, readers often find it more accessible than Hawthorne's Puritan tales. Despite that, "The Birth-Mark" shares many qualities with Hawthorne's other fiction. It is marked by the author's famous ambiguity, his complicated narrative voice, and his interest in dissecting characters' minds, hearts, and spirits. It also shares themes with much of Hawthorne's other work. A close reading of the story will help you identify these themes, and it is an important first step in crafting a strong, thoughtful paper. This section provides a model of close, analytical reading that should begin the writing process.

Often readers are tempted to rush through the opening of a story in order to get to the "meat" of the plot. Those who rush through the first paragraph of "The Birth-Mark," however, miss many details that alert them to Hawthorne's interests and themes. An alert reader will notice that even the story's first sentence conveys a great deal of information. It sets the action in the historical past and quickly sets up the central issue of the story, which the rest of the paragraph develops upon:

> In the latter part of the last century, there lived a man of science—an eminent proficient in every branch of natural philosophy—who not long before our story opens, had made experience of the spiritual affinity, more attractive than any chemical one. He had left

his laboratory to the care of an assistant, cleared his fine countenance from the furnace-smoke, washed the stain of acids from his fingers, and persuaded a beautiful woman to be his wife. In those days, when the comparatively recent discovery of electricity, and other kindred mysteries of nature, seemed to open paths in the region of miracle, it was not unusual for the love of science to rival the love of woman, in its depth and absorbing energy. The higher intellect, the imagination, the spirit, and even the heart, might all find their congenial ailment in pursuits which, as some of their ardent votaries believed, would ascend from one step of powerful intelligence to another, until the philosopher should lay his hand on the secret of creative force, and perhaps make new worlds for himself. We know not whether Aylmer possessed this degree of faith in man's ultimate control over nature. He had devoted himself, however, too unreservedly to scientific studies, ever to be weaned from them by any second passion. His love for his young wife might prove the stronger of the two; but it could only be by intertwining itself with his love of science, and uniting the strength of the latter to its own.

Such a union according took place, and was attended with truly remarkable consequences, and a deeply impressive moral.

Besides introducing the historical setting, the first sentence introduces the main character, Aylmer. The narrator doesn't initially name Aylmer but, instead, merely calls him "a man of science." Why is this description your first introduction to Aylmer? This question can be used as an entry into the story. It immediately opens up two lines of inquiry: the first about character, and the second about theme. How does this initial description help to characterize Aylmer? What does it mean to be "a man of science"? With these questions in mind, you are well prepared to analyze later descriptions of Aylmer and his science. Why does his laboratory leave him covered with "furnace-smoke"? Does the narrator's description of Aylmer devoting himself "too unreservedly to scientific studies" carry any hint of criticism?

This character description leads into an investigation of the theme of science, which plays such a large role in "The Birth-Mark." The midsection of this paragraph spends a good bit of time describing "the love of science" and the goal of its "ardent votaries," for the "philosopher to lay his hand on the secret of creative force, and perhaps make new worlds for himself." It further suggests that the final aim of science is "Man's control over nature." What does that description say about these scientists? Do their goals seem consistent with the goals of modern science? Why or why not? Take note of the language that surrounds science and scientists like Aylmer: "passion," "faith," "ardent," "miracle." Why does Hawthorne use particularly unscientific language—language of love and of religion—to describe Aylmer and his science? Such questions lead to broader philosophical questions about the intersection of faith and science and the nature of human relationships.

The tale's very long first sentence introduces the question of human relationships when it says that Aylmer had "made experience of a spiritual affinity, more attractive than any chemical one" and had asked a "beautiful woman to become his wife." The end of the paragraph focuses the conflict of the story around this division between the love of science and the love of a woman: "He had devoted himself, however, too unreservedly to scientific studies, ever to be weaned from them by any second passion. His love for his young wife might prove the stronger of the two; but it could only be by intertwining itself with his love of science . . ." In essence, Hawthorne's "man of science" has become the center of the story's experiment, which will test his love for his wife, the "spiritual affinity," against his passion for science. Which will prove "the stronger of the two"? You may have found hints about the story's outcome in the questions posed, but read the rest of the story with an attentive eye toward the relationship between Georgiana and Aylmer.

Finally, given the story's focus on the marriage, you may have questions about what the opening paragraph does *not* say. It doesn't say much of Georgiana, who is merely described as "a beautiful woman" and as Aylmer's "young wife." (She is not named until the third paragraph.) Why doesn't Hawthorne tell her name? Why does he introduce her through her relationship with Aylmer? What does this say about her role in the story? Does it reflect anything about Hawthorne's beliefs about marriage and women's roles? Questions about Georgiana's character and her place in the story may lead to broader explorations about gender roles and the position of women in Hawthorne's time and in our own.

Such a thorough examination of the story's opening paragraph supplies a number of issues to explore in the rest of the text. Examining Hawthorne's treatment of these characters, themes, and conflicts throughout the rest of story will provide you with sufficient evidence to build a strong, thoughtful essay.

TOPICS AND STRATEGIES

Building upon the reading of the story begun above, this section provides broad topic ideas that should help you develop an essay on "The Birth-Mark." Remember that the topic ideas below are just springboards for your own exploration; you will need to focus your analysis and develop your own specific thesis.

Themes

The introductory section of this chapter introduced some of the themes of this story. Clearly science and love/marriage emerge as central themes of "The Birth-Mark," though these are not the only themes that Hawthorne touches on in the story. The analysis of the story's opening paragraph also noted that the narrator uses the language of religion in the discussion of science. This language hints at another of the story's themes, faith. To write a paper about the themes of "The Birth-Mark" you should begin by identifying a theme and then deciding what you think the story had to say about it. Having identified science as a central theme of the story, for example, allows you to read Aylmer's beliefs about science and scientific discovery against the narrator's comments about science and its relation to the natural world. Additionally, Aylmer's experiments, including his treatment of the birthmark itself, coupled with the language that surrounds the laboratory and Aminadab, should help to develop a reading of Hawthorne's assessment of scientific advancement. Other themes worth considering are faith, love, or marriage. A comparison of Aylmer and Georgiana's attitudes toward each other, coupled with the narrator's word choice in describing their positions in the marriage, could help develop a paper on attitudes toward marriage in "The Birth-Mark." As this discussion indicates, the themes in this story are rooted in Hawthorne's characters; the section on philosophy and ideas will also show the connections between the story's themes and its philosophical outlooks.

Sample Topics:

1. **Science:** How does Hawthorne characterize the pursuit of science in "The Birth-Mark?" Does he seem to have faith in scientific advancement?

   To construct an essay on this topic, you will need to pay close attention to the language that surrounds both Aylmer's pursuit of science and his decision to remove Georgiana's birthmark. Why is he so determined to remove the birthmark? You should also be careful to sort out differing attitudes toward science in the story. Comparing and contrasting Aylmer's position with Georgiana's, Aminadab's, and the narrator's should help you develop a focused thesis. Similarly, the language used to describe both Aylmer's laboratory and his assistant, Aminadab, should be useful in developing your position, as should the ultimate failure of the experiment on the birthmark.

2. **Faith:** In the first paragraph, the narrator questions Aylmer's "degree of faith" in scientific discovery. How might this story be read as a story about faith?

   As the first section of this chapter noted, the story's opening paragraph uses language often associated with religion to describe Aylmer and his science. Why might Hawthorne use such language to describe what we often think of as a logical, strictly intellectual pursuit? In addition, you may find that the language of doubt is related to this theme, as is the language of trust. Toward the story's end, both Aylmer and Georgiana accuse each other of mistrust. The issue of faith and trust within the marriage might help to shed light on the theme of faith in this story.

3. **Love/marriage:** What does Hawthorne seem to be saying about the qualities of marriage? How are we to evaluate Aylmer and Georgiana as partners in a marriage?

In many ways, the whole story revolves around the question of the strength of Aylmer's love for Georgiana. A paper that assesses the "The Birth-Mark"'s perspective on marriage should take into consideration the interactions between Georgiana and Aylmer. Does either character change as a result of their relationship? Where and when do these changes occur? As the section of this chapter on faith indicates, the issue of trust within marriage is certainly relevant here. Similarly, you would also need to consider Aylmer's attitudes about the birthmark as well as his decision to remove it. A thorough investigation of the story's commentary on marriage should probably take into account the story's historical context, the time period in which Hawthorne lived and wrote. Gender expectations of the 1840s clearly affect both Georgiana's portrayal and the portrayal of marriage in this tale. Barbara Welter's famous article, "The Cult of True Womanhood: 1820–1860," which appeared in the journal *American Quarterly* 18 (1966), is an excellent source on gender roles and marriage in antebellum America.

Character

As the opening section of the chapter indicates, "The Birth-Mark" provides rich material for the exploration of character, and the characters help to give the reader a great deal of insight into the story's "deeply impressive moral." (And, despite the narrator's description, most readers would argue that there are a great many morals that can be drawn from this story.) Although the story seems to provide just three characters to analyze, there are many ways to develop thoughtful essays around Hawthorne's characters and their development. To begin, you will need to analyze what the characters say, what they do, how they interact, and what all these factors say about them. Additionally, since this story is told in the third person, you should examine what the narrator says about each character. The narrator's word choice and judgments about the characters have a strong effect on the reader's interpretation of these characters. In fact, since it is always important not to assume that the narrator is the voice of the author himself, you could even choose to analyze the narrator as a character.

Sample Topics:

1. **Aylmer as a character:** How is Aylmer presented, and what are readers to think of him? Aylmer means "noble." Is he noble? Would you agree with an assessment of Aylmer that calls him the protagonist?

   This topic is far too broad to write about without a good bit of narrowing, and there are numerous topics that you can develop about Aylmer. What do you think of his decision to remove Georgiana's birthmark, and why do you think he is unsuccessful? Answering these questions can provide a beginning for a closer analysis of Aylmer. To further assess Aylmer's motivations, you need to explore the story's central conflict—his love of science versus his love for Georgiana. This exploration leads directly to the birthmark. How does Aylmer feel about the birthmark? How do his feelings about the birthmark affect his love for his wife?

   While such explorations of Aylmer's character may allow you to write an essay that explores the role he plays in the story's outcome, remember, too, that you could write a strong, focused essay on Aylmer himself. This type of essay would make an argument about Aylmer's motivations and his psychology. You might explore what his obsession with the birthmark tells about him. (Do you even think that it is fair to call his relationship with the birthmark an "obsession"?) Examining the language the narrator uses about this relationship should also prove helpful.

   A related approach might focus on Aylmer's relationship with science. Why is Aylmer so passionate about science? How do his experiments help him to define his identity? How do they make him feel about himself? Once again, the opening paragraph provides a good starting place. You might also want to examine how Aylmer talks about his science and his experiments, including his reference to Pygmalion early in the story.

   Similarly, you might choose to evaluate Aylmer's self-knowledge. How well does he understand his own motivations? An essay on this topic should read the narrator's assessments of Aylmer closely.

2. **Georgiana as a character:** What is Georgiana's role in the story? How is she presented? What role does she play in her own death? Her name is the feminine form of George, which means farmer or earth worker. Is this relevant to her role in the story?

As with Aylmer, an analysis of Georgiana's character and her role in the story can lead to many good paper topics. In the first paragraph, Georgiana is described largely through her association with Aylmer: She is "a beautiful woman" who becomes Aylmer's "young wife." As the story continues, though, Georgiana develops as a character in her own right. One method of developing an essay on Georgiana might be to explore what her relationship with Aylmer reveals about her. What kind of a *woman* is she? What kind of a *wife* is she? Does her love for Aylmer change? How does it affect her decisions? How does it affect her sense of self and her self-esteem? An essay on this topic should also analyze her attitudes toward her birthmark. Do these attitudes change throughout the story? One particularly relevant question is why Georgiana drinks Aylmer's potion after she has read his notebook and discovered that "his most splendid successes were almost invariably failures, if compared with the ideal at which he aimed."

A related approach to writing about Georgiana might explore the language of perfection, or near perfection, that surrounds her. Early in the story the narrator remarks that some of her suitors "wished . . . away" the birthmark so "that the world might possess one living specimen of ideal loveliness, without the semblance of a flaw." Near the end of Aylmer's experiment he says to Georgiana, "There is no taint of imperfection on thy spirit. Thy sensible frame, too, shall soon be perfect." It seems that the narrator, and perhaps Hawthorne himself, sees Georgiana as a nearly perfect character. Do you agree? An essay that evaluates Georgiana's near perfection would need to analyze the story's language closely and consider its historical context. How might the 150 years between Hawthorne's time and now affect your assessment of Georgiana's character and her role?

3. **Aminadab as a character:** What is the significance of this apparently minor character in the story? Aminadab is "bad anima" spelled backward. (Anima means "inner self" or "soul.") How does this knowledge help you assess his role in the story?

An essay on Aminadab should evaluate his role as assistant to Aylmer, especially in light of the apparent meaning of his name. Similarly, it should note Aminadab's assessment of Aylmer's decision to remove the birthmark. Because Aminadab is what we might call a "flat" or symbolic character, an analysis of the language and symbolism that surrounds both Aminadab and his environment, the laboratory, would constitute an important part of a paper on his role in the story.

Philosophy and Ideas

As many of his well-known works demonstrate, Hawthorne was keenly interested in religion and related questions of sin. These are just two of the religious or philosophical ideas that he returned to again and again in much of his fiction. The theme of science and questions pertaining to scientific discovery and human responsibility that are so prevalent in this story are also important, recurring issues for Hawthorne. In fact, as you may have noticed in this chapter's discussions of the theme of science and the theme of faith, issues of science and religion are often interconnected in Hawthorne's works. You might, therefore, choose to explore the treatment of religious or philosophical ideas in a paper about "The Birth-Mark."

Sample Topics:

1. **Faith versus science:** The narrator often uses language associated with religion and faith in his discussions of science. Why? What is the relationship between scientific advancement and faith in "The Birth-Mark"?

A paper on this topic must closely examine much of what this chapter has already discussed—Aylmer's attitudes toward science, his attitudes toward the birthmark, the narrator's comments on Aylmer and on the birthmark, the language and imagery that surround the birthmark, Aylmer, Aminadab, and the laboratory. How do all these elements comment on science's relationship to religion and faith?

2. **Humanity's fallen nature:** The fall of Adam and Eve and the consequent mark of sin upon humanity is another religious subject that occupies much of Hawthorne's fiction. In "The Birth-Mark," the narrator says that Georgiana's birthmark is "the fatal flaw of humanity, which Nature . . . stamps ineffaceably on all her productions, either to imply that they are temporary and finite, or that their perfection must be wrought by toil and pain." If this is, in fact, what the birthmark represents, what does Aylmer's treatment of the birthmark say about the never-ending struggle for human perfectibility?

To address this question, you would need to address much of the same material that a paper on science and faith would address. You should also consider the relationship between Georgiana's body and her soul or spirit. How are the two related in the story? The language of perfection or near perfection that surrounds Georgiana is also important, and it connects the story to issues still relevant in modern society. How is Aylmer's desire to rid Georgiana of her birthmark related to issues in modern medicine like plastic surgery and genetic engineering?

3. **Scientific ethics and responsibility:** Both Aylmer and Georgiana know that most of Aylmer's "most splendid successes were almost invariably failures, if compared with the ideal at which he aimed." Knowing this, was it irresponsible for Aylmer to proceed with the experiment?

This is another topic that is related to both the quest for perfection and the relationship between science and faith. A paper that explores Aylmer's ethics also needs to consider the language of perfection along with the story's religious or theological commentary about the human condition. Is it always ethical to pursue scientific advancement? (One might question the very term "advancement." Is science leading us in the wrong direction?) Once again, an exploration of these issues connects the story to modern ethical dilemmas like those surrounding genetic engineering and cloning.

Language, Symbols, and Imagery

Hawthorne frequently uses symbols and imagery to communicate his points. Favorite images recur in much of his fiction: light and dark, sunlight versus shadow, moonlight, reflection, reality versus illusion. These images help you to interpret both setting and character. And while the scarlet *A* of *The Scarlet Letter* is Hawthorne's most famous symbol, his fiction is full of many allusive symbols (like Georgiana's birthmark). To prepare a paper on symbols or imagery, you need to identify and trace images and symbols that appear in the work and try to draw some conclusions about how they function. Like the scarlet *A*, Georgiana's birthmark cannot be contained in one single meaning, and like the *A*, it is interpreted differently by nearly everyone who looks at it. Clearly this inability of characters and readers to definitively interpret these symbols is part of Hawthorne's point. A strong paper on imagery and symbolism will thoroughly consider their use in the story and will try to reach some conclusions about how or why the author uses them as he does.

Sample Topics:

1. **The birthmark:** What is the significance of Georgiana's birthmark? Hawthorne seems to use it as a symbol. What does it represent? What is its relation to Georgiana herself?

   As pointed out above, every character in the story interprets or reads Georgiana's birthmark differently: "[T]he impression wrought by this fairy sign-manual varied exceedingly, according to the difference of temperament in the beholders." The narrator even recounts the reactions of observers outside of the plot—Georgiana's suitors and her rivals. You should explore what these interpretations say about the characters and what they say about the birthmark. Also, you need to ask what, if anything, they say about Georgiana herself. How is her birthmark related to her? Pay careful attention to the description of the birthmark (its shape and color) and to the language and comparisons used to describe it. (Aylmer at one point calls it "the stain.") In addition, weigh the narrator's comments about the birthmark carefully. Do these comments seem to carry more weight than the characters' interpretations?

2. **Georgiana's apartment and Aylmer's laboratory:** The action of the story takes place in just a few rooms. Why does Aylmer move Georgiana into these rooms as he begins his experiment on the birthmark? What does the description of Georgiana's apartment and the connecting laboratory say about the nature of Aylmer's experiment?

The description of the "extensive apartments occupied by Aylmer as a laboratory" spans a good bit of the story, and for readers who pay attention to Hawthorne's use of imagery, this description conveys a good deal of information. Georgiana's boudoir "looked like a scene of enchantment": the curtains "shut in the scene from infinite space" and kept out the "sunshine" so that it might be "a pavilion among the clouds." Here Aylmer entertains her with "light and playful secrets," "airy figures," and "forms of unsubstantial beauty . . . imprinting their momentary footsteps on beam of light." This boudoir is connected to the furnace room where Aylmer does his work. This room is marked by fire, vapors, grime, and inhabited by Aminadab. In order to address how the setting illuminates the story's action and/or character, you must read and analyze these descriptions carefully.

Compare and Contrast Essays

As this chapter's discussion of imagery and of science and religion indicates, "The Birth-Mark" shares thematic and philosophical concerns as well as stylistic similarities with much of Hawthorne's other work. It provides many opportunities to write compare and contrast papers about theses shared concerns and techniques. Remember, a strong compare and contrast thesis needs to comment on the *significance* of the similarities and/or the differences you observe. For example, one possibility for a compare and contrast paper about "The Birth-Mark" is to compare the main characters' assessments of the birthmark itself. Since Georgiana and Aylmer's interpretations of the mark are so obviously different, a good thesis would need to make an assertion about the significance of those differences. Why are their differences important? What do these differences tell us about the characters or about Hawthorne's philosophies or ideas? When you are developing a paper about the connections between works, an effective method of shaping a strong thesis and argument is to observe the similarities between the works, but to develop a thesis that asserts how these apparently similar elements are different. Many scholars, for example, have noted that Hawthorne created many "mad scientist" characters, men who are so devoted to their science or their art that they lose perspective on all else. Aylmer is one of these characters. A good thesis comparing Aylmer and Dr. Rappaccini of "Rappaccini's Daughter" would initially identify both characters as examples of Hawthorne's mad scientists, but would argue that their motivations for scientific experimentation differ.

Sample Topics:

1. **Hawthorne's "mad scientists"**: Aylmer and Dr. Rappaccini are just two of Hawthorne's "mad scientists." Others include Roger Chillingworth of The Scarlet Letter and Owen Warland of "The Artist of the Beautiful." Choose one of Hawthorne's scientists and compare him to Aylmer. How are they alike and/or different? What does Hawthorne seem to be arguing through his presentation of these men?

   A paper that tackles this topic will need to address the kinds of questions posed in the sections on character, themes, and religion and philosophy and apply them to both characters. Often Hawthorne's critiques of these characters are fairly biting. Why? Despite their shared obsessions with their science, not all of these characters are considered villains. Why? Does Hawthorne seem to see any redeeming value in science?

2. **Faith:** As the section on religious and philosophical ideas indicated, "The Birth-Mark," with its emphasis on scientific advancement, also considers related issues of faith or belief.

Choose another of Hawthorne's works that comments on faith and compare its methods and/or conclusions to those of "The Birth-Mark."

Once again, the works that include the mad scientist figures usually confront issues of faith and belief. "Rappaccini's Daughter" is an obvious example. In this story, it is not Rappaccini and his science, but the growing love between Giovanni and Beatrice, that initiates questions of faith and belief. Similarly, of course, issues of trust and doubt test the relationship of Young Goodman Brown and his young wife, Faith. What points does Hawthorne seem to be making through these relationships?

3. **Dreams and visions:** Early in the story, Aylmer dreams of removing the birthmark from Georgiana; that dream, in effect, serves as a premonition. The narrator says: "Truth often finds its way to the mind close-muffled in robes of sleep and then speaks with uncompromising directness of matters in regard to which we practise an unconscious self-deception, during our waking moments." Compare Hawthorne's use of dreams and/or vision in this and another story. Are dreams the messengers of truth in the author's work?

As a writer concerned with human perception and the difference between reality and appearance, Hawthorne often uses dreams to comment on the accuracy of human perception. A paper that addresses this topic would need to assess just how dreams or visions function in the context of the particular stories. Do they allow a character to see the world more accurately or do they, as products of the unconscious mind, merely cloud and confuse the character? Conversely, you might wish to take a more psychological approach and consider what the dreams reveal about the characters themselves. An analysis of how the characters use their dreams would provide another approach. You could argue, for instance, that if Aylmer and Young Goodman Brown responded to their dreams differently, their lives might have been much different.

4. **Women's positions and roles:** As the section on character noted, Georgiana is first introduced in the story only as
Aylmer's wife. In many ways, the story presents her as the ideal
wife who loves and trusts her husband. Modern readers have
begun to question such evaluations of Georgiana. Scholars have
also noted similarities between Georgiana and many of Hawthorne's other women, comparing their physical descriptions,
their characterizations, and their social positions. Compare
Georgiana to another of Hawthorne's women.

This topic includes character development. A thoughtful
paper would also place these characters in some historical
context and evaluate how the social expectations and gender
roles of Hawthorne's time helped to shape them. Additionally,
you could compare the gender expectations of the 1840s with
those of modern times in an attempt to analyze modern readers' assessment of these women.

Bibliography and Online Resources for "The Birth-Mark"

Baym, Nina. *The Shape of Hawthorne's Career.* Ithaca, NY: Cornell UP, 1976.

Browner, Stephanie P. *Profound Science and Elegant Literature: Imagining Doctors in Nineteenth-Century America.* Philadelphia: U of Pennsylvania P,
2005.

Dauber, Kenneth. *Rediscovering Hawthorne.* Princeton, NJ: Princeton UP, 1977.

Donovel, David. "Introduction to 'The Birthmark.'" Hawthorne in Salem. Available online. URL: http://www.hawthorneinsalem.org/Literature/Alienation
OfTheArtist/TheBirthMark/Introduction.html. Downloaded June 7, 2006.

Doubleday, Neal Frank. *Hawthorne's Early Tales: A Critical Study.* Durham,
NC: Duke UP, 1972.

Easton, Alison. "Hawthorne and the question of women." *The Cambridge Companion to Nathaniel Hawthorne.* Ed. Richard H. Millington. Cambridge:
Cambridge UP, 2004. 79–98.

Eckstein, Barbara. "Hawthorne's 'The Birthmark:' Science and Romance as
Belief." *Studies in Short Fiction* 20 (Fall 1989): 511–19. EBSCO Information
Services. Available online by subscription. URL: http://www.ebsco.com.
Accessed June 14, 2006.

Ellis, Barbara. "Some Observations About Hawthorne's Women." *WILLA* 2 (1993): 13–18. Available online. URL: http://scholar.lib.vt.edu/ejournals/old-WILLA/fall93/k-ellis.html. Downloaded June 15, 2006.

Fetterley, Judith. *The Resisting Reader: A Feminist Approach to American Fiction.* Bloomington: Indiana UP, 1978.

Fogle, Richard, *Hawthorne's Fiction: The Light and the Dark.* Norman: U of Oklahoma P, 1952; rev. ed., 1964.

Gollin, Rita. *Hawthorne and the Truth of Dreams.* Baton Rouge: Louisiana State UP, 1979.

Grusser. John. "Playing with the (Birth) Mark: Aylmer's Failed Attempt to Achieve Perfect Whiteness." Hawthorne in Salem. Available online. URL: http://www.hawthorneinsalem.com/ScholarsForum/MMD1309.html. Downloaded June 7, 2006.

Millington, Richard. *Practising Romance: Narrative Form and Cultural Engagement in Hawthorne's Fiction.* Princeton, N.J.: Princeton UP, 1992.

Pfister, Joel. "Hawthorne as cultural theorist." In *The Cambridge Companion to Nathaniel Hawthorne,* edited by Richard H. Millington, 35–59. Cambridge: Cambridge UP, 2004.

Rosenberg, Liz. "'the best that earth could offer': 'The Birth-mark', A Newlywed's Story." *Studies in Short Fiction* 30 (Spring 1993): 145–52. EBSCO Information Services. Available online by subscription. URL: http://www.ebsco.com. Accessed June 14, 2006.

Shakinovsky, Lynn. "The Return of The Repressed: Illiteracy and the Death of the Narrative in Hawthorne's 'The Birthmark.'" *ATQ* 9 (December 1995): 269–82. EBSCO Information Services. Available online by subscription. URL: http://www.ebsco.com. Accessed June 14, 2006.

Smith, Allan Gardner Lloyd. *Eve Tempted: Writing and Sexuality in Hawthorne's Fiction.* Totowa, NJ: Barnes and Noble, 1983.

Stoehr, Taylor. *Hawthorne's Mad Scientists.* Hamden, CT: Archon Books, 1978.

Turner, Arlin. *Nathaniel Hawthorne. A Biography.* New York: Oxford UP, 1980.

Waggoner, Hyatt. *Hawthorne: A Critical Study* Cambridge, MA: Harvard UP, 1955; rev. ed. 1963.

Weinstein, Cindy. "The Invisible Hand Made Visible: 'The Birth-Mark.'" *Nineteenth-Century Literature* 48.1 (June 1993): 44–73.

Welter, Barbara. "The Cult of True Womanhood: 1820–1860." *American Quarterly* 18 (Summer 1966): 151–74.

Whitaker, Albert Keith. "Neoconservative Nathaniel: Bioethics and 'The Birth-Mark.'" Hawthorne in Salem. Available online. URL: http://www.hawthorne insalem.com/ScholarsForum/MMD2448.html. Downloaded June 7, 2006.

Wineapple, Brenda. "Excerpt from *Hawthorne: A Life.*" Hawthorne in Salem. Available online. URL: http://www.hawthorneinsalem.com/Literature/ AlienationOfTheArtist/TheBirthMark/MMD237 0.html. Downloaded June 7, 2006.

———. *Nathaniel Hawthorne: A Life.* New York: Knopf, 2003.

Youra, Steven. "'The Fatal hand': A Sign of Confusion in Hawthorne's 'The Birth-Mark.'" *ATQ* 60 (1986): 43–51.

Zanger, Jules. "Speaking of the Unspeakable: Hawthorne's 'The Birthmark.'" *Modern Philosophy* 80 (1983): 364–71.

"RAPPACCINI'S DAUGHTER"

READING TO WRITE

EARLY IN "Rappaccini's Daughter," as Giovanni watches Beatrice from the window above her father's garden, the narrator remarks, "Her face being now more revealed than on the former occasion, he was struck by its expression of simplicity and sweetness; qualities that had not entered into his idea of her character, and made him ask anew, what manner of mortal she might be." Giovanni's question is the central issue of the story, what scholars have called "the problem of Beatrice." Throughout most of the work, both Giovanni and the reader must try to assess "what manner of mortal" Beatrice is. Yet, while Beatrice is the title character and the central problem, she is certainly not the story's only problem. Instead, she is the focal point from which the work's other issues radiate. Like "Young Goodman Brown," this tale focuses on questions of human perception and the evidence of the senses. For much of the tale, Giovanni can only observe Beatrice and try to piece together the puzzle of her nature. Readers, through the narrative voice, observe Giovanni as he watches, interacts with, and assesses Beatrice. Finally, it seems that Hawthorne seeks to interest readers less in "the problem of Beatrice" than in the problem of the other characters' treatment and assessment of her. Notice how the narrator, at Beatrice's initial entrance into the story, directs the reader's attention not only to the beautiful young girl in the garden, but to Giovanni's observations and assessment of her. As he walks among the flowers of his garden, Doctor Rappaccini calls his daughter, precipitating her entrance into the story:

> "Here am I, my father! What would you?" cried a rich and youthful voice from the window of the opposite house; a voice as rich as a tropical sunset, and which made Giovanni, though he knew not why, think of deep hues of purple or crimson, and of perfumes heavily delectable.—"Are you in the garden?"
>
> "Yes, Beatrice," answered the gardener, "and I need your help."
>
> Soon there emerged from under a sculptured portal the figure of a young girl, arrayed with as much richness of taste as the most splendid of the flowers, beautiful as the day, and with a bloom so deep and vivid that one shade more would have been too much. She looked redundant with life, health, and energy; all of which attributes were bound down and compressed, as it were, and girdled tensely, in their luxuriance, by her virgin zone. Yet Giovanni's fancy must have grown morbid, while he looked down into the garden; for the impression which the fair stranger made upon him was as if here were another flower, the human sister of those vegetable ones, as beautiful as they—more beautiful than the richest of them—but still to be touched only with a glove, nor to be approached without a mask. As Beatrice came down the garden path, it was observable that she handled and inhaled the odor of several of the plants, which her father had most sedulously avoided.
>
> "Here, Beatrice," said the latter,—"see how many needful offices require to be done to our chief treasure. Yet, shattered as I am, my life might pay the penalty of approaching it so closely as circumstances demand. Henceforth, I fear, this plant must be consigned to your sole charge."
>
> "And gladly will I undertake it," cried again the rich tones of the young lady, as she bent toward the magnificent plant, and opened her arms as if to embrace it. "Yes, my sister, my splendor, it shall be Beatrice's task to nurse and serve thee; and thou shalt reward her with thy kisses and perfumed breath, which to her is as the breath of life!"

Then, with all the tenderness in her manner that was so strikingly expressed in her words, she busied herself with such attentions as the plant seemed to require; and Giovanni, at his lofty window, rubbed his eyes, and almost doubted whether it were a girl tending her favorite flower, or one sister performing the duties of affection to another. The scene soon terminated. Whether Doctor Rappaccini had finished his labors in the garden, or that his watchful eye had caught the stranger's face, he now took his daughter's arm and retired. Night was already closing in; oppressive exhalations seemed to proceed from the plants, and steal upward past the open window; and Giovanni, closing the lattice, went to his couch, and dreamed of a rich flower and beautiful girl. Flower and maiden were different and yet the same, and fraught with some strange peril in either shape.

You will note that the first paragraph of this passage draws attention to three of the actors in the story—Beatrice, Giovanni, and the narrator himself. Initially Beatrice attracts the reader's attention just as she attracts Giovanni's. Even before we see her, the narrator describes her voice as "rich and youthful." Almost immediately, though, he shifts the focus from Beatrice to Giovanni. Her voice, the narrator says, "made Giovanni, though he knew not why, think of deep hues of purple or crimson, and of perfumes heavily delectable." Why would the narrator emphasize the effect that Beatrice's voice had upon Giovanni? Why does Giovanni associate Beatrice's voice with the color purple and with heavy perfumes? Within the context of the story, what do these associations imply about Beatrice? What parallels do they establish? Further, what do these associations suggest about Giovanni? Why might the narrator stress that Giovanni did not know why Beatrice's voice evoked such associations? Does this help you to assess either the accuracy of Giovanni's thoughts or the motivations for them?

As Beatrice moves into the young man's view two paragraphs later, the story seems to amplify these associations. The narrator once again describes her through the language of richness and abundance. He comments on the "richness of taste" with which she is arrayed and parallels this richness with that of "the most splendid of flowers, beautiful as the day, and with a bloom so deep and vivid that one shade more would have been too much." The narrator develops the language of richness and overabundance in the next sentence: "She looked redundant with life, health, and energy." What impression does this language create in the mind of the reader? While the narrator does not distinctly link this initial description with Giovanni's point of view, his perception does seem limited by Giovanni's point of view. The reader sees Beatrice only when she becomes visible to the young man, and the narrator's analogy linking the young woman with the flower seem to develop from Giovanni's initial reactions to Beatrice's voice. What is the effect of the narrator focusing the reader's view of Beatrice through Giovanni? As the paragraph continues, the narrator explicitly links the analogy between Beatrice and the flower with Giovanni's point of view, saying, "the impression which the fair stranger made upon him was as if here were another flower, the human sister of those vegetable ones, as beautiful as they—more beautiful than the richest of them—but still to be touched only with a glove, nor to be approached without a mask." Certainly this analogy should attract any reader's attention, for Giovanni's impression is a curious one, and it seems to tell the reader more about Giovanni than about Beatrice. Indeed, the narrator seems to cast some doubt on the correctness of Giovanni's impressions when he says that "Giovanni's fancy must have grown morbid." Why might a young man see a beautiful young woman who is apparently "redundant with life, health, and energy" as a "human sister" to the flowers in Rappaccini's garden, curiously concluding that this beauty was "to be touched only with a glove, nor approached without a mask"? What do such impressions suggest about Giovanni? Do they suggest anything about his attitudes toward women?

Of course, as the paragraph continues, the narrator suggests that Giovanni's impressions, strange as they are, might be grounded in fact, for Beatrice "handled and inhaled the odor of several plants, which her father had most sedulously avoided." As the passage continues, her father overtly asks Beatrice to tend the magnificent purple plant located at the center of the fountain, claiming that his "life might pay the penalty of approaching it so closely." Beatrice assents, embraces the plant, calls it "sister," and remarks that in exchange for her nursing, the plant "shalt reward her with [its] kisses and perfumed breath, which to her is as the breath of life." Does this passage cause you to reassess your opinion of

Giovanni and his curious reaction to the beautiful girl in the garden? Earlier, the young man observed the doctor donning gloves and a mask as he walked among the garden, "as if all this beauty did but conceal a deadlier malice." Might he be correct in assuming that the girl, like the plants, also conceals a "deadlier malice" underneath her beautiful exterior? You might think, too, about the narrator's word choice here. "Malice" implies volition, willful evil; plants are incapable of malice. If Beatrice, like the plant, is poisonous, is she also malicious, spreading this poison willfully? This passage provides still more insight into Beatrice's nature. If the magnificent plant is poisonous, as all the evidence so far suggests, what does Beatrice's assertion that the plant's "breath" is "as the breath of life" to her suggest about the young woman's relationship with the plant and her relationship with poison? How might knowing that poison is "as the breath of life" to Beatrice affect your analysis and assessment of her as you continue to read the story?

The next paragraph continues to complicate Giovanni's attempt to evaluate Beatrice, for the girl tends to the flower "with all the tenderness in her manner that was so strikingly expressed in her words." Certainly, you should be trying to balance the widely varied language that seems to describe Beatrice. Can she contain both "malice" and "tenderness"? Can she be both "redundant with life, health, and energy" and poisonous as well? Like Giovanni, who "rubbed his eyes, and almost doubted whether it were a girl tending her favorite flower, or one sister performing duties of affection to another," readers have no basis for evaluation, and thus must question the accuracy of their "observations" of Beatrice. Strikingly, though, this paragraph emphasizes that we do have access to more than just our observations of Beatrice, for one of the more positive qualities attributed to the young girl, tenderness, is expressed both in her "manner" and in her "words." Might an assessment of the girl's manner and her words provide a particular insight into Beatrice's nature? In what ways is the evidence provided by the young woman's "manner" and her "words" qualitatively different from the evidence that created Giovanni's initial impressions? Whatever the effects of Beatrice's words, Giovanni's initial doubts are manifest in his dreams, where his subconscious still links "the rich flower and beautiful girl," finding that "[f]lower and maiden were different and yet the same, and fraught with some strange peril in either shape." What does Giovanni's dream suggest about his assessment of Beatrice? At this point, are you inclined to agree with the evaluation of Giovanni's subconscious?

When you have carefully analyzed the early pages of "Rappaccini's Daughter," you will approach the rest of the text armed with a number of important questions and observations. While you, like Giovanni, will read to discover "what manner of mortal" Beatrice is, you will also be attuned to the judgments that other characters—particularly Giovanni—make about Beatrice. A close reading of the story's beginning should also alert you to the complicated narrative voice that guides and shapes your perspective. Close readers will stay alert to places where the narrator limits the reader's perspective to that of Giovanni, and to places where the narrator seems to separate from Giovanni's perspective. Such nuances in the narrative voice are important to your evaluation of Beatrice and, consequently, to the story's larger meanings.

TOPICS AND STRATEGIES

The following section should guide you in developing effective topics for papers on "Rappaccini's Daughter." Remember that the topics discussed are quite broad; they give you a general framework to guide you as you read, reread, and analyze the story. Use these topics as springboards. You will need to narrow the focus of your writing, constructing an analytical thesis, and bearing in mind the proposed length of your paper.

Themes

In Hawthorne's preface to "Rappaccini's Daughter," he claims that the story is a translation of a story entitled "Beatrice; ou la Belle Empoisonneuse" by M. de l'Aubépine (French for "Hawthorne"). Poking fun at himself, Hawthorne notes that Aubépine's writings "might have won him greater reputation but for an inveterate love of allegory." Indeed, "Rappaccini's Daughter," like many of Hawthorne's stories, supports more than one allegorical interpretation. The abundant language of faith, doubt, and skepticism has led many to read "Rappaccini's Daughter" as an allegory of faith. Other allegorical readings suggest different themes. Giovanni's situation as a "young man for the first time out of his native sphere" casts him as one of Hawthorne young male initiates. Consequently, many read the story of Giovanni's developing relationship with Beatrice as an examination of the young man's psychological attitudes toward women and sexuality. Still others read the story as another of Hawthorne's comments on the enticements and the dangers of scientific study. To write a paper about a particular theme in "Rappaccini's Daughter," you should begin by identifying a theme that you discovered during your initial reading of the story. Return to the story, noting the aspects of plot, language, or character that will help you develop your interpretation.

Sample Topics:

1. **Faith:** Toward the story's end, Baglioni tells Giovanni that Beatrice, like the woman sent to Alexander the Great, is "poisonous as she is beautiful." The professor's argument "gave instantaneous distinctness to a thousand dim suspicions, which now grinned at [Giovanni] like so many demons. But he strove hard to quell them, and to respond to Baglioni with a true lover's perfect faith." How might you read "Rappaccini's Daughter" as an allegory of a young man's struggle between faith and skepticism?

   Like most other topics about this story, this question requires that you reach some conclusions about Beatrice and Giovanni's assessment of her. As the story progresses, Giovanni comes to know that Beatrice is both poisonous and beautiful, but he cannot decide if "those dreadful peculiarities in her physical nature . . . could not be supposed to exist without some corresponding monstrosity of soul." What do you think of Giovanni's various judgments of Beatrice? What do you think of his decision to institute a "decisive test" that should allow him to decide about the nature of Beatrice's soul? You will need to pay close attention to the language of faith, doubt, and skepticism in the story. How does such language help to develop the story as an allegory of faith? The introductory section of this chapter stressed that much of the story seems to involve Giovanni's skills in observation. How is the story's treatment of the physical senses integral to an assessment of the story as an allegory of faith? Similarly, you will need to evaluate Hawthorne's use of narrative voice in the story. Where and how does the narrator allow insight into the characters and their motivations? How does this insight help to develop your study of faith in "Rappaccini's Daughter"?

2. **Sexuality:** When Giovanni first sees Beatrice in the garden, the narrator notes her beauty and then notes that "the impression which the fair stranger made upon [Giovanni] was as if here were another flower . . . more beautiful than the richest of them—but still to be touched only with a glove, nor to be approached without a mask." In what ways might Giovanni's strange reaction to Beatrice and her beauty be read as a response to her sexuality? How might you develop a reading of Hawthorne's story as a commentary on human sexuality in general and female sexuality in particular?

As with the previous theme, this topic asks you to consider Beatrice's dualism—the relationship between her body and her soul. Similarly, it asks that you evaluate Giovanni's reaction to Beatrice. You will need to trace their developing relationship. This investigation might take a psychological perspective. What do Giovanni's reactions to Beatrice's body say about his attitudes toward sexuality? Does the fact that Hawthorne has cast Beatrice's physical nature as poisonous say something about the author's view of female sexuality? You should also spend some time analyzing the imagery that surrounds Beatrice. What is the effect of the analogy between Beatrice and the flowers in her father's garden? Similarly, the story clearly associates Rappaccini's garden with the Garden of Eden. How do you assess these associations?

3. **Science:** The narrator refers to Doctor Rappaccini as a "man of science," and "Rappaccini's Daughter" clearly seems a cautionary tale about scientific pursuit. What elements or aspects of scientific pursuit does Hawthorne seem to criticize in the story? Why?

A paper that focuses on "Rappaccini's Daughter" as an indictment of science and scientific pursuit must explore both Rappaccini and Baglioni thoroughly. Rappaccini clearly seems to be the villain of the story. How do you assess Baglioni and his role in the tale's events? Is his assessment of Rappaccini accurate? Does Baglioni share any culpability in the final outcome of the story? Is his role tied to his position as a scientist? You should also evaluate why Hawthorne criticizes Rappaccini and his science. Is he representative of all scientists, or are there qualities particular to Rappaccini that Hawthorne emphasizes? In order to answer these questions, you must look closely at Rappaccini's achievements and his motivations. Be alert to the language that Hawthorne uses in describing the garden and its relationship with nature. How does this comparison help you assess the flaws in Rappaccini's pursuit of science? Many readers see parallels between Doctor Rappaccini and Victor Frankenstein from Mary Shelley's *Frankenstein*. If you know Shelley's work, you might try to think of the parallels between the scientific pursuits of Frankenstein and Rappaccini. Another (potentially related) line of inquiry could involve the relationships between Beatrice and her father and between Beatrice and the plants. Rappaccini's decision to use his daughter—as well as her lover—as experiments raises obvious ethical questions. Examine the language and the imagery at the end of the story very carefully. Together, Giovanni and Beatrice seem to represent the culmination of Rappaccini's lifework. What motivates Rappaccini to use his science to render Giovanni into Beatrice's "bridegroom" who will "[stand] apart from common men," as does Beatrice? Finally, the story never mentions Beatrice's mother. Is this omission in any way suggestive for an analysis of Rappaccini's role as scientist in this story?

Character

Because the story revolves around the question of Beatrice's character and because the story's narrative perspective allows you to watch and assess the other characters' estimations of Beatrice, "Rappaccini's Daughter" provides ample material for papers about character and character development. As you reread the story, be sure to focus on the language and the actions of your character and to remain alert to the narrator's commentary on your character.

Sample Topics:

1. **Beatrice as a character:** Hawthorne's preface claims that the story is a translation of M. de Aubépine's "Beatrice; ou la Belle Empoisonneuse" (which would translate as "Beatrice; or The Beautiful Poisoner"); Hawthorne's tale bears the title "Rappaccini's Daughter." Both titles invoke Beatrice as the title character, but they do so rather differently. Which title better portrays Beatrice and her role in the story? Why?

Each of the titles portrays Beatrice quite differently, and each seems to cast her in a different position within the story's plot. You might begin by noting that the "original" title gives the heroine a name, while Hawthorne's "translated" title does not. Why might this be significant? What does the title "Rappaccini's Daughter" imply about the young woman and her position in the tale that "Beatrice: or la Belle Empoisonneuse" does not? Similarly, the "original" title names, or labels, Beatrice twice—she is "Beatrice" or "the beautiful poisoner." What does the doubleness of the title suggest about Beatrice? Might either title help to guide your assessment of Beatrice's character in a particular way? Does either title suggest anything about Beatrice's intentions and her actions in the story? What does each title imply or suggest about Beatrice's relationships with the male characters within the text? Explain. Some readers see in Beatrice a representative of the place of women in 19th-century society. How do the story's titles help to develop such a reading of her character?

2. **Giovanni as a character:** Toward the story's end, Baglioni's claim that Beatrice is "poisonous as she is beautiful" causes Giovanni to doubt her. Yet, the narrator says that Giovanni

"strove hard to . . . respond to Baglioni with a true lover's perfect faith." Evaluate Giovanni as a "true lover."

While this question obviously asks you to consider some of the same issues addressed in the discussion of the theme of faith, it also asks you to analyze other aspects of Giovanni's character more fully. You must evaluate the strength of Giovanni's faith in Beatrice, but you must also consider what causes him to react to her the way he does. Does the narrator provide us with any insight into Giovanni's emotions or his evaluations of Beatrice? How do these insights help us to understand or evaluate Giovanni? You may find that your study of Giovanni's emotions and motivations shares some territory with the questions posed in the discussion of the theme of sexuality.

3. **Doctor Rappaccini as a character:** Clearly, Hawthorne has created another of his scientist figures in Doctor Rappaccini, and many readers see "Rappaccini's Daughter" as a cautionary tale about science and scientific pursuit. Rappaccini plays other roles in this story though. While he is a scientist, he is also a medical doctor, a father, and a kind of artist. Choose one of these roles as a lens through which to analyze Doctor Rappaccini and his role in the story.

Rappaccini's role as a medical doctor is clearly related to his work as a scientist, but medicine is a specific branch of science with particular responsibilities and ethical concerns. Much of what we learn about Rappaccini's medicine comes in the form of gossip through both Baglioni and Lisabetta. As you would with any piece of gossip, you must evaluate the reliability of the information. Similarly, you must evaluate Rappaccini's relationship with both Beatrice and Giovanni.

As with all of the characters in the story, Rappaccini's own words and his actions are the most reliable gauges of his character. Should you wish to evaluate Rappaccini's role as a father, you must closely analyze his largest speaking role—his conversation with Beatrice at the story's end. What do his words and his behavior suggest about his relationship with Beatrice? What do you learn of his motivations and his intentions?

When Doctor Rappaccini first appears in this final scene, the narrator remarks that he looked at Beatrice and Giovanni "as might an artist who should spend his life in achieving a picture or a group of statuary, and finally be satisfied with his success." Hawthorne uses the language of art and artistry elsewhere in the story, and you should examine this language if you choose to write a paper about Rappaccini as an artist.

4. **Doctor Baglioni as a character:** Like Rappaccini, Baglioni plays many roles in the story. Indeed, he seems to play nearly all the same roles that Rappaccini does—he is a scientist, a doctor, a kind of substitute father figure for young Giovanni, and a storyteller/artist. Given all these roles, how do you assess Baglioni's role or position in the story?

Perhaps the most interesting way to evaluate Baglioni's character is to evaluate his position as substitute father and guide to Giovanni. Does Baglioni prove to be a good father figure? Why or why not? While this question asks that you analyze his relationship with Giovanni, you must also evaluate his relationship with Rappaccini and his interpretation of Beatrice. What do you know of his motivations and his values? As you develop your assessment of him, you should be sure to evaluate his own words as well as the narrator's assessment of him.

5. **The narrator as a character:** Analyze the narrator's role in the story. How does the narrative voice shape the reader's interpretation of the story?

As the introductory section of this chapter points out, the narrator's perspective in the beginning of the tale seems limited to Giovanni's point of view, showing readers what Giovanni sees and telling us what Giovanni thinks. At other points, the narrator seems more omniscient, sharing information with readers that is beyond Giovanni's knowledge. As you reread the story, examine these apparent shifts in narrative perspective. How do they shape readers' responses to Beatrice and to Giovanni?

Philosophy and Ideas

Besides providing two ways to look at Beatrice, Hawthorne's two titles to the story—the "original" French title from the preface and the story's English title—also raise more philosophical questions about the nature of names. Like the scarlet *A* from *The Scarlet Letter,* names are signs that represent something else, and Hawthorne's playful preface asks readers to think about the use and the effect of names, signs, and symbols.

Sample Topics:

1. **Naming and representation:** Hawthorne's claim in the story's preface that "Rappaccini's Daughter" is a translation of a tale entitled "Beatrice; or la Belle Empoisonneuse" invites a question about the importance of names. Unlike the other Hawthorne titles translated into French for Hawthorne's playful satire, the title of this story is not a literal translation. Why? How might you read "Rappaccini's Daughter" as a story about the ability of names to adequately represent reality?

   This question clearly shares a good deal of territory with the discussion of Beatrice's character and her relation to the story's two titles. There are, however, other aspects of "Rappaccini's Daughter" that invite this kind of inquiry. Consider, for example, the way words like "poison" and "antidote" work in the story. When he first observes Beatrice, Giovanni hears her tell her poisonous "sister" plant that its "breath" "is to her as the breath of life." Similarly, Baglioni tells Giovanni about Rappaccini's theory that "all medicinal virtues are comprised within those substances which we term vegetable poisons." Should this knowledge not lead Giovanni to wonder about the wisdom of asking Beatrice to drink an "antidote" or "medicine" that "would have rendered the most virulent poisons . . . innocuous"? Do you see any evidence that Beatrice understands the insufficiency of such names and labels? Explain.

Form and Genre

While studies of Hawthorne's longer fiction often explore the distinction between novel and romance that Hawthorne forged in the prefaces to his longer works, many of his short stories are productively read as allegories, stories in which characters, objects, and events represent abstract principles. Hawthorne's humorous preface to "Rappaccini's Daughter" addresses his "love of allegory" and directs the reader's attention to his interest in allegorical representation, and this could provide a focus for a paper.

Sample Topics:

1. **Allegory:** In his self-deprecatory preface, Hawthorne claims that M. de Aubépine "might have won . . . a greater reputation but for an inveterate love of allegory." He claims that Aubépine's stories, "if the reader chance to take them in precisely the proper point of view, may amuse a leisure hour . . . if otherwise, they can hardly fail to look excessively like nonsense." Finally, Hawthorne identifies "Rappaccini's Daughter" as a translation of Aubépine's "Beatrice; ou la Belle Empoisonneuse." How might you read "Rappaccini's Daughter" as a story about allegory?

   To approach this rather difficult question, you need to focus on Beatrice and her position in the story. Like a story, she is subject to multiple interpretations. Each of the male characters reads and interprets her. And like Aubépine's allegory, "which is apt to invest his plots and characters with the aspect of scenery and people in the clouds" who are not held "within the limits of our native earth," so Beatrice seems outside "the limits of ordinary nature." How might you develop a reading of the story that suggests that the problem of Beatrice is also the problem of allegory?

Language, Symbols, and Imagery

Throughout this story, Hawthorne employs imagery and metaphor to embellish and develop his meaning. Given the story's allegorical nature, even the literal level of the story can represent something more abstract and intangible. A close examination of Hawthorne's language should help you develop a paper on the imagery in "Rappaccini's Daughter."

Sample Topics:

1. **Poison as a metaphor:** While Beatrice's physical nature is poisonous, Hawthorne clearly uses poison as a metaphor in "Rappaccini's Daughter." Analyze the language of poison and poisoning in the story. How does Hawthorne use the idea of poison both literally and metaphorically in the text?

A close reading of the story should clearly demonstrate just how thoroughly Hawthorne integrates the language of poison and poisoning into the text. Where and how is this language used? How does it reflect on the individual characters? While M. de Aubépine's title for the story, "Beatrice; ou la Belle Empoisonneuse," labels Beatrice "the beautiful poisoner," you might also want to consider who, finally, are the poisoners in the story. In a related approach, you might explore the language of monstrosity that also pervades the text and which the story often links to poison and poisonous natures.

2. **Language and imagery of Eden:** As Giovanni observes Doctor Rappaccini in his garden in the early pages of the story, the narrator remarks, "Was this garden, then, the Eden of the present world?—and this man, with such a perception of harm in what his own hands caused to grow, was he the Adam?" How does Hawthorne develop the imagery of Eden in this story? What seems to be his purpose in planting this analogy in Giovanni's thoughts?

Hawthorne includes more than this one reference to Eden in the story; much of the language and imagery of Rappaccini's garden seems to evoke thoughts of Eden. The analogy, though, is hard to sustain. You might think about which of Hawthorne's characters you would cast in which roles in the story of Eden. Is Rappaccini, as Giovanni speculates, Adam? What role does Beatrice play? In what ways is Beatrice like a resident of Eden? Does Giovanni also have a part in the drama of Eden within the story? What of Baglioni, who never actually sets foot within the garden? Further, you might consider what it means to be "the Eden of the present world." How might "the Eden of the present world" compare to the paradise of Adam and Eve?

3. **The fountain and the shrub as symbols:** Two symbols, the fountain and the purple-blossomed shrub that stands in the midst of the fountain, dominate the story. Both stand at the center of the garden; both seem closely linked with Beatrice. How do the fountain and the shrub help characterize Beatrice?

To answer this question thoroughly, you will not only need to examine the shrub and the fountain, but you will need to identify the language and imagery used elsewhere in the story that evokes either of these elements. As the question itself indicates, you should explore the connections between Beatrice and these two symbols and then consider how these connections help develop your answer.

Compare and Contrast Essays

The treatment of character, faith, science, and representation in "Rappaccini's Daughter" provides ample material for comparison with other works by Hawthorne. Giovanni, for example, is just one of many inexperienced young men in Hawthorne's fiction who venture into the wider world. You could productively compare him with Robin Molineux of "My Kinsman, Major Molineux," Young Goodman Brown, Reuben Bourne from "Roger Malvin's Burial," or with Donatello from *The Marble Faun.* Doctor Rappaccini, of course, shares a great deal with Hawthorne's other scientist characters—Aylmer from "The Birth-Mark" and Roger Chillingworth from *The Scarlet Letter.* You might also compare him with Hawthorne's artist characters like Owen Warland from "The Artist of the Beautiful" or Holgrave from *The House of the Seven Gables.* Similarly, Beatrice Rappaccini seems to prefigure some of the stronger heroines of Hawthorne's novels. Whether you compare Hawthorne's treatment of character or his use of a particular theme, be sure that your paper constructs an argument about why and how the similarities and differences are important.

Sample Topics:

1. **Faith and skepticism:** "Rappaccini's Daughter" is one of Hawthorne's later stories and in it he returns to a theme that occupied him throughout most of his career—faith. How is Hawthorne's treatment of faith in "Rappaccini's Daughter" different from his consideration of faith in another of his works?

   You might immediately think of "Young Goodman Brown" in response to this question, for the story is an obvious allegory of faith. Numerous other stories would work just as well here. "The Artist of the Beautiful," for example, is another of Hawthorne's later tales that explores issues of faith and skepticism. You might also examine "The Birth-Mark" or "The Minister's Black Veil."

2. **Relationships:** Compare Hawthorne's treatment of male-female relationships in "Rappaccini's Daughter" and another of his works.

   You could focus this topic in a number of ways. Comparing Beatrice and Georgiana from "The Birth-Mark" as female subjects of male experiments should provide plenty of material for a thoughtful paper. Similarly, comparing the relationship of Beatrice and Giovanni with that of Georgiana and Aylmer could be quite suggestive. You could compare the relationship between Hester Prynne and Arthur Dimmesdale with that of Beatrice and Giovanni. You might think about how the human relationships in the stories are linked to questions of faith.

3. **Hawthorne's women:** Some critics see Beatrice Rappaccini as a precursor of Hawthorne's strong, "dark" women from his novels. Choose one of these women and explore the relationship that she bears to Beatrice.

In a paper such as this, you would do well to do more than just compare the women's personalities or qualities. Hawthorne seemed to have a particular interest in the place that these women had in society. Since many readers see Beatrice as a victim of male misunderstanding, you might fruitfully compare her to Hester Prynne (*The Scarlet Letter*), Zenobia (*The Blithedale Romance*), or Miriam (*The Marble Faun*). How might these women be said to be victims of the men who surround them? If you choose to compare Beatrice with Zenobia, you might consider the similar imagery that surrounds both women. What does it suggest? You might also choose to compare their deaths. Zenobia commits suicide; does Beatrice? Critics comment that Beatrice's name invokes Beatrice Cenci, a 16th-century Italian noblewoman who was allegedly imprisoned and raped by her father and later participated in his murder. Miriam in *The Marble Faun* is frequently compared to Beatrice Cenci. This, too, could provide a fruitful area for investigation.

4. **The progeny of science and of art:** Scholars have focused quite a bit of attention on Hawthorne's men of science and his artist figures. Readers have spent less time comparing the progeny or offspring of these characters. Beatrice tells Giovanni that her "sister" plant is the "offspring of [Rappaccini's] science, of his intellect, while I was but his earthly child." Compare Rappaccini's "offspring"—his plants and Beatrice—with the creations of another of Hawthorne's artist or scientist figures. What point does Hawthorne seem to be making through their portraits?

Owen Warland's mechanical butterfly seems to present a particularly interesting comparison. Both Beatrice and the butterfly are the culmination of their creators' lifelong labor. Neither the butterfly nor Beatrice survives. Why? While Georgiana from "The Birth-Mark" is not Aylmer's progeny, he means her "perfected" body to be his crowning achievement. You could write an interesting comparison of Georgiana and

Beatrice as the subjects of—and embodiments of—Rappaccini and Aylmer's science.

Bibliography and Online Resources for "Rappaccini's Daughter"

Baym, Nina. *The Shape of Hawthorne's Career.* Ithaca NY: Cornell UP, 1976.

Bell, Millicent. *Hawthorne's View of the Artist.* Albany: SUNY P, 1962.

———, ed. *New Essays on Hawthorne's Major Tales.* New York: Cambridge UP, 1993.

Bensick, Carol Marie. *La Nouvelle Beatrice: Renaissance and Romance in "Rappaccini's Daughter."* New Brunswick, NJ: Rutgers UP, 1985.

Bradley, Judy, Fred Brown, John Robinson, Chris Sykes, and Joe Westfield. "Rappaccini's Daughter: An Online Study Guide." Plymouth Public Schools. Available Online. URL: http://www.plymouthschools.com/Rappaccinis_ Daughter/index.html. Downloaded November 9, 2006.

Brown, Gillian. "Hawthorne and Children in the Nineteenth Century: Daughters, Flowers, Stories." *A Historical Guide to Nathaniel Hawthorne.* Ed. Larry J. Reynolds. New York: Oxford UP, 2001. 79–108.

Browner, Stephanie P. *Profound Science and Elegant Literature: Imagining Doctors in Nineteenth-Century America.* Philadelphia: U Pennsylvania P, 2005.

Christophersen, Bill. "Agnostic Tensions in Hawthorne's Short Stories." *American Literature* 72 (2000): 595–624.

Colacurcio, Michael. "A Better Mode of Evidence." *Emerson Society Quarterly* 54 (1969): 12–22.

Crews, Frederick C. *The Sins of Fathers: Hawthorne's Psychological Themes.* New York: Oxford UP, 1966.

Dryden, Edgar. *Nathaniel Hawthorne: The Poetics of Enchantment.* Ithaca NY: Cornell UP, 1977.

Easton, Alison. "Hawthorne and the question of women." *The Cambridge Companion to Nathaniel Hawthorne.* Ed. by Richard H. Millington. Cambridge: Cambridge UP, 2004. 79–98.

Eaton, Cathy, and Melissa Pennell. "Introduction to 'Rappaccini's Daughter.'" Hawthorne in Salem. Available online. URL: http://www.hawthornein salem.com/Literature/Hawthorne&Women/Rappaccini/Introduction.html. Downloaded November 8, 2006.

Fogle, Richard Harter. *Hawthorne's Fiction: The Light and the Dark.* Norman: U of Oklahoma P, 1952.

Fossum, Robert H. *Hawthorne's Inviolable Circle: the Problem of Time.* Deland, FL: Everett/Edwards Inc., 1972.

Gilmore, Michael T. *American Romanticism in the Marketplace.* Chicago: U of Chicago P, 1988.

Herbert, T. Walter. *Dearest Beloved: The Hawthornes and the Making of the Middle-Class Family.* Berkeley: U of California P, 1993.

Idol, John L., and Melinda M. Ponder. *Hawthorne and Women: Engendering and Expanding the Hawthorne Tradition.* Amherst, MA: U of Massachusetts P, 1999.

Male, Roy R. *Hawthorne's Tragic Vision.* New York: Norton, 1957.

Mancall, James N. *"Thoughts Painfully Intense": Hawthorne and the Invalid Author.* New York: Routledge, 2002.

Millington, Richard H. "The Meanings of Hawthorne's Women." Hawthorne in Salem. Available Online. URL: http://www.hawthorneinsalem.com/Literature/Melville/LiteraryLinks/MMD1210.html. Downloaded November 8, 2006.

Mitchell, Thomas. *Hawthorne's Fuller Mystery.* Amherst: U of Massachusetts P, 1998.

Reynolds, Larry J. *A Historical Guide to Nathaniel Hawthorne.* New York: Oxford UP, 2001.

Walker, Pierre A. "Why We Still Read Hawthorne 150 Years Later." Hawthorne in Salem. Available online. URL: http://www.hawthorneinsalem.com/ScholarsForum/MMD2004.html. Downloaded November 8, 2006.

Waggoner, Hyatt H. *Hawthorne: A Critical Study.* Cambridge, MA: Belknap Press of Harvard University, 1955.

"THE ARTIST OF
THE BEAUTIFUL"

READING TO WRITE

IN "THE Artist of the Beautiful" Hawthorne explores quite a few of the
themes and issues that he addresses elsewhere in his fiction. Art and the
artist, faith, and idealism all play important roles in this story. And, as in
"The Birth-Mark" and *The Scarlet Letter,* Hawthorne also grapples with the
nature of symbolism. Literary scholars often note that a series of contrasting elements fuel this story. Just as the tale seems to set Owen Warland
and Robert Danforth in opposition, so it establishes clear tensions between
spirit and matter, time and transcendence, beauty and utility, the ideal and
the real. You must work to sort out the value system of the story and to
decide if Hawthorne celebrates or critiques Owen Warland and his creative
impulse. As is the case with most of Hawthorne's artist figures, the author's
assessment is both complicated and elusive. Early in the story, after Owen
has inadvertently destroyed his artistic project, he spends a "few sluggish
weeks" in an apparent depression. During this time, his old master and
nemesis, Peter Hovenden, visits Owen and examines the young artist's delicate, mechanical creation. Hovenden warns Owen, "in this small piece of
mechanism lives your evil spirit." The ensuing passage provides insight into
both the characters' motivations and the story's themes and values:

> "You are my Evil Spirit," answered Owen, much excited—"you, and
> the hard, coarse world! The leaden thoughts and the despondency

that you fling upon me are my clogs. Else, I should long ago have achieved the task that I was created for."

Peter Hovenden shook his head, with the mixture of contempt and indignation which mankind, of whom he was partly a representative, deem themselves entitled to feel toward all simpletons who seek other prizes than the dusty ones along the highway. He then took his leave with an uplifted finger, and a sneer upon his face, that haunted the artist's dreams for many a night afterwards. At the time of his master's visit, Owen was probably on the point of taking up the relinquished task; but, by this sinister event, he was thrown back into the state whence he had been slowly emerging.

But the innate tendency of his soul had only been accumulating fresh vigor, during its apparent sluggishness. As the summer advanced, he almost totally relinquished his business, and permitted Father Time, so far as the old gentleman was represented by the clocks and watches under his control, to stray at random through human life, making infinite confusion among the train of bewildered hours. He wasted the sunshine, as people said, in wandering through the woods and fields, and along the banks of streams. There, like a child, he found amusement in chasing butterflies, or watching the motions of water-insects. There was something truly mysterious in the intentness with which he contemplated these living playthings, as they sported on the breeze; or examined the structure of an imperial insect whom he had imprisoned. The chase of butterflies was an apt emblem of the ideal pursuit in which he had spent so many golden hours. But, would the Beautiful Idea ever be yielded to his hand, like the butterfly that symbolized it? Sweet, doubtless, were these days, and congenial to the artist's soul. They were full of bright conceptions, which gleamed through his intellectual world, as the butterflies gleamed through the outward atmosphere, and were real to him for the instant, without the toil, and perplexity, and many disappointments, of attempting to make them visible to the sensual eye. Alas, that the artist, whether in poetry or whatever other material, may not content himself with the inward enjoyment of the beautiful, but must chase the flitting mystery beyond the verge of his ethereal domain, and crush its frail being in seizing it with a material grasp! Owen

Warland felt the impulse to give external reality to his ideas, as irresistibly as any of the poets or painters, who have arrayed the world in a dimmer and fainter beauty, imperfectly copied from the richness of their visions.

You might begin your analysis of this passage by examining Hovenden. Why does he believe that Owen's artistic impulse, as represented in the "small piece of mechanism," is Warland's "evil sprit"? Does this assertion tell you something about Hovenden's values, or does it provide more insight into Owen? Are you inclined to agree with Hovenden? Why or why not? Owen's response to his old master requires examination as well—he turns the tables and says, "You are my Evil Spirit." Why might the young man view Hovenden in this way? Further, in Warland's part of the dialogue, the words "evil" and "spirit" are capitalized; in Hovenden's, they are not. What might be the implications of this difference? Consider, too, that Warland tells the old man that his artistic work is "the task that I was created for." Owen seems to see his work as divinely ordained. Consider how such a belief might shape Owen's commitment to his work as well as his responses to his critics. Owen also identifies his old master with the "hard, coarse world," and the narrator seems to echo this sentiment when he says that Hovenden was "partly a representative" of "mankind." If this is so, what does Hawthorne seem to be saying about the values of the world? Why does the world in which Owen lives seem to be at odds with him? What "prizes" does Owen seek that the world deems worthy of "contempt and indignation"? What are the "dusty [prizes] along the highway" that those like Hovenden value? Further, why is Hovenden *partly a representative* of "mankind"? Does the story provide the reader with other representatives of "mankind" or society at large? How do they compare to the old watchmaker? You might pursue this line of inquiry further by examining Hovenden's effect upon the young artist. The narrator says that the old man's "sneer . . . haunted the artist's dreams for many a night afterwards," and that this encounter throws Owen into his state of sluggish depression. Why does the old man affect Warland as he does? Examine the language that Owen uses as he hurls this accusation at the old man. How does the artist's assertion that his old master flings "leaden thoughts" that are his "clogs" work within the larger patterns of language and imagery in the story?

Once Owen begins to emerge from his state of inactivity, he seems transformed. Now, instead of concentrating on the business of his clock and watch shop, he "totally relinquished his business" and spends a great deal of time in the woods. Examine the language that the narrator uses to describe the transformation in Owen. After this encounter with Hovenden, "he was thrown back into the state whence he had been slowly emerging." The narrator continues: "But the innate tendency of his soul had only been accumulating fresh vigor, during its apparent sluggishness." What does the narrator's description imply about Owen? How does it connect to the larger patterns of imagery in the story? Further, as you analyze Owen and the change he undergoes, you should pay careful attention both to the oppositions that Hawthorne establishes and to the language he uses to describe these oppositions. The "business" that Owen relinquishes is his watchmaker's shop. What is the significance of Owen's profession? How is the rather fanciful description of Owen's neglect of his business significant? Further, examine what stands in opposition to Owen's business. Instead of minding time, Owen "*wasted* the sunshine, as people said, in *wandering* through the woods and fields, and along the banks of streams. There, *like a child,* he found *amusement* in chasing butterflies, or watching the motions of water-insects" (italics mine). How does the language of this passage, which reflects the sentiments of the townspeople who observe Owen, provide a contrast between the world of business and the world of the artist? Does the narrator's voice seem to agree with the people's assessment of Owen? Why or why not? Is the parallel between Owen and the child positive or negative? Why?

Most readers will also note that this passage incorporates the story's central symbol—the butterfly. The passage mentions butterflies a few times. In the sentences quoted in the previous paragraph the butterflies become the objects of Owen's "amusement[s]"—he "wasted" his time "chasing butterflies." As the passage continues, however, you can see that the butterflies and other insects are not so much a source of amusement for Owen as they are a subject of study: "There was something truly mysterious in the intentness with which he contemplated these living playthings, as they sported on the breeze; or examined the structure of an imperial insect whom he had imprisoned." Look closely at this description. What is the effect of the narrator using both the language of play and the language of study/observation? What does this linkage imply about the nature of Owen's art? Further, thoughtful readers might wonder if this passage asks the reader to explore the ethical dimensions of Owen's art. Is there something potentially troubling about the idea of Owen "imprison[ing]" these "living playthings?"

In the sentence that follows, the narrator invokes the butterfly quite differently. He says, "The chase of butterflies was an apt emblem of the ideal pursuit in which he had spent so many golden hours. But, would the Beautiful Idea ever be yielded to his hand, like the butterfly that symbolized it?" Perhaps the first question you might ask of this important sentence is what the narrator implies about Owen's artistic endeavors through this analogy. Does he condemn them, arguing that they are as wasteful and childlike as catching butterflies, or does he mean something more positive with this analogy? Further, you should notice that the narrator twice invokes the butterfly as a symbol in this passage, noting that chasing butterflies "was an apt emblem" of Owen's pursuit of the ideal, and observing that the butterfly itself "symbolized" the "Beautiful Idea" that Owen pursued. Why might Hawthorne purposely call attention to the symbolic value of the central symbol of his story? Might you argue that the story is about the very act of representation, the artist's project of rendering the abstract tangible to the senses? Consider how the rest of this passage develops this idea, while still focusing on the image of the butterfly. During this time, Owen's days were "full of bright conceptions, which gleamed through his intellectual world, as the butterflies gleamed through the outward atmosphere, and were real to him for the instant, without the toil, and perplexity, and many disappointments, of attempting to make them visible to the sensual eye." The narrator ends this passage with a commentary on artists' endeavors to "give external reality to his ideas" with a lament: "Alas, that the artist, whether in poetry or whatever other material, may not content himself with the inward enjoyment of the Beautiful, but must chase the flitting mystery beyond the verge of his ethereal domain, and crush its frail being in seizing it with a material grasp!" How do you interpret this passage? Is he saying that art and the artist, by their very nature, are inadequate? Does he imply, consequently, that artists waste their time trying to capture their visions and ideas of beauty? Do you think, finally, that this lament condemns or praises Owen? How does the passage—and the story as a whole—support your assessment?

TOPICS AND STRATEGIES

This section of the chapter should help you develop ideas for essays on "The Artist of the Beautiful" by providing suggestions for writing topics. Remember that the topics discussed are quite broad; they give you a general framework to guide you as you read, reread, and analyze the story. Use these topics as springboards. You will need to narrow the focus of your writing, constructing an analytical thesis, and bearing in mind the proposed length of your paper.

Themes

As the opening section of this chapter makes clear, "The Artist of the Beautiful" clearly presents art and the artist as its central focuses. The title of the story, alone, asks readers to see the story as a work about art and its creators, and Hawthorne's overt discussion of the process of artistic creation and representation draw the reader even further into these issues. Indeed, the very artistry of Hawthorne's text assures that these two related themes can provide for a myriad of essay topics.

Sample Topics:

1. **Art:** Early in the story, the narrator says that, even as a child, Owen was "remarkable for a delicate ingenuity." He continues, saying that "Those who discovered such peculiarity in the boy ... sometimes saw reason to suppose that he was attempting to imitate the beautiful movements of Nature. ... It seemed, in fact, a new development of the love of the beautiful." As the paragraph closes, the narrator observes that Owen's family apprenticed him to the watchmaker Peter Hovenden, "hoping that his strange ingenuity might thus be regulated, and put to utilitarian purposes." This passage sets up an apparent contrast between beauty and usefulness. According to the story, does art have a "use," or are art and utility polar opposites? Does art need to have a use, or does it have a value that is separate from utility?

To assess the story's comments on art's value and the apparent contrast between beauty and utility, you will need to analyze the characters and their attitudes and pay close attention to the language of beauty, use, practicality, and value in the story. As the opening section of the chapter implies, "the hard, coarse world" seems always to oppose Owen and his artistry. Examine Owen and his art carefully. Explore the relationship between Owen's "utilitarian" work as a watchmaker and his pursuit of the beautiful. How are the two related, and how are they different? Examine Peter Hovenden's attitudes toward Warland and his art. In the story's fourth paragraph, the old man says that his former apprentice "has not the sort of ingenuity to invent anything better than a Dutch toy," and he repeats, "He would turn the sun out of its orbit and derange the whole course of time, if, as I said before, his ingenuity could grasp anything bigger than a child's toy." How are Hovenden's comments significant? Do you agree with his assessment? Is Owen's butterfly, finally, no better than "a Dutch toy"? While the story clearly sets Peter Hovenden, Owen's master and a master clockmaker, in opposition to Owen, Robert Danforth may provide a more helpful contrast in your examination of this question. In what ways is Robert like Owen, and in what ways is he different? Look, especially, at their work. Examine Robert's attitudes toward Owen's work as well, looking closely at his part in the final scenes when Owen presents his butterfly to Annie.

2. **The artist:** As the story's title implies, the artist Owen is the central focus of the story, and the story's central theme focuses on the artist and his/her role in society. Does "The Artist of the Beautiful" finally condemn or praise the artist? What elements in the text allow you to develop your interpretation of the story's statement about the artist?

The story focuses so intently on Owen and his role as an artist that you can approach this question in a number of ways. Like many of Hawthorne's artist figures, Owen is an isolate; he does not seem to fit into his society. Where, finally, does Hawthorne place the blame for Owen's isolation? Does society cling to the wrong values, refusing to truly see and appreciate Owen and his talents, or does Owen, himself, bear the blame for his own isolation? What do you think about some of Warland's decisions? Do you think that it is fair to label Warland, like Aylmer of "The Birth-Mark," obsessive, and overly focused on his art?

Another way to approach an analysis of Owen as artist is to focus on the language Hawthorne uses to describe Owen and the links between this language and the descriptions of his art. As he does in some of his other discussions of art and artists, most notably in his self-portrait in "The Custom-House," Hawthorne seems to cast doubt on Warland's masculinity through his word choice. Carefully examine the language that the author uses to characterize Owen. You might also find it helpful to compare this language to that used to characterize Robert Danforth. How do they compare? What does this contrast imply about Owen and his artistic endeavors? How does the story's plot further enhance this contrast, especially as it contrasts the fruits of the two men's creative efforts—the butterfly and the baby?

Yet another way to focus this inquiry is through the lens of Mary Shelley's *Frankenstein*. When Owen presents the butterfly to Annie at the story's end, she asks three times whether it is alive. And, indeed, as her husband indicates, it seems to be a living creature. Has Owen managed, like Shelley's Victor Frankenstein, to unlock the secret of life? If so, is this an accomplishment to be praised, or has Warland overstepped the proper boundaries of humanity? Examine the language of paternity, maternity, creation, and procreation in the text in order to develop an essay that examines the artist from this perspective. Additionally, you might develop the ethical questions contained in such an inquiry by examining Warland's treatment of his own creation. When the butterfly seeks to return to Owen's hand, Owen will not allow it, saying, "Thou hast gone forth out of thy master's heart. There is no return for thee." Does Warland bear any responsibility for the butterfly's destruction, or is his comment merely an accurate reflection of the artist's relationship with his/her art—once it has left its creator, it is dependent upon the kindly reception of its audience.

Character

Hawthorne's characters provide another focus for paper topics. Examine the individual characters in "The Artist of the Beautiful." What do you learn of them through their dialogue and through the narrator's descriptions? How does the portrayal of characters connect to the story's themes? How does Hawthorne's language develop the implications of character? Such investigations should help you develop a strong paper about a specific character.

Sample Topics:

1. **Owen Warland as a character:** Examine Owen Warland as an embodiment of spirit in the story. How does the language of the story encourage or develop such an assessment of Owen? What, finally, does the story say about the relationship between spirit and matter? What is the relationship between spirit and art?

   While it is impossible to consider the themes of art or the artist without some evaluation of Owen Warland's character, the story provides for another way to assess Warland's role in the story. The contrasts that fuel this story allow for a number of allegorical readings of this text, and reading the story as an allegory of the relationship between spirit and matter should prove fruitful. Assessing Owen as a representation of the spirit will obviously ask you to consider some of the questions discussed in the treatment of art and the artist, and you will probably also want to consider his relationship with other characters, particularly Robert Danforth and Peter Hovenden. Similarly, considering Owen as an embodiment of spirit may help you assess his relationship with Annie.

2. **Robert Danforth as a character:** How do you assess Robert Danforth's role in the story? He provides an obvious contrast to Owen and he proves to be Owen's rival for Annie, and yet the story does not portray Danforth as hostile to Owen. Why?

   You might address this question through an investigation of the allegory of spirit versus matter discussed above. If you choose this approach to Danforth, you should be sure to examine the nature of the relationship between Danforth and Owen. Examine the interactions of the two characters carefully. What do these interactions suggest about the relationship between matter and spirit? Another way of focusing an investigation into Danforth's character and his role in the story is to examine his job as a blacksmith. While his occupation is clearly tied to Danforth's characterization as the "man of main strength," what other roles does it play? Often blacksmiths, because of the fires of their forges, are associated with the infernal. Is this the case with Danforth? Why or why not? Does Danforth share any qualities with Owen that might explain their relationship?

3. **Peter Hovenden as a character:** Consider Peter Hovenden's role in the story. He clearly functions as Owen's nemesis, continually disparaging and casting doubt on Owen's skills and abilities. What might Hovenden represent? Why does he prove so hostile to Owen Warland and his artistic endeavors?

Hovenden plays an important allegorical role in the story. In order to assess his role and its importance, you need to consider his profession as watchmaker as well as his relationship with Owen. As a watchmaker, Hovenden is everything that Owen is not. Owen takes over old Peter's shop after the older man was "compelled . . . to relinquish" it. "[T]hen," the narrator says, "did people recognize how unfit a person was Owen Warland to lead old blind Father Time along his daily course." What does Hoevenden's success as a watchmaker say about his values and his worldview? Why does Hovenden give up his shop? What does Hovenden himself say about his job as a watchmaker? Taken together, how do these factors help to characterize Peter Hovenden? How do they help to explain his reaction to Owen and his artistry? Examine Hovenden's role in the final scenes of the story when Owen presents the mechanical butterfly to Annie. How are the old man's reaction to, and his treatment of, the butterfly significant? How do these factors help to develop your assessment of Hovenden's role in the story?

4. **Annie Hovenden as a character:** How do you assess Annie Hovenden's role in the story? What does she seem to represent?

Annie is less developed than the male characters in the story. In fact, the story's richest description of her comes from Owen's perceptions. After he learns of her engagement to Robert Danforth, Owen sinks into another "fit of illness." Warland had "persisted in connecting all his dreams of artistical success with Annie's image." The narrator quickly asserts, though, "Of course he had deceived himself; there were no such attributes in Annie Hovenden as his imagination had endowed her with. She, in the aspect which she wore to his inward vision, was as much a creation of his own as the mysterious piece of mechanism would be were it ever realized . . . had he won Annie to his bosom, and there beheld her fade from angel into ordinary woman, the disappointment might have driven him back, with concentrated energy, upon his sole remaining object." The story repeatedly seems to invoke Annie as a representation of something else—later she is called "the representative of the world." What do you make of the fact that Annie seems to function more as a representation in this story than as a real woman? Does her role as representation have any relevance in a story about art and representation? Is there a way to connect Annie's role in the story with the roles of women in Hawthorne's time?

5. **Annie and Robert's baby as a character:** What is the role of Annie and Robert's baby in the story? Why is the infant, finally, cast in the role of the destroyer of the butterfly?

The baby and the butterfly provide another apparent contrast in this story, and yet, finally, their relationship is far more complicated than this initial, apparent contrast implies. While the baby and the butterfly are clearly set at odds, they also share a great many similarities. What similarities do they share? You might find it helpful to explore the language of paternity and maternity as well as images of birth in the story. How does such an investigation help to develop the parallels between baby and butterfly? In light of this investigation, what does Hawthorne seem to imply through the baby's destruction of the butterfly?

Philosophy and Ideas

Hawthorne's treatment of philosophical ideas can provide another way to focus a paper on this story. As in many of his works, Hawthorne asks difficult questions about the nature of faith and belief in "The Artist of the Beautiful." Similarly, the story shows his interest in the nature of symbolism and representation that would take its fullest form in *The Scarlet Letter.*

Sample Topics:

1. **Transcendentalism/romanticism:** Coming in the wake of transcendentalists like Ralph Waldo Emerson, Hawthorne often wrote about their ideas and philosophies. Hawthorne knew Emerson and Thoreau, and he wrote "The Artist of the Beautiful" while he was living in a home owned by Emerson, the Old Manse. Consider "The Artist of the Beautiful" as a statement on transcendentalist beliefs about the abilities of the artist and the artists' role in society. Does Hawthorne seem to bolster the arguments of romantic transcendentalism or does he oppose them?

   Drawing from the philosophies of the British romantic thinkers, transcendentalists like Emerson believed that the artist was a kind of seer who could see beauty and the transcendent in the world. Further, transcendentalists like Emerson (as well as British romantics like Wordsworth and Coleridge) believed that our abilities to see and understand the world are much stronger in our infancies and childhoods. In his essay *Nature*, Emerson says, "To speak truly, few adult persons can see nature. Most persons do not see the sun. At least they have a very superficial seeing. The sun illuminates only the eye of the man, but shines into the eye and heart of the child. The lover of nature is he whose inward and outward senses are still truly adjusted to each other; who has retained the spirit of infancy even into the era of manhood." You can learn more about transcendentalist thought and read more of Emerson's philosophies online on the American transcendentalism Web: http://www.vcu.edu/engweb/transcendentalism/. Clearly, this question also asks you to consider many of the questions posed in the thematic discussions about art and the artist. You might find Owen's childlike qualities and his relationship with the rest of his community particularly relevant to this topic.

2. **Faith:** Early in the story, the narrator claims that "It is requisite for the ideal artist to possess a force of character that seems hardly compatible with its delicacy; he must keep his faith in himself, while the incredulous world assails him with its utter disbelief." Later, after his mechanism is destroyed for the third time and Owen falls into "a fit of illness," the narrator says, "Poor, poor, and fallen Owen Warland! . . . He had lost his faith in the invisible, and now prided himself, as such unfortunates invariably do, in the wisdom which rejected much that even his eye could see, and trusted confidently in nothing but what his hand could touch." How might you read "The Artist of the Beautiful" as a story about faith and skepticism?

   As the question indicates, you could approach this topic through an investigation of Owen himself, exploring his vacillations between self-confidence and self-doubt. A close reading of the story will demonstrate that Hawthorne has woven the language of faith and doubt into the fabric of the entire story. Where else do you see language of faith and doubt and of the invisible versus the tangible? Besides Owen, who else seems to embody doubt? In the second passage cited above, Hawthorne seems clearly to be echoing the theological dimensions of this topic when he calls Owen Warland "fallen" and when he uses the language of sight and touch. You might think about biblical stories of faith and doubt as you focus a paper on this topic. Biblical passages on doubting Thomas (John 20: 24–29) and on Jesus' insistence that believers have the faith of a child (Mark 10:13) should prove particularly helpful as you explore the treatment of faith in this story.

3. **Ethics and responsibility:** Does "The Artist of the Beautiful" comment upon the ethical dimensions of art and the artist? Does Owen Warland bear any blame for the destruction of the butterfly in the final scene?

   In the final scene, Hawthorne's characters discuss the nature of Owen's butterfly. Three times Annie asks, "Is it alive?" Both Owen and Danforth assent that the butterfly is, indeed, alive. As the opening section of this chapter indicates, one approach to this topic might question whether Owen's dedication to his artistic creation causes him to sport with life. Examine how the story uses the word "plaything(s)" in reference to both the butterflies that Owen observes and the butterfly he creates. You might also question whether Owen knows the fate that will befall his butterfly when he presents it to Annie and her family. A related approach, which was discussed in the section or theme, might consider whether Owen, in creating a living creature, has overstepped the proper boundaries of humanity. Robert Danforth innocently remarks of the butterfly, "Well, that does beat all nature!" Might the author, though, imply something less innocent and more accusatory through Danforth's exclamation?

4. **Symbolism and representation:** Like the scarlet *A* in *The Scarlet Letter*, the butterfly in "The Artist of the Beautiful" serves as a symbol. In another parallel between this story and Hawthorne's story of Hester Prynne, the central symbol of the tale appears repeatedly in different forms. How might Hawthorne be using the symbol of the butterfly to comment on the nature of symbolism and representation?

As the introductory section of this chapter pointed out, Hawthorne invokes butterflies frequently throughout the text and he even makes overt references to the butterflies' positions as symbols or emblems. Might you argue that the story is about the very act of representation, the artist's project of attempting to render the abstract tangible to the senses? If so, what does Hawthorne seem to argue about the artist's project by the story's end? You should, of course, examine the last few sentences of the story in detail. Here, the narrator claims that "the ruin of [Owen's] life's labor ... was yet no ruin," once again evoking the nature of symbolism: "When the artist rose high enough to achieve the Beautiful, the symbol by which he made it perceptible to mortal senses became of little value in his eyes, while his spirit possessed itself in the enjoyment of the Reality." What happens to the relationship between the real, the tangible, and the abstract—between the sign and the signified—in this passage? Which, finally, seems more "real"? Similarly, you might consider the passage, just prior to the story's end, in which the narrator argues, "Not at this latest moment, was he to learn that the reward of all high performance must be sought within itself, or sought in vain." How might this comment help to explain Owen's final reaction to the destruction of the symbol of his achievement?

Language, Symbols, and Imagery

Hawthorne's focus on artistry and representation in this story provides a solid basis for papers about symbolism and imagery. The butterfly serves as the story's primary symbol, but clocks, watches, and the language of time also play an important role in the dynamic of the story.

Sample Topics:

1. **The butterfly:** In his preface to *The House of the Seven Gables*, Hawthorne invokes the image of the butterfly in order to discuss his treatment of the novel's moral: "The Author has considered it hardly worth his while, therefore, relentlessly to impale the story with its moral, as with an iron rod—or rather, as by

sticking a pin through a butterfly—thus at once depriving it of life, and causing it to stiffen in an ungainly and unnatural attitude." Similarly, in "The Artist of the Beautiful" he refuses to skewer his central symbol, the butterfly, with a single meaning. Instead he provides it with a breadth of representational value. What might the butterfly be said to represent in "The Artist of the Beautiful"?

The Philosophy and Ideas section of this chapter considered the butterfly as a commentary on the nature of representation, but you can also focus a paper on the butterfly as a symbol. Hawthorne's story allows for a number of different approaches to this question. You can analyze Owen's mechanical butterfly as a symbol of Owen himself. What does the butterfly say about the artist, his abilities, and his relationship to the world? How is Owen himself similar to a butterfly? How does the story develop this parallel? The story frequently asserts that the butterfly is the embodiment of the "Beautiful Ideal." How does Hawthorne develop on this more abstract idea through his use of the butterfly? Some scholars have argued that the butterfly is a representation of the feminine. How could you develop a paper on this assessment of the butterfly's role in the story? Further, how might this argument connect to an argument that the butterfly represents Owen? Finally, you might wish to focus your paper around the fact that Owen's butterfly is a mechanical butterfly, made of watch and clock parts. How is this aspect of the butterfly's creation significant?

2. **Clocks and watches:** Owen is a watchmaker by trade. Examine the imagery and the language of clocks, watches, and time in "The Artist of the Beautiful." What is their significance?

Like the image of the butterfly, the language of time, clocks, and watches is thoroughly integrated into the story. A paper that addresses this question should consider Owen's relationship with his profession. Similarly, you might think about the relationship between Owen's art, his "strange ingenuity," and his trade as a watchmaker. Clearly, the story sets the two in contrast, and yet it is because of his "strange ingenuity" that his family apprentices Owen to the watchmaker Peter Hovenden. Further, is it significant that Owen's mechanical butterfly is made of the elements of his watchmaker's trade? Obviously, Peter Hovenden warrants your consideration too. What makes him good at his trade? What effects does his trade have upon Hovenden? Consider Hovenden's treatment of Owen and his effect upon Owen. How are these related to the two men's relationship with their business? As you focus your paper, you should also examine the way that Hawthorne uses the language of both clocks and of time in his treatment of other elements in the story. How and why does he use this language evocatively?

Compare and Contrast Essays

Since "The Artist of the Beautiful" yokes contrasting elements together, it provides plenty of opportunity for writing compare and contrast essays. The discussions of Owen Warland and Robert Danforth suggest paper topics that would allow for comparison of these characters. Similarly, Peter Hovenden and Owen Warland provide much opportunity to compare and contrast, as the discussion of their characters and their profession suggests. Beyond the opportunities within the story, you should find that "The Artist of the Beautiful" shares topical and thematic concerns with many of Hawthorne's other works. This chapter has already suggested how you might examine the story's treatment of symbolism in relation to *The Scarlet Letter*. The story, though, presents other possibilities for comparison with Hawthorne's other work. As you formulate a compare and contrast paper, remember that your thesis should make an assertion about the significance of the similarities and differences that you discuss.

Sample Topics:

1. **Hawthorne's artists:** Compare Owen Warland with one of Hawthorne's other artist figures. What does the author say about the role and the position of the artist though these figures?

   Aylmer from "The Birth-Mark" provides a particularly strong subject for this topic. While Aylmer might more properly be

termed one of Hawthorne's scientist figures, he and Hawthorne's other men of science share a great many qualities
with Hawthorne's artists. You might think about questions of
creation, of obsession, and of responsibility in an investigation
of Aylmer and Owen. Similarly, Clifford from *The House of the
Seven Gables* could provide a fruitful comparison with Owen,
especially if you consider their love of beauty and their relationships with the world that surrounds them. Dr. Rappaccini
and Roger Chillingworth might also prove good subjects for
this topic.

2. **Faith:** Consider "The Artist of the Beautiful" as a statement on
faith and skepticism. How is Hawthorne's commentary on faith
similar or different from that in one of his other works?

Clearly, "Young Goodman Brown" considers Brown's relationship with his faith. It, too, considers the importance of the
tangible and the intangible. "Rappaccini's Daughter" also provides a statement about faith and what can be known through
the senses.

Bibliography and Online Resources for "The Artist of the Beautiful"

American transcendentalism Web. Available online. URL: http://www.vcu.edu/
engweb/transcendentalism/. Downloaded August 2, 2006.

Baym, Nina. *The Shape of Hawthorne's Career.* Ithaca, NY: Cornell UP, 1976.

Bell, Millicent. *Hawthorne's View of the Artist.* Albany: SUNY P, 1962.

Crews, Frederick C. *The Sins of Fathers: Hawthorne's Psychological Themes.* New
York: Oxford UP, 1966.

Donavel, David. "Alienation in 'The Artist of The Beautiful': Introduction."
Hawthorne in Salem. Available online. URL: http://www.hawthornein
salem.com/Literature/AlienationOfTheArtist/TheArtist/Introduction.
html. Downloaded October 25, 2006.

———. "Passages Related to Alienation in 'The Artist of the Beautiful.'" Hawthorne in Salem. Available online. URL: http://www.hawthorneinsalem.
com/Literature/AlienationOfTheArtist/TheArtist/Literature.html. Downloaded October 25, 2006.

Erlich, Gloria. *Family Themes and Hawthorne's Fiction: The Tenacious Web.* New Brunswick, NJ: Rutgers UP, 1984.

Fogle, Richard Harter. *Hawthorne's Fiction: The Light and the Dark.* Norman: U of Oklahoma P, 1952.

Fossum, Robert H. *Hawthorne's Inviolable Circle: the Problem of Time.* Deland, FL: Everett/Edwards Inc., 1972.

"Learning Activities Related to 'The Birth-Mark.'" Hawthorne in Salem. Available online. URL: http://www.hawthorneinsalem.com/Literature/AlienationOfTheArtist/TheBirthMark/Explorations.html. Downloaded October 25, 2006.

Male, Roy R. *Hawthorne's Tragic Vision.* New York: Norton, 1957.

Miller, Edwin Haviland. *Salem Is My Dwelling Place: A Life of Nathaniel Hawthorne.* Iowa City: U of Iowa P, 1991.

Newbury, Michael. *Figuring Authorship in Antebellum America.* Palo Alto, CA: Stanford UP, 1997.

Pfister, Joel. "Hawthorne as cultural theorist." *The Cambridge Companion to Nathaniel Hawthorne.* Ed. Richard H. Millington. Cambridge: Cambridge UP, 2004. 35–59.

Reynolds, Larry. "Hawthorne's labors in Concord." *The Cambridge Companion to Nathaniel Hawthorne.* Ed. Richard H. Millington. Cambridge: Cambridge UP, 2004. 10–34.

Wineapple, Brenda. *Hawthorne: A Life.* New York: Knopf, 2003.

THE SCARLET LETTER

READING TO WRITE

THE BEST-KNOWN of Hawthorne's novels (or romances, as he called them), *The Scarlet Letter* occupies a prominent place in American literary history, and it has been the subject of scores of books and essays since its publication in 1850. The novel's artistry easily warrants all this critical attention, and it continues to invite interpretation and reevaluation. Indeed, the very process of interpretation and evaluation is one of the novel's subjects. In "The Custom-House," the lengthy introduction to *The Scarlet Letter*, Hawthorne claims to have found the letter *A* made "of fine red cloth, much worn and faded." He speculates that "Certainly there was some deep meaning in it, most worthy of interpretation, and which, as it were, streamed forth from the mystic symbol subtly communicating itself to my sensibilities, but evading the analysis of my mind." Hester's scarlet *A* is replicated and reflected repeatedly throughout the novel, and readers are quickly enveloped in a veritable maze of *A*s and drawn into questions of symbolism, representation, and meaning. In addition to this complex philosophical thread, *The Scarlet Letter* draws readers into Puritan history, a frequent and fraught topic for Hawthorne. In the second chapter, "The Market-Place," Hawthorne introduces three of the novel's main characters—Hester, Pearl, and the scarlet letter itself—thereby introducing the complex issue of meaning and representation.

Careful readers can find a great deal in these opening chapters to guide their analysis of the novel and help them develop topics for essays.

Consider the following passage from the second chapter where the town beadle leads Hester, with the infant Pearl, from the prison:

> Stretching forth the official staff in his left hand, he laid his right upon the shoulder of a young woman, whom he thus drew forward; until, on the threshold of the prison-door, she repelled him, by an action marked with natural dignity and force of character, and stepped into the open air, as if by her own free will. She bore in her arms a child, a baby of some three months old. . . .
>
> When the young woman—the mother of this child—stood fully revealed before the crowd, it seemed to be her first impulse to clasp the infant closely to her bosom; not so much by an impulse of motherly affection, as that she might thereby conceal a certain token, which was wrought or fastened into her dress. In a moment, however, wisely judging that one token of her shame would but poorly serve to hide another, she took the baby on her arm, and, with a burning blush, and yet a haughty smile, and a glance that would not be abashed, looked around at her townspeople and neighbours. On the breast of her gown, in fine red cloth, surrounded with an elaborate embroidery and fantastic flourishes of gold thread, appeared the letter *A*. It was so artistically done, and with so much fertility and gorgeous luxuriance of fancy, that it had all the effect of a last and fitting decoration to the apparel which she wore; and which was of a splendor in accordance with the taste of the age, but greatly beyond what was allowed by the sumptuary regulations of the colony.
>
> The young woman was tall, with a figure of perfect elegance, on a large scale. She had dark and abundant hair, so glossy that it threw off the sunshine with a gleam, and a face which, besides being beautiful from regularity of feature and richness of complexion, had the impressiveness belonging to a marked brow and deep black eyes. She was lady-like, too, after the manner of the feminine gentility of those days; characterized by a certain state and dignity, rather than by the delicate, evanescent, and indescribable grace, which is now recognized as its indication. And never had Hester Prynne appeared more lady-like, in the antique interpretation of the term, than as she issued from the prison. Those who had

known her, and had expected to behold her dimmed and obscured by a disastrous cloud, were astonished, and even startled, to perceive how her beauty shone out, and made a halo of the misfortune and ignominy in which she was enveloped. It may be true, that, to a sensitive observer, there was something exquisitely painful in it. Her attire, which, indeed, she had wrought for the occasion, in prison, and had modeled much after her own fancy, seemed to express the attitude of her spirit, the desperate recklessness of her mood, by its wild and picturesque peculiarity. But the point which drew all eyes, and, as it were, transfigured the wearer,—so that both men and women, who had been familiarly acquainted with Hester Prynne, were now impressed as if they beheld her for the first time,—was that SCARLET LETTER, so fantastically embroidered and illuminated upon her bosom. It had the effect of a spell, taking her out of the ordinary relations with humanity, and inclosing her in a sphere by herself.

Astute readers will note that even though this is the first time Hester actually appears in the novel, she has been introduced just a few paragraphs earlier through the conversation of the women who have gathered in the marketplace to witness Hester standing on the scaffold. In that conversation, as they do just after this passage, the women assess Hester's sin and her punishment. Even before Hester is introduced, then, she and her sin are assessed in the marketplace, and we learn that the community's assessment of Hester and her sin is not stable or uniform. Hawthorne has already introduced the paramount theme of his novel, the question of interpretation or the assignation of meaning.

The narrator's description of Hester in the passage above will allow you to begin to form your own opinion of the heroine. The first thing the narrator describes is not her physical appearance, but her demeanor and actions. These seem to be the key to understanding Hester's character. Despite being led from the prison to the scaffold for a public shaming, Hester displays a "natural dignity and force of character." Understandably, her first response to being fully displayed in the marketplace seems to be one of shame: "[I]t seemed to be her first impulse to clasp the infant closely to her bosom; not so much by an impulse of motherly affection, as that she might thereby conceal a certain token, which was wrought or fastened into her dress." Quickly, though, Hester's demeanor changes, and the narrator says that she faced the townspeople with "a burning blush, and yet a haughty smile, and a glance that would not be abashed." Think about how this introduction helps to characterize Hester. Though there is a hint of embarrassment in her blush, Hawthorne repeatedly emphasizes her strength of will. Immediately you can see that she is a complicated character; she is strong, but she is subject to the laws of her community. Perhaps her blush even indicates that she respects these laws as well. Here Hawthorne has introduced another important theme—the relationship between the individual and her society. As the passage continues we learn more about Hester. The third paragraph provides a physical description that emphasizes her "lady-like" beauty along with her dark hair and eyes, and it reinforces the perception of Hester's strength, telling us that she was "characterized by a certain state and dignity."

The other two characters introduced in this passage are Pearl and the scarlet *A* itself; both are intimately connected to Hester's adultery. In her initial shame, Hester tries to conceal the *A* by holding Pearl close to her chest. The narrator remarks, "In a moment, however, wisely judging that one token of her shame would but poorly serve to hide another, she took the baby on her arm." A careful reader should realize that Hester's gestures and the narrator's comment reveal a good deal about the relationships in the novel. Clearly the linkage between Pearl and the scarlet letter is particularly striking here. The narrator asserts an identity between them, describing both as "token[s] of [Hester's] shame," and Hawthorne develops this parallel throughout the course of the novel. But these sentences tell a good bit more. Careful readers might inquire how this description serves to characterize Pearl, the *A*, the relationship between them, and Hester's relationship with each of them. What does it mean to call a human child "a token of . . . shame"? On the most basic level, you might recognize the truth of the narrator's statement here. Like the letter, Pearl is a very real and palpable reminder of Hester's sin; she is a physical sign of Hester's adultery. How does her status as a double of the scarlet *A* affect the relationship between mother and daughter? Further, does this label reflect anything more about her character? A "token" is a sign or a symbol. Does Hawthorne use Pearl as a symbol or a symbolic character? Pearl is, quite clearly, a strange and enigmatic child. How should you, respond to her? Whatever your response to Pearl, Hawthorne is clearly inviting readers to evaluate the response of the Puritan community.

While the passage gives much to speculate about, it tells little about Pearl. It does, however, spend considerable time describing the scarlet letter. Hester's *A* is made of "fine red cloth, surrounded with an elaborate embroidery and fantastic flourishes of gold thread." The narrator further adds: "It was so artistically done, and with so much fertility and gorgeous luxuriance of fancy, that it had all the effect of a lasting and fitting decoration to the apparel which she wore; and which was of a splendor in accordance with the taste of the age, but greatly beyond what was allowed by the sumptuary regulations of the colony." A careful analysis of this first description of the scarlet *A* helps to shed light on both character and theme.

Perhaps the first line of approach might be to explore what Hester's embellishment of the *A* reveals about her character or personality. After all, the Puritan leaders of her community clearly meant to label the heroine with the scarlet letter. The *A* marks her as an adulteress. Does Hester, through her "fantastically embroidered" embellishment of the *A*, seek to label or mark herself differently? Careful attention to Hawthorne's language should prove fruitful. Hawthorne emphasizes Hester's talent with the needle. Her needlework is "artistically done . . . with . . . fertility and gorgeous luxuriance of fancy." In other words, Hester is an artist, and needlework is her medium. She is a creative force, and she produces not only a beautiful child, but beautiful needlework. Further, the passage suggests that the laws of her society leave little room for Hester to express her creativity, for her embellishment of the *A* is "beyond what was allowed by the sumptuary regulations of the colony." Why does Hawthorne portray Hester as a kind of artist? Does his portrayal of Hester say anything about the nature of the artist?

Beyond these initial questions about Hester and her artistry, you might also ask why Hester chose to decorate the sign of her sin with gold embroidery and why she chose to embellish it "beyond what was allowed by the sumptuary regulations of the colony." This line of inquiry could lead to a question about Hester's place within her society. Is Hester making a statement about her sin? Is she, as one of the matrons assumes, proud of her *A*? Is she making a statement about the repression of the Puritan code of law? Or, is she commenting on her relationship with her society? Does she believe that, having broken one law of the colony, she is now outside the community?

Lastly, look at the effects of the scarlet letter. Hawthorne notes that it "transfigured the wearer,—so that both men and women, who had been familiarly acquainted with Hester Prynne, were now impressed as if they beheld her for the first time. . . . It had the effect of a spell, taking her out of the ordinary relations with humanity, and enclosing her in a sphere by herself." It does seem, then, that one of the effects of the *A* is to remove Hester from her society and place her outside of "ordinary relations" with others. In addition, it is worth noting that while "transfigure" means to alter the appearance of something, it can also mean to glorify or exalt. Hawthorne's sentence seems to invoke both meanings of the word. Clearly the fanciful and "fantastically embroidered" letter drastically alters Hester's appearance, but it also seems to set her apart and make her appear special. Indeed, as the novel progresses, we learn that visitors to Boston mistake Hester's *A* for a mark of honor, and later the narrator remarks that Hester and Pearl might remind "a Papist" of "the image of Divine Maternity." As the novel progresses the theme of transfiguration or transformation appears repeatedly. Nearly all the major characters undergo at least one important transformation.

Similarly, Hawthorne's assertion that the *A* has the effect of a "spell" conjures thoughts of witchcraft, a topic that, because of their harsh punishment of purported witches, is often linked to discussions of Puritan history. Further, since Hawthorne's great-grandfather, John Hathorne, was a magistrate who presided over the Salem witch trials in 1692, Hawthorne frequently returned to the topic of the Puritans and witchcraft. Does the language in this passage hint that the scarlet letter might be tied to magic and witchcraft? If so, is it the Puritans, as the originators of the scarlet letter, or Hester, who embellishes and wears the *A*, who bears responsibility for the scarlet letter's spell?

Finally, it is worth exploring whether the scarlet letter has the desired effect upon the community. The Puritan magistrates have marked Hester as an adulteress, intending that "the infliction of a legal sentence would have an earnest and effectual meaning" (*The Scarlet Letter*, chapter 2) and that Hester would become "a living sermon against sin" (*The Scarlet Letter*, chapter 3). Hester's time on the scaffold in chapter 2 is framed by the conversations of some of the women of Boston. In their initial conversation they debate the appropriateness of her punishment. Then Hester "show[s her] scarlet letter in the market-place," and the women continue to debate the appropriateness of the punishment in light of Hester's decoration of the *A*. One woman notes that Hester's needlework seems already to have transformed the meaning of the scarlet letter, arguing that she has "made a pride out of what they . . . meant for a punishment." Another more sympathetic observer rebukes the woman, arguing that "not a stitch in that embroidered letter, but she has felt in her heart." If the scarlet *A* is a fitting punishment of Hester and it allows her to serve as a living sermon, the meaning of the *A* should be clear, stable, and undisputable. Why, then, before chapter 2 is concluded, does the community already question the meaning and the value of the scarlet letter? What does Hawthorne seem to be saying about the nature of signs and symbols? Is the setting of chapter 2 important? The Puritan leaders may have a particular meaning behind the sign that they mark Hester with, but once she enters into the marketplace, a community center where goods are bartered and exchanged, that meaning inevitably becomes the subject of reevaluation. It enters into circulation in the community. How does this community evaluation (or reevaluation) of Hester, her sin, and her punishment reflect upon the larger theme of symbols and representation in the novel?

Before the end of chapter 2, Hawthorne has already introduced some of his most important thematic and philosophical concerns, as well as three major figures in the novel. Take note of Hawthorne's language, descriptions, and the dynamics between his characters in the early chapters and you will approach the rest armed with questions and ideas that should help generate and develop thoughtful essays on *The Scarlet Letter*.

TOPICS AND STRATEGIES

This section provides broad topic ideas that should help develop a paper on *The Scarlet Letter*. Remember that the topics below are just springboards; you will need to focus your analysis and develop your own specific focus and thesis.

Themes

As already noted, the relation between the individual and society is one of the most readily apparent themes of *The Scarlet Letter*. Another apparent theme, discussed in the **Philosophy and Ideas** section, is that of symbols and representation. This rich text explores many more themes, including the nature of sin, art and the imagination, and paternity, among others. If you want to write about themes, you should begin by identifying a theme that you find interesting. As you examine the text, note what it has to say about that particular theme. If you choose to explore the relationship between the individual and society in *The Scarlet Letter*, for example, you might begin by examining how the text characterizes the Puritan society of Boston. A paper on this topic would also need to study Hester's character and her role in society. Additionally, you might want to evaluate Dimmesdale's relationship with his society as well, since he provides a striking contrast to Hester. Because many of the themes in this novel are tied to Hawthorne's beliefs about Puritan history and to complex questions of symbolism and representation, strong papers on theme will also include examination of the philosophical concerns discussed in the **Philosophy and Ideas** section.

Sample Topics:

1. **The individual and society:** If living in society, as part of a human community, involves taking part in an explicit or implicit compact or agreement, what are the rights and obligations of the parties involved in this agreement? What does Hawthorne have to say about the relationship between the individual and society in *The Scarlet Letter*?

   As the previous paragraphs suggest, there are a great many ways to approach this multifaceted subject. Inevitably, though, your investigation will involve an assessment of both the community and Hester. You might focus your investigation of this relationship on a thorough examination of the Puritan society of Boston, and it should begin with chapter 1. What kind of impression does this introduction to Puritan Boston create? How does Hawthorne's imagery and word choice work to create this impression? You should also consider how Hawthorne develops the characterization of the community throughout the novel. Remember that Massachusetts Bay Colony was, a theocracy, a place where "religion and law were almost identical" (*The Scarlet Letter*, chapter 2). This comment seems to require that you also examine the society's penal system. In a related vein, you might choose to examine the sympathy and insight of the community at large versus the sympathy and insight of the governmental leaders and their law. How does each change in its assessment of Hester as the novel progresses? Further, is it relevant that the members of the community and their laws often seem to be in disagreement throughout the novel?

Another way to approach this topic might be to evaluate the effects the scarlet letter has on Hester. If one of its purposes is to bring her in line with community laws and values, how successfully does it achieve this goal? In order to assess its success you should analyze Hester's ongoing relationship with the community of Boston. Remember that chapter 2 tells that initially the letter had "the effect of a spell, taking her out of the ordinary relations with humanity, and inclosing her in a sphere by herself." Does this effect continue throughout the novel? There are a number of passages that should help with this evaluation. (*The Scarlet Letter*, chapters 5, 8). Toward the end of chapter 8, Hawthorne allows a single sentence to stand as a paragraph: "The scarlet letter had not done its office." In light of all the meditations on Hester's relationship with society, how do you read this declaration? Is Hawthorne critiquing the efficacy of the magistrates' punishment or is he commenting on Hester's ability to learn the proper lessons and become amenable to society's laws and values?

2. **Sin:** In chapter 2, the beadle calls Massachusetts Bay Colony a place "where iniquity is dragged out into the sunshine," and in chapter 3, a townsman characterizes the colony as a place where "iniquity is searched out and punished in the sight of rulers and people." What is the effect of this insistence on public confession and punishment of sin in *The Scarlet Letter*? What does Hawthorne seem to be saying about the values of Puritan New England?

Because "religion and law were almost identical" in Hester's society, the theme of sin is closely related to the previously discussed theme of the individual and society. Numerous approaches to the theme of sin could provide substantial paper topics, but perhaps the most fruitful approach might be an investigation into publicly acknowledged sin versus private sin. What is the effect of the public nature of Hester's sin and punishment? In contrast, Dimmesdale grapples with his sin privately. When they meet in the forest, he tells Hester, "Happy are you, Hester, that wear the scarlet letter openly upon your bosom! Mine burns in secret!" (*The Scarlet Letter,* chapter 17). While Dimmesdale seems to desire public confession and the chance to share his secret, such public acknowledgment remains elusive until the novel's end. He makes halfhearted or, as the narrator calls them, hypocritical attempts at "confession" from his pulpit in chapter 11, and he and Chillingworth discuss the virtues and attributes of the confession of sins in Chapter 10. Taken together, what do all these reflections on sin and public confession say about the nature of sin, punishment, and confession? While Hester's sin is "dragged out into the sunshine," her role in the community is forever altered. Dimmesdale, on the other hand, tortures himself with his private guilt. Does Hawthorne seem to be advocating for the necessity of publicly acknowledged sin? Is he commenting on the hypocrisy of Puritan society in their treatment and handling of sinners?

A slightly different approach to the question of sin in the novel might be to explore Hawthorne's assessment of the Puritan notion of sin. Does the author seem to view sin in the same way as the Puritans did? In their conversation in the forest, Dimmesdale says to Hester, "We are not, Hester, the worst sinners in the world." And Hester replies, "Never, never! . . . What we did had a consecration of its own. We felt it so! We said so to each other! Hast thou forgotten it?" (*The Scarlet Letter,* chapter 17). Does Hawthorne seem to agree with their assessment? If so, what does the novel seem to argue is a worse type of sin?

3. **Art and imagination:** Hawthorne clearly portrays Hester as an artist. What is the role of art and the artist in the novel? Does his portrayal say anything about the nature of the artist?

The theme of art and the imagination is important to Hawthorne, and artist figures appear in much of his work. Frequently, they seem to be methods of reflecting on the author's own vocation. While chapter 2 establishes Hester's artistry, chapter 5 provides a good deal of insight into Hester's needlework. Clearly, her needlework serves a number of roles for Hester. Analyze this chapter carefully. What does it tell us about the function of Hester's art? Similarly, consider Hester's embellishment of the *A* and of Pearl. Why does she choose to embellish both of them? What does this say about the relationship between Pearl and the *A?* About Hester's relationship with both of them?

In a related approach, you may explore Pearl's potential status as an artist. Decorated by her mother's art, Pearl seems to embody Hester's artistry and spirit. In addition, Pearl's imaginative force seems to share much with Hester's artistry. How might you consider Pearl a type of artist? Examining Pearl's play in chapter 6 should prove helpful in developing this topic.

4. **Paternity:** As chapters 2, 3, and 4 clearly demonstrate, the question of Pearl's paternity is a central theme of the novel, at least for the community at large. How and why does Hawthorne develop this theme?

This question is twofold. On one level, the Puritan leaders clearly wish to learn the identity of Hester's "fellow sinner" (*The Scarlet Letter*, chapter 3), and they also argue that her confession would benefit her soul and her salvation. On a more metaphorical level, the community leaders come to fear that, just as she does not know her earthly father, Pearl is "in the dark" about her heavenly father (*The Scarlet Letter*, chapter 8). How does Hawthorne develop this theme of religious paternity? Clearly, an investigation of this theme will lead you into a thorough investigation into Pearl's characterization and her role in the novel.

Character

Hawthorne's characters and their development are closely related to important themes in the text. For example, a paper on Hester might explore Hester's position as an artist. Any thorough investigation of character should pay close attention to Hawthorne's methods of character development. Examine the descriptions of the characters, their language and dialogue. In Hawthorne's fiction, it is always especially important to note what the narrator has to say about a particular character—Hawthorne's narrators often provide particularly insightful assessments of his characters.

Sample Topics:

1. **Hester as a character:** How are we to evaluate Hester? Does Hawthorne seem to admire her or condemn her? Why does she choose to remain in Boston, despite the harsh punishment of that community?

Even a cursory reading of the text quickly demonstrates just how complex Hester is. Most papers that analyze Hester will probably deal, at least in part, with her complicated, and sometimes perplexing, relationship with her society. These papers, though, should focus more on explaining or illuminating Hester herself. For example, you might choose to analyze what Hester's needlework and her use of her art says about her character. Clearly, though, an essay on Hester will need to be narrowly focused. There are a number of strategies you could use to begin focusing such a paper.

You might find that Hester's relationship with the scarlet letter is a potentially rewarding focus for an essay. Early in the novel the narrator comments on Hester's decision to remain in Boston after her public humiliation: "It may seem marvelous, that, with the world before her . . . this woman should still call that place her home, where, and where only, she must needs be the type of shame" (*The Scarlet Letter*, chapter 5). Why does Hester choose to remain in Boston and wear her scarlet letter? Once she thinks about escaping to a new life, and later she and

Pearl disappear from the community for a long period of time. In the conclusion, though, the narrator tells us that Hester returns to her seaside cottage and continued to wear the scarlet *A*. "She had returned, therefore," the narrator says, "and resumed,—of her own free will, for not the sternest magistrate of that iron period would have imposed it,—resumed the symbol of which we have related so dark a tale" (*The Scarlet Letter*, chapter 24). Why does she return? Why does she continue to wear the *A* long after the community would have forced her to? What do her actions tell us about Hester?

Alternately, you could focus on the transformative power of the scarlet letter. In chapter 2, the narrator tells us that it "transfigured" or transformed Hester. And at the conclusion the scarlet *A* had been transfigured: "the scarlet letter ceased to be a stigma which attracted the world's scorn and bitterness, and became a type of something to be sorrowed over, and looked upon with awe, yet with reverence too." Like all the major characters in *The Scarlet Letter*, Hester undergoes a significant transformation. Hester, in fact, undergoes many transformations during the course of the novel, and you may develop a thoughtful thesis by drawing a conclusion about the nature and cause of her transformations. For example, in chapter 13, the narrator says that, "The effect of the symbol—or rather, of the position in respect to the society that was indicated by it—on the mind of Hester Prynne herself, was powerful and peculiar. . . . Some attribute had departed from her, the permanence of which had been essential to keep her a woman." The narrator continues: "She who has once been a woman, and ceased to be so, might at any moment become a woman again, if there were only the magic touch to effect the transfiguration. We shall see whether Hester Prynne were ever afterwards so touched, and so transfigured." With Dimmesdale, when Hester throws the scarlet *A* to the forest floor, Hester seems to undergo just such a transformation. Hester's transformation is accompanied by a transformation of the surrounding woods: "All at once, as with a sudden smile of heaven, forth burst the sunshine, pouring a very flood into the obscure forest." The narrator comments on this transformation: "Such was the sympathy of Nature—that wild, heathen Nature of the forest, never subjugated by human law, nor illumined by higher truth—with the bliss of these two spirits!" (*The Scarlet Letter,* chapter 18). An exploration of this series of transformations could lead in more than one direction. First of all, consider what Hawthorne seems to be saying about womanhood here. What, in his opinion, seems to be essential to womanhood? Another type of investigation could explore the nature of these transformations. Is Hester redeemed or saved by this meeting with Dimmesdale? Has she been transformed back into a woman? Is it significant that this transformation happens in the forest, outside of the boundaries of her community? What do you make of the apparent sympathy between the natural world and the two lovers? Is Hawthorne condoning or condemning Hester's transformation here? Similarly, you might ask if this transformation is tied in any way to the "wildness" in Hester's nature that the narrator so often remarks upon.

In a related vein, Hawthorne also spends some time describing Hester as a proponent of social reform. Chapter 13 speaks a good deal about this element of Hester's character. At one point the narrator remarks, "It is remarkable, that persons who speculate most boldly often conform with the most perfect quietude to the external regulations of society.... So it seemed to be with Hester.... Yet, had little Pearl never come to her ... [t]hen she might have come down to us in history hand in hand with Ann Hutchinson, as the foundress of a religious sect. She might, in one of her phases, have been a prophetess." The narrator continues, "Indeed, the same dark question often rose into her mind with reference to the whole race of womanhood. Was existence worth accepting, even to the happiest among them?" Even at the end of the novel, Hester's revolutionary impulse has not left her, for she often serves as a counselor, especially of women. How do you assess Hester's revolutionary or prophetic impulse? Does Hawthorne seem to be advocating for a kind of feminist philosophy through Hester or is he condemning her reformist ideas?

2. **Pearl as a character:** Pearl is a particularly strange character. Like Hester, she is complex, but her behavior is more inexplicable. What is her role in *The Scarlet Letter*? Why has Hawthorne drawn her in such a strange, almost inhuman way?

Pearl's complexity lies less in her psychological development than in her position as both character and symbol. Drawn in part from Hawthorne's observations of his daughter Una, Pearl does, at times, seem to act like a human child. However, the novel frequently emphasizes her role as a symbol, and her symbolic function is multilayered: "Pearl's spirit was imbued with a spell of infinite variety; in this one child there were many children" (*The Scarlet Letter*, chapter 6). Most obviously, Pearl is a double for the scarlet letter itself, and Hawthorne emphasizes this role in numerous ways. When we first meet Pearl she is compared to the scarlet letter both by Hester's gesture of hiding the *A* behind the infant and by the narrator's reference to Pearl as a "token" of Hester's sin. Similarly, Hawthorne repeatedly emphasizes that Hester dresses Pearl to reflect the color and the embroidery of the scarlet letter. And Hester says to Governor Bellingham, "she is the scarlet letter, only capable of being loved" (*The Scarlet Letter*, chapter 8).

But, like the scarlet letter, Pearl's meaning and function is multivalent and forever shifting. This multiplicity of meanings and functions provides material for a number of different paper topics. Essays on Pearl, then, like essays on Hester, must choose a specific aspect of Pearl to analyze.

Like the *A*, Pearl is a "token of [Hester's] shame." Consequently, like the *A*, she seems in many ways to represent or embody elements or qualities of Hester. The narrator says that she represents her "mother's impassioned state" and "the warfare of Hester's spirit" (*The Scarlet Letter*, chapter 6). How might you analyze Pearl as an extension of Hester, as an embodiment of one element of Hester's character? Conversely, Hester maintains, as does the narrator, that Pearl is the one thing that saves Hester. How might you develop that argument?

Alternatively, you could choose to focus on the Puritan's evaluation of Pearl as a "token of shame." Some in the community see her as an "emblem and product of sin" (*The Scarlet Letter,* chapter 6), and in this capacity they see an answer to the question of Pearl's paternity: "[T]he neighboring towns-people . . . seeking vainly elsewhere for the child's paternity, and observing some of her odd attributes, had given out that poor little Pearl was a demon offspring." The narrator and Hester sometimes seem to concur. Chapter 6 alone refers to Pearl as an "airy sprite," "a little elf," a "spirit," and a "little laughing image of a fiend," and it asserts that much of Pearl's strange behavior is attributable to her conception: "Her nature . . . lacked reference and adaptation to the world into which she was born. The child could not be made amenable to rules. In giving her existence, a great law had been broken; and the result was a being, whose elements were perhaps beautiful and brilliant, but all in disorder; or with an order peculiar to themselves" (*The Scarlet Letter,* chapter 6). How and why does Pearl act in the novel as an "emblem . . . of sin"?

Another focus could be on Pearl's associations with wild-ness, nature, and sunshine. While the chapters that take place in the forest emphasize this particularly, many other spots in the novel show this close relation between Pearl and elements of the natural world. Why does the novel emphasize this rela-tionship? What light does it shed on Pearl's character or her role in the novel?

Finally, like Hester, Pearl undergoes significant transfor-mations in the novel, and these could form the basis of an analytical paper. These transformations come at the hands of others. Her first transformation, or promise of transformation, happens after Dimmesdale publicly acknowledges her as his daughter in the final scaffold scene (*The Scarlet Letter,* chap-ter 23). The novel's final chapter describes the transformation that she undergoes when Chillingworth leaves her a substan-tial fortune. How would you describe the transformations that Pearl undergoes? How do these transformations reflect upon the other themes in the novel (like Hawthorne's commentary on Puritan society or Pearl's status as a symbolic character)?

3. **Chillingworth as a character:** How are we to evaluate Chillingworth's role in the novel? Although he is in some ways the "wronged" character, he transforms into the novel's villain. Why?

Like Pearl, Chillingworth seems to occupy two realms in *The Scarlet Letter*. He seems both a realistically drawn character and an allegorical or symbolic one. Just as Pearl's symbolic value is underlined by Hester's explanation of her name, "'Pearl,' as being of great price," so Chillingworth's name communicates something of his role in the novel. What connotations or associations does his name carry? Other imagery surrounds the physician too. In chapter 4, Hester says to Chillingworth, "Why does thou smile so at me? . . . Art Thou like the Black Man that haunts the forest round about us? Hast thou enticed me into a bond that will prove the ruin of my soul?" How does the imagery of the novel help to support Hester's description of her husband? Examining Chillingworth's role in the novel can help underscore this examination of the imagery that surrounds him. It is especially worth examining the relationship between Chillingworth and Dimmesdale. How would you describe their relationship? How would you describe Chillingworth's motivation in befriending the young minister? Chapter 9 is dedicated largely to Chillingworth and his role as physician to Dimmesdale. Why might Hawthorne have chosen to title that chapter, "The Leech"? How does the novel comment further on Chillingworth's motivations? Why does Chillingworth try to prohibit Dimmesdale from acknowledging Hester and Pearl in chapter 23?

In still another approach to Chillingworth, you could study the alterations in his character. Like many of Hawthorne's male characters, including Aylmer from "The Birth-Mark" and Dr. Rappaccini from "Rappaccini's Daughter," Chillingworth is a scientist and a scholar. How does his role as scientist and scholar help to define his character? You should pay particular attention to how his scholarly and scientific pursuits change over the course of the novel. He and Hester discuss his former character in chapter 4. How does Chillingworth use his science differently once he discovers Hester and Pearl?

4. **Dimmesdale as a character:** How are we to assess Dimmesdale's apparent weakness in the novel? He claims to love truth, but cannot bring himself to confess until the end of the novel. What does this failure say about his character?

As the discussion about Hester indicates, Dimmesdale's character provides a marked contrast to hers, both in relation to society and in relation to their sin. Perhaps the best place to begin an investigation into the minister's character is his public address to Hester in chapter 3. Here, Mr. Wilson has pressed the young minister to convince Hester to confess the name of her lover, and Dimmesdale urges Hester to speak. In this speech Dimmesdale labels himself a hypocrite—if Hester does not name him, he says, he will be "compel[led]" to "add hypocrisy to sin." Later, after Dimmesdale tells his congregants that he is "utterly a pollution and a lie," the narrator says, "The minister well knew—subtle, but remorseful hypocrite that he was!—the light in which his vague confession would be viewed" (*The Scarlet Letter*, chapter 11). Many readers see hypocrisy or a kind of doublespeak even in Dimmesdale's initial address to Hester. Do you agree that Dimmesdale is a hypocrite?

Further, if he truly "loved the truth, and loathed the lie," why does Dimmesdale not confess? To develop an essay on Dimmesdale and the issue of confession you would need to examine his numerous "confessions" throughout the text. What do they tell us about his character? About his relationship with society? What other aspects of his character help to support your assessment of his relationship with society? Finally, you should consider the scarlet letter that Dimmesdale bears on his chest. What does it tell us about his conception of sin?

History and Context

Some familiarity with Puritan New England and with Hawthorne's attitudes toward the Puritans (and toward his family history) will help you understand the historical context of *The Scarlet Letter*. You could use this historical context to help shape an analytical paper on the novel. Biographies of Hawthorne might be a good place to start exploring his attitudes toward Puritanism. Further historical research that could help to illuminate the text might include research on the history of Anne Hutchinson and the history of the Salem witch trials, both of which have some bearing on *The Scarlet Letter*. Remember that a paper that addresses the history and context of a work should use the history as a tool to shed light on the work and should not focus only on the history.

Sample Topics:

1. **Anne Hutchinson:** In chapter 1, the narrator refers to the rosebush that grows by the prison door, and comments that "there is fair authority for believing [that] it had grown up under the footsteps of the sainted Ann Hutchinson, as she entered the prison door." The rosebush is linked to both Hester and Hutchinson, and the narrator reiterates this link again in chapter 13, when he asserts that Hester might have "come down to us in history, hand in hand with Ann Hutchinson, as the foundress of a religious sect" had it not been for Pearl. Why does Hawthorne make these comparisons between Hester and Anne Hutchinson? How do these comparisons comment on Hester's character? Is it significant that Hawthorne's first reference to Hutchinson refers to her as "sainted"?

   Hutchinson was a Puritan woman who gained a following when she began to hold weekly meetings to discuss sermons in her home. Eventually, the magistrates of Massachusetts Bay Colony challenged her religious beliefs and her public preaching and she was banished from the colony for Antinomianism. In addition to Hawthorne's overt references to Hutchinson,

Hester and Hutchinson are linked through their children. As noted above, the Puritan community insisted on reading Pearl as a sign of her mother's transgressions when they call her a "demon offspring." Similarly, Hutchinson's community read one of her misshapen, stillborn children as a sign of her heretical theology.

2. **Salem witch trials:** Throughout the novel Hawthorne makes references to witches and witchcraft. The author apparently felt great guilt about his great-grandfather's role in the trials and even changed the spelling of his last name to distance himself from this element of his family's past. Is the history of Salem and its treatment of purported witches relevant to Hawthorne's points in *The Scarlet Letter*? How does Hawthorne use witchcraft and the supernatural in the novel to comment on Puritan beliefs and attitudes?

A close reading of *The Scarlet Letter* will show that, even though the novel is set in Boston rather than Salem, the topic of magic and witchcraft is well represented in the novel, as are Puritan beliefs about witches and witchcraft—Pearl's strange behavior is frequently attributed to the supernatural and witchcraft; Hester is reputed by some to be a witch; and the novel frequently mentions the character of Mistress Hibbins who was later executed for witchcraft. A paper that addresses the theme of witchcraft with all its historical resonance for Puritan New England must be sure to have a solid understanding of the dynamics of the historical trials as well as the dynamics of the novel. You will probably find that the most fruitful investigation will use the historical events to explain Hawthorne's attitudes toward Puritan beliefs and values in the novel.

Philosophy and Ideas

As discussed in the beginning of this chapter, one of the central themes of *The Scarlet Letter* is a philosophical inquiry into the nature of signs, symbols, and representation. Since this is a complex issue, you could approach it in a number of ways, each yielding plenty of material for a short interpretative paper.

Sample Topics:

1. **Signs and representation:** Hester's scarlet *A* is replicated and reflected throughout the novel, and readers are quickly enveloped in a veritable maze of *A*'s. What does Hawthorne seem to be saying about the nature of signs and symbols? Is it important that the sign in question is a letter of the alphabet (and beyond that, the very first letter of the alphabet)? Is Hawthorne commenting on the representational ability of language?

   Obviously, this is one of the central themes of the novel, and arguably, its most complex topic. Careful attention to the text demonstrates that the scarlet *A* is replicated incessantly throughout the novel. As already noted, Pearl quite clearly functions as a kind of double for the scarlet letter. In addition, when Hester and Pearl visit Governor Bellingham's mansion they seem to find themselves in a house of mirrors. Hester's scarlet *A* and Pearl are both reflected in the breastplate and the headpiece of the governor's suit of armor. In chapter 15, Pearl decorates her own chest with a green *A* made of eelgrass. Additionally, before the novel is over, Dimmesdale reveals the scarlet letter on his own chest, saying that Hester's scarlet letter "is but the shadow of what he bears on his own breast, and that even this, his own red stigma, is no more than the type of what has seared his inmost heart" (*The Scarlet Letter*, chapter 23). The first time that Dimmesdale stands on the scaffold, under the cover of darkness, the narrator says that a meteor created a "great red letter in the sky,—the letter A" (*The Scarlet Letter*, chapter 12). Even the novel's last line creates another visual incarnation of Hester's *A* as it describes Hester's tombstone: "On a field, sable, the letter *A*, gules."

   All these *A*'s and the repeated attempts to interpret them raise a number of questions that you could explore in a paper. The question that this multitude of scarlet *A*'s first raises is the issue of primacy. The title of the novel is *The Scarlet Letter*, but we find not one, but a multitude of scarlet letters in the text.

Why? Which is *the* scarlet letter? While we meet Hester's *A* first, and it certainly seems to be the *A* to which the novel's title refers, Dimmesdale's comments when he reveals his scarlet letter seem to claim that the letter "seared on his inmost heart" is *the* scarlet letter, and Hester's *A* and the *A* on his own chest, he claims, are but "types" of this letter. Indeed, chapter 23's title, "The Revelation of the Scarlet Letter," seems to reinforce his point. How does this proliferation of *A*'s reflect on the novel's other themes? Is it a reflection about the Puritan way of thinking?

A second line of inquiry involves the issue of interpretation and representation. What is the meaning of a symbol or a sign? What does it stand for? Hawthorne calls Pearl "the living hieroglyphic." Similarly, the narrator calls the "great red letter" in the sky one of the "awful hieroglyphics" that people often interpreted as a sign about "the destiny of nations" (*The Scarlet Letter*, chapter 12). Like hieroglyphs, though, the meaning of these symbols proves elusive. Clearly, the Puritan leaders seek to mark Hester as an adulteress when they impose the scarlet *A*. The *A* stands for "adultery." (Or does it stand for "adulteress"?) Hester cannot be contained by any one label, though, and before the novel's end the community has broadened that meaning considerably. Hester's *A*, they claim, comes to stand for "Able." Similarly, readers quickly see a great disparity of interpretation surrounding any of the scarlet letters that appear in the text. What does this proliferation of symbols, meanings, and interpretations say about the nature of representation? What does it say about the human ability to communicate? Obviously, a paper that addresses this topic must narrow the focus. You might, for example, decide to focus on just one incarnation of the *A* within the text. Clearly, there are a multitude of directions in which such an inquiry could lead you.

Language, Symbols, and Imagery

While the scarlet letter stands as the most significant symbol in the text, any paper that seeks to deal with its significance must also grapple with the larger philosophical issues of signs and representation. The novel incorporates a number of images and patterns that prove significant throughout. You might choose to examine Hawthorne's contrasting use of sunshine and shadow. Similarly, a brief paper could address his use of the rosebush that grows at the prison door. Finally, you could choose to investigate Hawthorne's use of setting. While most of the tale takes place in Boston or at Hester's seaside cottage, the forest plays a significant role in the action.

Sample Topics:

1. **The forest:** While nearly all of the action of the novel takes place in Boston or in Hester's seaside cottage on the outskirts of town, four chapters take place well outside the boundaries of the town in the forest. What is the role of the forest in *The Scarlet Letter*?

   An investigation that considers Hawthorne's use of setting and the imagery that surrounds it might also help shed light on the relationship between the individual and society. You might examine the action, the dialogue, and the imagery associated with the forest in these chapters. Why is it that this is the only place in the novel where Hester and Dimmesdale have a private conversation? Why does Hester remove the scarlet letter and throw it to the forest floor here?

   Furthermore, if the forest is so dark and deep (and often associated with the devil, as Pearl's questions about meeting "the Black Man" in the forest suggest), why does sunshine figure so prominently in these chapters? Examine Hawthorne's use of sunshine in these chapters carefully. With whom is it most associated? Why? How do the other characters in these chapters relate to the sunshine? How might Hawthorne's contrast of the forest and the town shed light on other issues and themes of the novel?

2. **The Rosebush:** In the first chapter, we meet the "wild rosebush" that grows at the prison door. The narrator seems to contrast the bush with the prison, which he calls, "the dark flower of civilized society." The rosebush enters into the dialogue again

when Pearl tells Mr. Wilson that "she had not been made at all, but had been plucked by her mother off the bush of wild roses, that grew by the prison-door" (*The Scarlet Letter*, chapter 8). How does Hawthorne use the image of the rosebush, and how does it reflect other themes of the novel?

It is worth noting that the narrator mentions the rosebush in the short introductory chapter that deals, at least in part, with the more philosophic question of the nature of human community and society. The prison, which stands in contrast to the rosebush, is a sad necessity of civilized society. Similarly, you should pay close attention to the way that the rosebush participates in the color imagery that Hawthorne uses in the text. Inquiries into these issues, as well as the rumored link between the rosebush and Anne Hutchinson, amplify the bush's significance within the text.

Compare and Contrast Essays

The Scarlet Letter shares thematic and philosophical concerns with much of Hawthorne's other work. "The Custom-House," because of its close connection with the novel, provides a particularly rich ground for comparative papers. Hawthorne's introductory essay is thematically linked to the novel through its concern with art and the artist and through its treatment of paternity. The chapter on "The Custom-House" provides a more thorough discussion about writing on these matters. Beyond these connections, though, you will likely find that many of Hawthorne's short stories provide interesting connections to *The Scarlet Letter*. "Young Goodman Brown," for example, shares an interest in the nature of human sinfulness and human community. Remember that your goal in these types of papers is to draw conclusions about the significance of the similarities or differences that you observe.

Sample Topics:

1. **Sin and community:** In chapter 5, the narrator remarks on Hester's isolation, noting that she sometimes believed that she could sense the hidden sin of others. The lengthy passage concludes: "Such loss of faith is ever one of the saddest results of

sin. Be it accepted as a proof that all was not corrupt in this poor victim of her own frailty, and man's hard law, that Hester Prynne yet struggled to believe that no fellow mortal was guilty like herself." In some ways, this second sense about the sin of others is the same knowledge that Young Goodman Brown gains in his encounter in the forest. How do the reactions of Hester and Brown compare? How does their knowledge of sin affect their relationship with others? What does Hawthorne seem to be saying about the nature of sin, the nature of human community, and the nature of faith through these two characters?

An essay that seeks to address this topic should thoroughly examine both texts, making special note of the narrator's commentary in chapter 5. You should also find the conclusion of "Young Goodman Brown" helpful in formulating a response to this question.

You could also reshape or expand this topic to consider Dimmesdale's response to his meeting with Hester in the forest. Examine his thoughts and his confusion in chapter 20, particularly his query, "Am I mad? Or am I given over utterly to the fiend?" In addition, analyze his discussion with Mistress Hibbins in this same chapter along with his response to those he meets on his way back to town. You could fruitfully compare his response to this encounter in the forest with Young Goodman Brown's and/or Hester's and consider how they reflect upon Hawthorne's assessment of human sinfulness. In addition, you might find that "The Minister's Black Veil" provides suitable material for an essay examining the responses of Reverend Hooper and Dimmesdale to their recognition of their own sinfulness.

2. **Scientists:** As a scientist and a scholar, Chillingworth shares qualities with other scientist figures in Hawthorne's fiction, including Aylmer in "The Birth-Mark" and Dr. Rappaccini of "Rappaccini's Daughter." Scholars have often drawn a connec-

tion between Hawthorne's scientists and his artist figures, like Owen Warland in "The Artist of the Beautiful" and Holgrave in *The House of the Seven Gables.* All of these figures reflect on Hawthorne's conception of his own role as artist. What qualities does Chillingworth share with these other characters? How does a comparison of Chillingworth and these characters help to shed light on Chillingworth's character?

A response to this question would require a good deal more narrowing, and you would do well to limit your comparison to just one or two of the other characters listed. An assessment of Chillingworth's role would benefit from a careful assessment both of his relationship with Dimmesdale and of Hawthorne's descriptions of the physician's motivations. Consider Chillingworth's propensity for close, careful observation. Additionally, you might find that an inquiry like this also connects to issues of sin in the novel. Keep in mind Hawthorne's story "Ethan Brand." In this story, Brand goes in search of the "Unpardonable sin," which he describes as "The sin of an intellect that triumphed over the sense of brotherhood with man, and reverence for God, and sacrificed everything to its own mighty claims." How does this language reflect some of the language of sin found in *The Scarlet Letter?*

Bibliography and Online Resources for *The Scarlet Letter*

"Anne Hutchinson." Available online. URL: http://www.annehutchinson.com/Default.htm. Downloaded June 15, 2006.

Arac, Jonathan. "The Politics of *The Scarlet Letter.*" In *Ideology and Classic American Literature.* Ed. Sacvan Bercovich and Myra Jehlen, Cambridge MA: Harvard UP, 1986. 247–66.

Barlowe, Jamie. *The Scarlet Mob of Scribblers: Rereading Hester Prynne.* Carbondale: Southern Illinois UP, 2000.

Baym, Nina. "The Significance of Plot in Hawthorne's Romances." In *Ruined Eden of the Present: Hawthorne, Melville, and Poe.* Ed. G. R. Thompson and Virgil L. Lokke. West Lafayette, IN: Purdue UP, 1981. 49–70.

———. *The Scarlet Letter: A Reading.* Boston: Twayne, 1986.

———. *The Shape of Hawthorne's Career.* Ithaca, NY: Cornell UP, 1976.

———. "Thwarted Nature: Nathaniel Hawthorne as Feminist." In *American Novelists Revisited: Essays in Feminist Criticism.* Ed. Fritz Fleischmann. Boston: Hall, 1982. 58–77.

Bell, Michael Davitt. *Hawthorne and the Historical Romance of New England.* Princeton, NJ: Princeton UP, 1971.

Bell, Millicent, ed. *Hawthorne and the Real, Bicentennial Essays.* Columbus: Ohio State UP, 2005.

———. *Hawthorne's View of the Artist.* Albany: SUNY P, 1962.

Bensick, Carol M. "Partly Sympathy and Partly Rebellion: Mary Ward, *The Scarlet Letter,* and Hawthorne." *Hawthorne and Women: Engendering and Expanding the Hawthorne Tradition.* Ed. John L. Idol, Jr., and Melinda M. Ponder. Amherst: U of Massachusetts P, 1999.

Benstock, Shari. "The Scarlet Letter (a)dorée, or the Female Body Embroidered." *The Scarlet Letter: Case Studies in Contemporary Criticism.* Ed. Ross C. Murfin. Boston: Bedford, 1991. 288–303.

Bercovitch, Sacvan. "The Scarlet Letter: A Twice Told Tale." *Nathaniel Hawthorne Review.* Available online. URL: http://www.eldritchpress.org/nh/sb1. html. Downloaded June 15, 2006.

———. *The Office of the Scarlet Letter.* Baltimore/London: John Hopkins UP, 1991.

Bloom, Harold. *Nathaniel Hawthorne's* The Scarlet Letter. New York: Chelsea House, 1998.

Boyer, Paul, and Stephen Nissenbaum. *Salem Possessed: The Social Origins of Witchcraft.* Cambridge, MA: Harvard UP, 1974.

Brodhead, Richard. *Hawthorne, Melville, and the Novel.* Chicago: U of Chicago P, 1973.

Carrez, Stephanie. "Symbol and Interpretation in *The Scarlet Letter.*" Hawthorne in Salem. Available online. URL: http://hawthorneinsalem.org/Scholars Forum/MMD2575.html. Downloaded June 7, 2006.

Carton, Evan. *The Rhetoric of the American Romance.* Baltimore: Johns Hopkins UP, 1985.

Chase, Richard. *The American Novel and Its Tradition.* Garden City, NY: Doubleday, 1957.

Colacurcio, Michael. "Footsteps of Ann Hutchinson: The Context of *The Scarlet Letter.*" *ELH* 39 (1972): 459–94.

———, ed. *New Essays on* The Scarlet Letter. Cambridge: Cambridge UP, 1985.

Crews, Frederick C. *The Sins of Fathers: Hawthorne's Psychological Themes.* New York: Oxford UP, 1966.

Crowley, J. Donald, ed. *Hawthorne: The Critical Heritage.* New York: Barnes, 1971.

Eldred, Eric. Nathaniel Hawthorne (1804–1864) home page. Available online. URL: http://www.eldritchpress.org/nh/hawthorne.html. Downloaded June 15, 2006.

Fiedler, Leslie. *Love and Death in the American Novel.* Rev. ed. New York: Stein and Day, 1966.

Fogle, Richard Harter. *Hawthorne's Fiction: The Light and the Dark.* Norman: U of Oklahoma P, 1952.

Fryer, Judith. *The Faces of Eve: Women in the Nineteenth-Century American Novel.* New York: Oxford UP, 1976.

Goddu, Teresa, and Leland Person, editors. The Scarlet Letter *after 150 Years: A Special Issue. Studies in American Fiction* 29 (2001): 2–128.

Gomes, Peter G. "Anne Hutchinson." Harvard Magazine online. Available online. URL: http://www.harvardmagazine.com/on-line/1102194.html. Downloaded June 29, 2006.

Hawthorne, Nathaniel. "Mrs. Hutchinson." Nathaniel Hawthorne (1804–1864) home page. Available online. URL: http://www.ibiblio.org/eldritch/nh/mrsh.html. Downloaded June 15, 2006.

Herbert, T. Walter. *Dearest Beloved: The Hawthornes and the Making of the Middle Class Marriage.* Berkeley: U of California P, 1993.

Irwin, John. *American Hieroglyphics: The Symbol of the Egyptian Hieroglyphics in the American Renaissance.* New Haven, CT: Yale UP, 1980.

Kopley, Richard. *The Threads of the Scarlet Letter: A Study of Hawthorne's Transformative Art.* Newark, DE: U of Delaware P, 2003.

Levin, Harry. *The Power of Blackness.* New York: Knopf, 1958.

Male, Roy R. *Hawthorne's Tragic Vision.* New York: Norton, 1957.

Matthiessen, F. O. *American Renaissance: Art and Expression in the Age of Emerson and Whitman.* New York: Oxford UP, 1941.

Miller, Edwin H. *Salem Is My Dwelling Place: A Life of Nathaniel Hawthorne.* Iowa City: U of Iowa P, 1991.

Millington, Richard H., ed. *The Cambridge Companion to Nathaniel Hawthorne.* Cambridge: Cambridge UP, 2004.

Millington, Richard. "The Meanings of Hawthorne's Women." Hawthorne in Salem. Available online. URL: http://hawthorneinsalem.org/Literature/ Melville/LiteraryLinks/MMD1210.html. Downloaded June 7, 2006.

Pearce, Roy Harvey. *Hawthorne Centenary Essays.* Columbus: Ohio State UP, 1964.

Pease, Donald E. *Visionary Compacts: American Renaissance Writings in Cultural Context.* Madison: U of Wisconsin P, 1987.

Pennell, Melissa. "Subverting the Subversive: Hawthorne's Containment of Hester Prynne in *The Scarlet Letter.*" Hawthorne in Salem. Available online. URL: http://hawthorneinsalem.org/ScholarsForum/MMD2451.html. Downloaded June 7, 2006.

Person, Leland S. *Aesthetic Headaches: Women and a Masculine Poetics in Poe, Melville, and Hawthorne.* Athens: U of Georgia P, 1988.

Ponder, Melinda. "Hawthorne and 'The Sphere of Ordinary Womanhood.'" Hawthorne in Salem. Available online. URL: http://hawthorneinsalem. org/ScholarsForum/Hawthorneandwomanhood.html. Downloaded June 7, 2006.

Ragussis, Michael. "Silence, Family Discourse, and Fiction in *The Scarlet Letter.*" *The Scarlet Letter: Case Studies in Contemporary Criticism.* Ed. Ross C. Murfin. Boston: Bedford, 1991. 316–29.

Reynolds, Larry J. *A Historical Guide to Nathaniel Hawthorne.* New York: Oxford UP, 2001.

Rueben, Paul P. "Nathaniel Hawthorne." PAL: Perspectives in American Literature—A Research and Reference Guide—An Ongoing Project. Available online. URL: http://www.csustan.edu/english/reuben/pal/chap3/hawthorne. html. Downloaded March 17, 2006.

———. "Anne Hutchinson." PAL: Perspectives in American Literature—A Research and Reference Guide—An Ongoing Project. Available online. URL: http://www.csustan.edu/english/reuben/pal/chap1/hutchinson.html. Downloaded June 15, 2006.

"Salem Witchcraft Hysteria." National Geographic.com. Available online. URL: http://www.nationalgeographic.com/features/97/salem/. Downloaded June 26, 2006.

"The Salem Witch Trials 1692: A Chronology of Events." Salem Web. Available online: URL: http://www.salemweb.com/memorial/. Downloaded July 1, 2006.

Sterling, Laurie A. "Paternal Gold: Translating Inheritance in *The Scarlet Letter.*" *ATQ* 6 (1992): 17–31.

Stuart, John W. "Christian Imagery in Hawthorne's *The Scarlet Letter.*" Hawthorne in Salem. Available online. URL: http://hawthorneinsalem.org/ScholarsForum/MMD1824.html. Downloaded June 7, 2006.

Turner, Arlin. *Nathaniel Hawthorne: A Biography.* Oxford: Oxford UP, 1980.

Waggoner, Hyatt H. *Hawthorne: A Critical Study.* Cambridge, MA: Belknap-Harvard University Press, 1955.

Wineapple, Brenda. *Hawthorne: A Life.* New York: Knopf, 2003.

"THE CUSTOM-HOUSE"

READING TO WRITE

OFTEN, READERS are tempted to skip over "The Custom-House" and move right to *The Scarlet Letter,* claiming that the introductory essay is long, boring, and irrelevant. For many, its connection to *The Scarlet Letter* seems tenuous at best. A little more than halfway through the sketch, Hawthorne claims to have found "a certain affair of fine red cloth, much worn and faded.... It was the capital letter *A*." Additionally, he claims to have found the account of the *A* and its wearer, Hester Prynne, written by a former Custom-House Surveyor, Mr. Surveyor Pue. Hawthorne admits to "dressing up" Pue's tale and shaping it into the novel that follows. These claims, of course, are fictitious, further frustrating some readers. While "The Custom-House" is rich enough to be studied of its own accord, a careful reading of the sketch can also shed a great deal of light on both *The Scarlet Letter* and on Hawthorne's history and character.

The sketch is steeped in Hawthorne's own history. In March 1846, Hawthorne was appointed to the post of Surveyor of the Custom-House in his hometown of Salem, Massachusetts. Badly in need of a salary, Hawthorne had pressed his political connections for the position, and he remained at Customs until he was removed from the post in June 1849 in the midst of a political scandal. The Democrats had been voted out of office, and Hawthorne, a Democratic political appointee, had become entangled in partisan politics while in Customs. He was implicated in a Democratic plan to channel kickbacks to his party. As it became apparent that he would most likely lose his position, Hawthorne staged a counteroffensive to try to save his job. The political upheaval resulted in a war of words that kept him, as he says in "The Custom-House," "careering through the public prints." The Whigs accused Hawthorne of political wrongdoing and Hawthorne claimed he was just a nonpartisan writer. In the end, after a bitter public battle, Hawthorne lost his post.

Growing from this history, "The Custom-House" sketch, which is subtitled "Introductory to *The Scarlet Letter*," actually serves two functions. It is, as its subtitle suggests, a lengthy introduction to *The Scarlet Letter.* In addition, though, it serves as Hawthorne's attempt to try to have the last word on his dismissal. It is his attempt to regain control over his name, his reputation, and his history. Remembering this dual purpose can help you understand and analyze this piece. "The Custom-House" rewards the tenacious reader by illuminating and enhancing many of the novel's themes and providing insight into Hawthorne's artistry and writing.

Early in the sketch, Hawthorne tells the reader of his hometown, Salem, and he draws brief portraits of two of his ancestors in order to establish his ties to the town and to explain its "hold on [his] affections." He first tells of his "first ancestor," a "grave, bearded, sable-cloaked" man who immigrated to the new world: "He was a soldier, legislator, judge; he was a ruler in the Church; he had all the Puritanic traits, both good and evil." Hawthorne calls this man "a bitter persecutor" whose "hard severity" is remembered in history. In addition, Hawthorne writes that "His son, too, inherited the persecuting spirit, and made himself so conspicuous in the martyrdom of the witches, that their blood may fairly be said to have left a stain upon him." With his family ties to Salem so established, Hawthorne continues:

> Doubtless, however, either of these stern and black-browed Puritans would have thought it quite a sufficient retribution for his sins that, after so long a lapse of years, the old trunk of the family tree, with so much venerable moss upon it, should have borne, as its topmost bough, an idler like myself. No aim, that I have ever cherished, would they recognize as laudable; no success of mine— if my life, beyond its domestic scope, had ever been brightened by success—would they deem otherwise than worthless, if not posi-

tively disgraceful. "What is he?" murmurs one gray shadow of my forefathers to the other. "A writer of story-books! What kind of a business in life,—what mode of glorifying God, or being service-able to mankind in his day and generation,—may that be? Why, the degenerate fellow might as well have been a fiddler!" Such are the compliments bandied between my great-grandsires and myself, across the gulf of time! And yet, let them scorn me as they will, strong traits of their nature have intertwined themselves with mine.

Attentive readers should find that this passage raises a number of questions. In turn, these questions could help develop paper topics on Hawthorne's themes in "The Custom-House" or on its ties to *The Scarlet Letter*.

The reader's first questions might concern Hawthorne's profile of his Puritan ancestors. Why does he choose to sketch these characters for us, and how does he characterize them? These initial questions could lead the reader to two distinct lines of investigation—the first about Hawthorne's self-portrait and the second about the sketch's relationship with *The Scarlet Letter*. On one level, this is clearly an autobiographical sketch. How, then, do the portraits of these Puritans reflect upon Hawthorne's literary self-portrait? In response to this question, the reader might ask if it is significant that the Puritan predecessors Hawthorne profiles are both men. Clearly Hawthorne was descended from women as well as men, but it is the figure of that "first ancestor" that "haunts" the author. The reader might ask if Hawthorne's decision to focus on these two men in some way speaks to questions of gender and gender roles in the 19th century. These questions should clearly lead back to investigations of how Hawthorne paints his ancestors. Certainly the language that describes them might be regarded as traditionally masculine: "grave," "hard," "strong," "stern." You should also explore the relationship that Hawthorne envisions between these "stern and black-browed Puritans" and himself. Why do these ghostly incarnations chide Hawthorne about his vocation? Further, examine the content of their chidings: "What is he? . . . A writer of story-books! What kind of a business in life . . . may that be? Why the degenerate fellow might as well have been a fiddler!"

What does their language reveal about their expectations and their value system? Even today, we often hear about the Puritan work ethic (also known as the Protestant work ethic). How might the language of Hawthorne's ancestors reflect a culture that disdains idleness and sees hard work as necessary? Additionally, examine Hawthorne's self-description when he says that his forefathers "would have thought it quite a sufficient retribution for his sins that, after so long a lapse of years, the old trunk of the family tree, . . . should have borne, as its topmost bough, an idler like myself. No aim, that I have ever cherished, would they recognize as laudable; no success of mine . . . would they deem otherwise than worthless, if not positively disgraceful." How does Hawthorne's language in this passage help to underline this value system? Further, how does this imagined dialogue "bandied between" Hawthorne and his ancestors "across the gulf of time" characterize his work as a writer or artist? Why is Hawthorne's vocation as a writer not an acceptable "business in life"? What connotations does the analogy between Hawthorne and a fiddler carry? Why does Hawthorne characterize himself as an "idler"? Taken together, what do these comments say about Puritan attitudes toward art and creativity? Further, how do they reflect on Hawthorne's own conception of himself? As you continue to investigate the character of Nathaniel Hawthorne that this passage paints, you should look to the apparent contrast provided by the passage's final line: "[S]corn me as they will, strong traits of their nature have intertwined themselves with mine." How does this sentence modify the portrait of Hawthorne sketched until now? Finally, you might also question why Hawthorne uses the metaphor of the "family tree" to describe his lineage. Granted, it is common and familiar, but you might ask if the writer chooses it purposely here. How might it amplify his description of his relationship with Salem?

A second line of inquiry suggested by this passage concerns the relationship between the introductory sketch and the novel. Why, in an introduction to *The Scarlet Letter,* would Hawthorne choose to profile the "stern and black-browed Puritans" of his own ancestry? Quite clearly, Hawthorne's characterization of his "grave, bearded, sable-cloaked, and steeple-crowned progenitor[s]" begs comparison with the "throng of bearded men, in sad-colored garments and gray, steeple-crowned hats" described in the very first line of *The Scarlet Letter.* Careful readers of both texts should note the likeness and realize that the Puritanic Hathornes of Salem ("Hathorne" is the original spelling of Hawthorne's name) and the leaders of Boston who figure so prominently in *The Scarlet Letter* are reflections of one another. This realization easily leads to a series of questions about the relationship between the texts. If Hawthorne so clearly establishes a connection between his forefathers and the Puritan leaders of old Boston, how does he develop upon this connection, and why does he draw this parallel? How does this correspondence help to illuminate the relationship between the texts? This line of questioning could lead you back to an examination of the values of Hawthorne's Puritan forefathers. Their imagined dialogue clearly reflects their attitudes about Hawthorne's vocation as an artist. Do the Puritan leaders of *The Scarlet Letter* display the same kinds of attitudes about art and its value? How might you develop this link between "The Custom-House" and the novel? Further, does this parallel suggest any potential comparison between any other figures in the two texts? How might you develop these parallels? Hawthorne also expresses some anxiety or concern about his relationship with his forefathers and seems to question his position on the family tree. Does *The Scarlet Letter* develop upon the theme of ancestry and inheritance at all? How might you build an analysis of the theme of ancestry or paternity in these two texts?

Such a thoughtful reading allows the reader to see connections between "The Custom-House" and *The Scarlet Letter* that might not be apparent to a more casual or impatient reader. In addition, it allows you to see the depth and significance of "The Custom-House" itself. Realizing that this lengthy introductory sketch, like Hawthorne's other works of fiction, incorporates both character and thematic development should help you to find a foothold for developing thoughtful paper topics on the piece.

TOPICS AND STRATEGIES

Building upon the reading of the sketch begun above, this section of the chapter provides broad topic ideas that should help you develop an essay on "The Custom-House." Remember that the suggestions below are just springboards for your own exploration; you will need to focus your analysis and develop your own specific thesis.

Themes

"The Custom-House" deals with themes such as paternity, inheritance, art, and the imagination. In fact, you will discover that these themes are closely linked. You may find that exploring Hawthorne's treatment of paternity in the essay soon leads you to questions about the importance of art and the imagination. Other themes include the notion of home and Hawthorne's thoughts about business and work. These themes prove to be interconnected. As you develop a paper on one of these themes, then, be sure to think about its relation to other major themes in the essay. Consider how they amplify or modify each other. Remember, too, that you will need to consider other elements of the essay, including the character sketches and Hawthorne's own history. Analyzing the intersection of theme with character and/or history should prove helpful in developing a strong analytical paper.

Sample Topics:

1. **Paternity and inheritance:** In the opening pages of the essay Hawthorne seems to doubt his own place on the family tree. He tells us that the figure of his first ancestor "was present to my boyish imagination, as far back as I can remember," adding, "It still haunts me." Why does Hawthorne envision both his familial forefathers and, late in the essay, Surveyor Pue as kinds of ghosts or apparitions? What kind of relationship does he envision with his ancestors? With Pue? How does the language he uses in his discussions of Pue help to develop your understanding of his relationship with the Surveyor? As you compare Hawthorne's relationship with his biological ancestors to that he envisions with Pue, what can you conclude about Hawthorne himself, about his abilities and his values?

An essay on this topic will be dependent on both a close, careful analysis of Hawthorne's language in these passages and on some understanding on Hawthorne's biography. You will probably need to consider his own attitude toward his literary career. "The Custom-House" provides some information on how the author balanced (or failed to balance) his literary career with his job in Customs. As with any autobiographical writing, though, you need to consider how accurate and honest Hawthorne's self-portrait is. Additionally, you might read from some of the biographies on Hawthorne to explore his attitudes about being a professional writer. (He was among the first of what we might consider "professional" writers in our country.) Exploration of these issues, coupled with careful attention to his language in this passage should help elucidate Hawthorne's purpose.

2. **Art and the imagination:** Hawthorne imagines that his career as a writer would be "quite a sufficient retribution" for the sins of his Puritan forefathers. He claims, though, that his work in Customs compromised his abilities as a writer. Why does Hawthorne argue that his job in Customs and his work as a "literary man" were incompatible? What value does he find in writing, art, and the work of the imagination? Why is it important to him that he regain control over the "tribe of unrealities"?

Clearly, this topic is related to the issues of paternity and inheritance. You should probably consider why Hawthorne believes that his ancestors would not value his work as an artist. A thorough investigation of this topic should also analyze the language that Hawthorne uses in these passages and others to describe his literary efforts. The image of the tarnished mirror, the "tribe of unrealities," the forge, the stiff, unmalleable characters of his imagination are all provocative. Hawthorne discusses his abilities and inabilities as an artist often throughout this essay, and there are many more passages you should take into account.

3. **Home/ "home-feeling":** In the third paragraph of "The Custom-House," Hawthorne introduces "my native town of Salem." Salem's status as Hawthorne's ancestral home plays an important role in this sketch. Repeatedly, Hawthorne talks of his family's position in the town and of his own relationship with it. He begins the seventh paragraph by saying, "This old town of

Salem—my native place, though I have dwelt much away from it, both in boyhood and maturer years—possesses, or did possess, a hold on my affections." He continues, "And yet, though invariably happiest elsewhere, there is within me a feeling for old Salem, which, in lack of a better phrase, I must be content to call affection. The sentiment is probably assignable to the deep and aged roots which my family has struck into the soil." Both this description and that in the following paragraph—"It still haunts me, and induces a sort of home-feeling"—seem to indicate a kind of ambivalence about his home: it is both haunting and homey; he is happier elsewhere, but holds an affection for the town. Why is Hawthorne's attitude toward Salem so complicated and, at times, contradictory? What does this complex attitude tell us about Hawthorne? About his values? About his attitudes toward Salem's past (and his own past)?

There are many more passages to examine if you are to thoroughly consider the topic of home in "The Custom-House." And, once again, you must be certain to pay close attention to the language and images that Hawthorne uses in his descriptions of both Salem and his relationship with the town. Clearly, the eighth paragraph ties Hawthorne's "home-feeling" to his family tradition in the town: "I seem to have a stronger claim to a residence here on account of this grave, bearded, sable-cloaked, and steeple-crowned progenitor." Are Hawthorne's attitudes about his family and his town linked? He uses the metaphor of the "family tree" to discuss relationship with his ancestors. How is the imagery he uses to describe his relationship to Salem related to this metaphor? Remember that your goal in a paper on this topic is to analyze Hawthorne's feelings about his home and to draw some conclusions about it. You should, therefore, think about why he feels as he does or why he chooses the patterns of imagery that he uses.

4. **Business and the Puritan work ethic:** Hawthorne imagines that his stern ancestors would condemn him as an "idler" whose

literary work was "worthless." By contrast, Hawthorne implies that his work in Customs is real work, work that his ancestors would be proud of. Despite this, Hawthorne claims that his time in the Custom-House sapped his abilities as a writer. He claims, "I had ceased to be a writer of tolerably poor tales and essays, and had become a tolerably good Surveyor of the Customs." Why does Hawthorne paint his work in the Custom-House and his work as a writer as incompatible? How does his assessment of the Custom-House and his assessment of his writing serve to comment on the work ethic and the values held by his ancestors? How does his time in Customs help to define Hawthorne's own values and his own work ethic?

A paper on this topic must closely examine Hawthorne's portrayal of Customs and of the Custom-House officers. His description of Customs begins in the third paragraph with his physical description of the building and of the American eagle who "hovers" over the entry door. Similarly, he spends a good deal of time midway through the essay creating his "gallery of Custom-House portraits." Like the description of the building and the eagle, these portraits of individual employees work to characterize Customs itself. Pay particular attention to Hawthorne's word choice. How does he characterize Customs, the government, and governmental employees? Compare this language to the language he uses to describe his art. How, and when, is the language similar? How and when is it different? You should also consider how Hawthorne portrays his abilities as a writer. This investigation might overlap with some of the questions posed by the section on art and the imagination.

Character

Since people often classify "The Custom-House" as an essay, they are not inclined to approach the work through a discussion of character. If we think of the piece as a "sketch" (and that is the term that Hawthorne used to describe the work), we are more likely to recognize Hawthorne's use of character in "The Custom-House." Because of the work's autobiographical focus, Hawthorne himself is the most interesting and developed character. In addition, Hawthorne includes a number of engaging and often humorous portraits of the other employees of Customs. While these later portraits might provide adequate substance for an essay, they are more productively studied as part of Hawthorne's portrait of Salem and of the working of Customs. Hawthorne's self-portrait, though, is complex enough to provide material for quite a few different paper topics.

Sample Topics:

1. **Hawthorne as a character:** In the opening paragraphs of "The Custom-House," Hawthorne discusses the "autobiographical impulse" that led him to write the sketch. He envisions an audience of "the few who will understand him" and yet concludes that he can "still keep the inmost Me behind its veil." Recognizing that all autobiography involves some shaping of character and some editing and selecting of events, how would you describe the persona that the author shapes for himself in this essay? Why do you think he paints his own portrait as he does?

   Clearly, one important purpose of "The Custom-House" is to provide a sketch of Hawthorne himself. And while there are a number of ways to analyze Hawthorne's character sketch, all of these approaches rely on the realization that Hawthorne shapes his own literary portrait in this work. As the following section on history and context will show, Hawthorne's political enemies surely believed that Nathaniel Hawthorne was someone quite different from the self-portrait he sketches here. Without grappling with the political history that underlies the sketch, you can still shape a number of responses to this type of topic. You might ask yourself how many versions of Nathaniel Hawthorne there are in this text. Alert readers will notice that Hawthorne, in effect, refers to a number of different selves throughout the essay. Similarly, as he contemplates the effect of Customs on his literary skills, he observes, "A gift, a faculty, if it had not departed was suspended and inanimate within me." He continues, "It might be true, indeed, that this was a life which could not, with impunity, be lived too long; else, it might make me permanently other than I had been, without transforming me into any shape which it would be worth my while to take." How does the experience in Customs transform Hawthorne? Why, according to the author, does it transform him as it does? A paper that approaches the topic from this angle will need to closely analyze Hawthorne's discussion of his work and of his "official" self—Surveyor Hawthorne—in relation to Nathaniel Hawthorne the writer. You should find numerous passages that will prove helpful for this kind of essay.

Another way to address this topic would be to use a psychoanalytic approach. At another point in the sketch, Hawthorne contemplates the effect of public office upon individual character. He asserts that political appointment, metaphorized as "Uncle Sam's gold," "has . . . a quality of enchantment like that of the Devil's wages. Who-ever touches it should look well to himself, or he may find the bargain go hard against him, involving, if not his soul, yet many of its better attributes . . . and all that gives the emphasis to a manly character." In the ensuing paragraph he begins to apply this belief to himself, saying, "I endeavoured to calculate how much longer I could stay in the Custom-House, and yet go forth a man." Do you see evidence in these passages of some anxiety over gender and manhood? You might also consider his stern forefather's opinion of Hawthorne's career as a writer too. How does their opinion reflect upon questions of gender and manhood?

History and Context

Clearly, a good bit of "The Custom-House" is built upon historical circumstance. Hawthorne draws from his experience in the Salem Custom-House and from his family history. Consequently, familiarity with Hawthorne's background and his family's ties to Salem provides a good deal of insight into the dynamics of this text. While the introductory section of this chapter provides a brief introduction to Hawthorne's experiences in Customs, you should learn more about his time there before you shape a paper on the biographical or historical dimensions of the sketch. Biographies of Hawthorne, like Wineapple's or Turner's, should prove helpful, as should Nevins and Nissenbaum's articles listed in the bibliography of this chapter. As the introductory section of this chapter indicates, this sketch appears, at least in part, to be Hawthorne's attempt to regain control of his name and reputation after the public fray that surrounded his dismissal from the Custom-House. Considering the literary self-portrait that he paints here, then, should provide rich material for an analytical paper.

Sample Topics:

1. **Hawthorne's experience in the Custom-House:** Hawthorne's dismissal from his position at the Salem Custom-House became a very public issue. Toward the end of the sketch, Hawthorne describes this public dispute, noting, "the press had taken up my affair, and kept me, for a week or two, careering through the public prints." Indeed, two different versions of the firing circulated in the public realm—one put forth by Hawthorne and his Democratic friends and supporters, and another circulated by Charles Upham and the Whigs. Clearly dismayed by the portrait painted by his political enemies, Hawthorne called them "slang-whangers" in his private correspondence. Given Hawthorne's distress over his public persona, how can "The Custom-House" be read as an attempt by Hawthorne to regain control over his name and his reputation?

   Besides requiring some historical investigation, this topic requires close attention to Hawthorne's self-characterization in the text, and this literary self-portrait is complex. Quite clearly, he takes up the scandal surrounding his dismissal, and he pays particular attention to his portrayal of both the execution of his work as Surveyor and his relationship with the Democratic Party. You would be wise, too, to consider Hawthorne's description of the management, effectiveness, and efficiency of the work at Customs as well as to his lengthy, sometimes amusing, portraits of his fellow employees at Customs. How do these description help to advance Hawthorne's version of himself and his history?

Another way to shape a response to this question involves Hawthorne's concern with his reputation as a writer. In the opening paragraphs of the sketch, he discusses the difficulty of finding a reader who will understand him when he "casts his leaves forth upon the wind." Later he comments "literary fame" flourishes only in a "narrow circle." A productive topic for an essay, then, might involve Hawthorne's treatment of his literary reputation in this sketch.

Finally, you could approach this topic by considering the balance of fact and fiction in "The Custom-House." In his preface to the Second Edition of *The Scarlet Letter*, Hawthorne claimed that he had intended to amend or revise the introductory sketch because of the "unprecedented excitement" that surrounded its publication. In the end, he says, he chose not to alter the work because "it appears to him, that the only remarkable features of the sketch are its frank and genuine good-humor, and the general accuracy with which he has conveyed his sincere impressions." He could not, he concludes, have written "with a livelier effect of truth." An analytical research paper might evaluate the relative truth of Hawthorne's portrait of himself or of the Salem Custom-House.

Form and Genre

Hawthorne called his longer works of fiction romances, and he drew a firm distinction between novels and romances. American writers in the 19th century generally accepted the distinction between novel and romance, and the latter was widely perceived as an American form. "The Custom-House," through its concern with Hawthorne's abilities and reputation as a writer, addresses the qualities of romance and provides us with one of Hawthorne's most famous definitions of the genre. Examining Hawthorne's theory of romance in "The Custom-House" could provide the basis for papers on Hawthorne's definition of romance as a genre or papers on his beliefs about the role and purpose of romance.

Sample Topics:

1. **Romance:** "The Custom-House" provides one of Hawthorne's most famous descriptions of romance. He says that "moon-

light, in a familiar room . . . is a medium the most suitable for a romance-writer." Through the agency of moonlight, "The floor of our familiar room has become a neutral territory, somewhere between the real world and fairy-land, where the Actual and the Imaginary may meet, and each imbue itself with the nature of the other." While Hawthorne did not classify "The Custom-House" as a romance, how might you apply this definition of romance to the sketch? In what ways is "The Custom-House" a "neutral territory, somewhere between the real world and fairy-land, were the Actual and the Imaginary . . . meet"?

Like Hawthorne's novel-length romances, this sketch blends history and fiction, and this question requires that you analyze the relationship between the two. You might want to ask why Hawthorne felt the need to introduce his own history into his introductory sketch for *The Scarlet Letter*. Similarly, you could question why Hawthorne uses this sketch to create a fictional history for *The Scarlet Letter*, manufacturing the story of finding the scarlet *A* and Surveyor Pue's manuscript. Does this blending of the "Actual and the Imaginary" tell us something about Hawthorne's art, about his audience, or about his confidence in his abilities?

Language, Symbols, and Imagery

Like the novel that it precedes, "The Custom-House" uses patterns of imagery that Hawthorne is famous for. Just as mirrors and reflections populate *The Scarlet Letter*, the author calls his imagination a "tarnished mirror" late in the sketch. Similarly, his concern with light and dark, moonlight, sunshine, firelight, ghosts, and visions is evident throughout this piece. The richest imagery in "The Custom-House," though, is that which Hawthorne uses to discuss romance. While his comparison of moonlight to the workings of the romance-writer is the most famous image found in "The Custom-House," Hawthorne uses a good many other images in his consideration of the operation of romance. If you examine his images carefully and see what they have in common, you should be able to draw some conclusions about his choice of images.

Sample Topics:

1. **Moonlight:** Through the agency of moonlight, Hawthorne writes, "The floor of our familiar room has become a neutral territory, somewhere between the real world and fairy-land, where the Actual and the Imaginary may meet, and each imbue itself with the nature of the other." Think about your own experience of seeing things by moonlight. Do you agree with Hawthorne's assertion that everyday objects are "spiritualized" by moonlight and "invested with a quality of strangeness and remoteness"? What does moonlight share with the other images Hawthorne uses to describe romance in the middle portion of "The Custom-House"? Why is moonlight so apt a comparison to the workings of romance?

   While this question clearly shares much territory with the discussion of romance, it asks you to focus your paper differently. It asks you to think much more about the logic behind Hawthorne's imagery and the analogy he creates between romance and moonlight. Remember that figurative language should provide a tangible, physical reference for something intangible. Thinking of your own experience with moonlight and firelight should prove helpful in developing your response to this question. Similarly, you might approach this question differently by thinking about more modern uses of these images. Modern movies, especially horror movies, make much of the effects of moonlight. While their ultimate aim is different and they use darkness and moonlight to frighten, they associate darkness and moonlight with many of the same things that Hawthorne does—the unreal, ghosts, the transformation of the familiar. How is Hawthorne's use of this imagery similar to more modern uses? How is it different?

2. **The second story of the Custom-House:** Hawthorne claims that he found the scarlet *A* and Surveyor Pue's manuscript on the second story of the Custom-House. Examine his description of the second floor carefully. How might the second story serve as a symbol? What might it be said to represent?

A paper on this topic must closely examine much of what this chapter has already discussed. You should be prepared to discuss Hawthorne's beliefs about art, his theory of romance, and his characterization of the business of Customs. How does the second story compare to the first floor of the Custom-House? Why, according to Hawthorne, was Pue's manuscript left on the second floor? What other documents remain on the second floor?

Compare and Contrast Essays

Quite clearly, *The Scarlet Letter* provides the richest ground for thematic and topical comparisons with "The Custom-House." But as this chapter has indicated, this sketch also shares much with the larger body of Hawthorne's writing. Because of Hawthorne's focus on his writing and his discussion of romance in this piece, you should find that it affords comparison to other discussions of writing and romance in Hawthorne's work. As you find grounds for comparison between texts, be sure to think about the purpose of your paper. Your thesis should make an assertion about the significances of the similarities and differences that you note.

Sample Topics:
1. **Paternity and home:** As this chapter has indicated, "The Custom-House" expresses anxiety about Hawthorne's place on the family tree. He does not seem the rightful heir to his stern, Puritanical ancestors and he does not seem entirely at home in his ancestral home of Salem. At the same time, he clearly establishes a parallel between his own Puritan ancestors and the Puritans who govern Boston in *The Scarlet Letter.* How does *The Scarlet Letter* share this interest in paternity and inheritance from the Puritans? How does it develop or change this focus? Do these parallels suggest that any of the novel's characters could reflect Hawthorne and his concerns about lineage, paternity, and home?

To address this topic you need to consider the questions posed in the section of this chapter on themes. Similarly, you will need to consider thematic concerns and character development in *The Scarlet Letter.* Another text that you could use in a compare and contrast essay on Hawthorne's treatment of home and inheritance is his last novel, *The Marble Faun.* Two of the characters in this novel, Hilda and Kenyon, are American artists living in Rome. They return to America at the novel's end. Drawn in large part from Hawthorne's own experiences living in Rome, this novel provides plenty of good material for comparison.

2. **Art and the imagination:** Just as Hawthorne's language develops a parallel between the Puritan leaders of Boston and his own Puritan ancestors, his description of his treatment of Hester's scarlet *A* and Surveyor Pue's manuscript is suggestive. Upon finding the "worn and faded" letter *A,* Hawthorne tells us, "I happened to place it on my breast. It seemed to me . . . that I experienced a sensation not altogether physical, yet almost so, as a burning heat; and as if the letter were not of red cloth, but red-hot iron. I shuddered, and involuntarily let it fall upon the floor." Later, discussing Pue's manuscript, he describes his reworking of the story as "the dressing up of the tale." Taken together, what do these passages suggest about Hawthorne's relationship with his book? About his relationship with the characters in the novel? What do these parallels say about Hawthorne's beliefs about art and the imagination?

3. **Romance:** In "The Custom-House," Hawthorne makes much of the transformative power of moonlight and of romance. Where do you see such transformative power at play in *The Scarlet Letter*? What do the parallels between the texts suggest about Hawthorne's perception of his art and of his role as artist?

While the previous question asks you to focus your paper on the parallels between Hester and Hawthorne, both Pearl and Chillingworth prove more useful in forging a response to this question. Clearly, though, the parallel between Hawthorne and Pearl and that between Hawthorne and Chillingworth should produce very different conclusions. You may want to focus your paper on the author's relationship with one of these characters, or you might ask why he would choose to portray the transformative power of art so differently in the novel.

Another approach to the topic of romance writing is more theoretical. You could compare Hawthorne's theory of romance as he expresses it in "The Custom-House" to his theory of romance in the prefaces to *The House of the Seven Gables* and *The Marble Faun.* How are they similar? Does Hawthorne's description of the genre seem to have evolved or changed?

4. **Hawthorne's editorial pose:** Hawthorne claims that he wrote "The Custom-House" to "put myself in my true position of editor" of *The Scarlet Letter.* While this claim is, of course, fictional, it is a rhetorical tactic that he uses frequently. Perhaps the other most interesting use of Hawthorne's editorial pose is the introduction to "Rappaccini's Daughter." Here, Hawthorne claims to be the translator of a story by a M. de l'Aubépine ("Aubépine" is "Hawthorne" in French). Why might Hawthorne be anxious to present his tales as reworkings of others' works or "twice-told tales" (the title of another of his collections of short stories)? Does this editorial pose reveal Hawthorne's anxieties about the reception of his own art? Does it tell us something about the expectations of the reading audience in the 19th century? Does it tell us something about Hawthorne's beliefs about the nature of storytelling?

As the final questions in the previous paragraph suggest, this topic could lead you in a number of very different directions. At the very base of the question, though, Hawthorne seems to be addressing the very nature of storytelling. If *The Scarlet Letter* is a novel about interpreting language, it is certainly suggestive that Hawthorne claims to be "dressing up" or changing and reinterpreting Pue's tale. Similarly, the very act of translating a tale, as he claims to do with "Rappaccini's Daughter," necessarily involves interpretation, since literal translation is rarely accurate or adequate. Consider that Hawthorne, in essence, provides two French titles for "Rappaccini's Daughter," since the "original" French version bears a subtitle. The story is "Beatrice: ou la Belle Empoisonneuse." "Rappaccini's Daughter" is a direct, literal translation of neither. Why does Hawthorne seem to insist that all his works are "twice told tales"?

Bibliography and Online Resources for "The Custom-House"

Anderson, D. "Jefferson, Hawthorne and 'The Custom House.'" *Nineteenth-Century Literature* 46 (1991): 309–26.

Baym, Nina. *The Shape of Hawthorne's Career*. Ithaca, NY: Cornell UP, 1976.

Becker, John E. *Hawthorne's Historical Allegory*. Port Washington, NY: Kennikat Press, 1971.

Colacurcio, Michael J., ed. *New Essays on The Scarlet Letter*. Cambridge: Cambridge UP, 1985.

Crowley, J. Donald, ed. *Hawthorne: the Critical Heritage*. New York: Barnes and Noble, 1970.

Dawson, Hugh. "*The Scarlet Letter*'s Angry Eagle and the Salem Custom-House." Hawthorne in Salem. Available online. URL: http://www.hawthornein salem.com/Literature/customhousesketch/factsandfantasy/angryeagle. html. Downloaded June 7, 2006.

Eakin, Paul John. "Hawthorne's Imagination and the Structure of 'The Custom-House.'" *American Literature* 43 (1971): 346–59.

Easton, Alison. "Hawthorne and the Question of Women." *The Cambridge Companion to Nathaniel Hawthorne*. Ed. Richard H. Millington. Cambridge: Cambridge UP, 2004. 79–98.

Eldred, Eric. "Notes to 'The Custom-House'—*The Scarlet Letter*." Eldritch Press. Available online. URL: http://www.biblio.org/eldritch/nh/slcus-n.html. Downloaded June 7, 2006.

Fossum, Robert H. *Hawthorne's Inviolable Circle: the Problem of Time*. Deland, FL: Everett/Edwards Inc., 1972.

Gollin, Rita. "Figurations of Salem in 'Young Goodman Brown' and 'The Custom-House.'" Hawthorne in Salem. Available online. URL: http://www.hawthorne insalem.com/ScholarsForum/FigurationsofSalem.html. Downloaded June 7, 2006.

Irwin, John. *American Hieroglyphics: The Symbol of the Egyptian Hieroglyphics in the American Renaissance*. New Haven, CT: Yale UP, 1980.

Johnson, Claudia Durst. "Excerpts from *The Custom-House: Hawthorne, the Nineteenth Century and The Scarlet Letter, Chapter 7.*" Hawthorne in Salem. Available online. URL: http://www.hawthorneinsalem.org/Literature/custom housesketch/factsandfantasy/MD1052.html. Downloaded June 7, 2006.

McCall, Dan. *Citizens of Somewhere Else: Nathaniel Hawthorne and Henry James.* Ithaca, NY, and London: Cornell UP, 1999.

Nevins, Winfield S. "Nathaniel Hawthorne's Removal from the Custom-House." *Historical Collections of the Essex Institute* 53 (1917): 97–132.

Nissenbaum, Stephen. "The Firing of Nathaniel Hawthorne." *Essex Institute Historical Collections* 114 (1978): 57–86.

Pease, Donald E. "Hawthorne in the Custom-House: The Metapolitics, Postpolitics, and Politics of *The Scarlet Letter.*" *boundary 2* 32 (2005): 53–70.

Schieber, Andrew J. "Public Force, Private Sentiment: Hawthorne and the Gender of Politics." *ATQ* 2 (1988): 285–99.

Traister, Bryce. "The Bureaucratic Origins of *The Scarlet Letter.*" *Studies in American Fiction* 29 (2001): 77–93.

Turner, Arlin. *Nathaniel Hawthorne: A Biography.* Oxford: Oxford UP, 1980.

West, Harry C. "Hawthorne's Editorial Pose." *American Literature* 44 (1972): 208–21.

Whitney, Teri. "The Custom-House Chapter of *The Scarlet Letter:* Introduction." Hawthorne in Salem. Available online. URL: http://www.hawthorne insalem.org/Literature/customhousesketch/factsandfantasy/Introdciion. html. Downloaded June 7, 2006.

Wineapple, Brenda. *Hawthorne: A Life.* New York: Knopf, 2003.

THE HOUSE OF THE SEVEN GABLES

READING TO WRITE

HAWTHORNE FELT that *The Scarlet Letter* was a dark tale and found it "impossible to relieve the shadows of the story with so much light as I would gladly have thrown in." But his next novel, *The House of the Seven Gables,* functions, finally, as a testament to brightness and sunshine, despite the gothic gloom that pervades much of the book. In the novel's preface, Hawthorne sets out a moral that prepares readers for a narrative of darkness and gloom: "[T]he Author has provided himself with a moral;—the truth, namely, that the wrong-doing of one generation lives into the successive ones, and, divesting itself of every temporary advantage, becomes a pure and uncontrollable mischief;—and he would feel it a singular gratification, if this Romance might effectually convince mankind . . . of the folly of tumbling down an avalanche of ill-gotten gold, or real estate, on the heads of an unfortunate posterity, thereby to maim or crush them." In the opening chapter of the narrative, "The Old Pyncheon Family," the narrator recounts the history of the titular House of the Seven Gables, highlighting the dark, gloomy character of the house, its owners, and its history. Readers quickly understand that the house, whose "very timbers were oozy," embodies the "ill-gotten . . . real estate" of Hawthorne's preface, and we learn that its owners, the Pyncheon family, are, consequently, haunted by the lurid curse of the reputed wizard Matthew Maule: "God will give him blood to drink!" This seems a dark

270

beginning for a book that will bear a rather conventional happy ending marked by a marriage and the reconciliation of this longstanding family feud. But in the first chapter's history of the House of the Seven Gables, readers find the keys to both the novel's gloom and its sunshine, for as the narrator tells of the dispute that surrounds the house, readers can discern the competing value systems that drive the plot of Hawthorne's novel. Consider how much information the narrator conveys in the following history:

The House of the Seven Gables, antique as it now looks, was not the first habitation erected by civilized man, on precisely the same spot of ground. Pyncheon-street formerly bore the humbler appellation of Maule's Lane, from the name of the original occupant of the soil, before whose cottage-door it was a cow-path. A natural spring of soft and pleasant water—a rare treasure on the sea-girt peninsula, where the Puritan settlement was made—had early induced Matthew Maule to build a hut, shaggy with thatch, at this point, although somewhat too remote from what was then the centre of the village. In the growth of the town, however, after some thirty or forty years, the site covered by this rude hovel had become exceedingly desirable in the eyes of a prominent and powerful personage, who asserted plausible claims to the proprietorship of this, and a large adjacent tract of land, on the strength of a grant from the legislature. Colonel Pyncheon, the claimant, as we gather from whatever traits of him are preserved, was characterized by an iron energy of purpose. Matthew Maule, on the other hand, though an obscure man, was stubborn in the defence of what he considered his right, and, for several years, he succeeded in protecting the acre or two of earth which with his own toil he had hewn out of the primeval forest, to be his garden-ground and homestead. No written record of this dispute is known to be in existence. Our acquaintance with the whole subject is derived chiefly from tradition. It would be bold, therefore, and possibly unjust, to venture a decisive opinion as to its merits; although it appears to have been at least a matter of doubt, whether Colonel Pyncheon's claim were not unduly stretched, in order to make it cover the small metes and bounds of Matthew Maule. What greatly strengthens such a suspicion is the fact, that this controversy between two ill-matched antagonists—at a period, moreover, laud it as we may, when personal influence had far more weight than now—remained for years undecided, and came to a close only with the death of the party occupying the disputed soil. The mode of his death, too, affects the mind differently, in our day, from what it did a century and a half ago. It was a death that blasted with strange horror the humble name of the dweller in the cottage, and made it seem almost a religious act to drive the plough over the little area of his habitation, and obliterate his place and memory from among men.

Old Matthew Maule, in a word, was executed for the crime of witchcraft. He was one of the martyrs to that terrible delusion which should teach us, among its other morals, that the influential classes, and those who take upon themselves to be leaders of the people, are fully liable to all the passionate error that has ever characterized the maddest mob. Clergy-men, judges, statesmen—the wisest, calmest, holiest persons of their day—stood in the inner circle roundabout the gallows, loudest to applaud the work of blood, latest to confess themselves miserably deceived. If any one part of their proceedings can be said to deserve less blame than another, it was the singular indiscrimination with which they persecuted, not merely the poor and aged, as in former judicial massacres, but people of all ranks; their own equals, brethren, and wives. Amid the disorder of such various ruin, it is not strange that a man of inconsiderable note, like Maule, should have trodden the martyr's path to the hill of execution, almost unremarked in the throng of his fellow-sufferers. But, in after days, when the frenzy of that hideous epoch had subsided, it was remembered how loudly Colonel Pyncheon had joined in the general cry, to purge the land from witchcraft; nor did it fail to be whispered, that there was an invidious acrimony in the zeal with which he had sought the condemnation of Matthew Maule. It was well known, that the victim had recognized the bitterness of personal enmity in his persecutor's conduct toward him, and that he declared himself hunted to death for his spoil. At the moment of execution— with the halter about his neck, and while Colonel Pyncheon sat on horseback, grimly gazing at the scene—Maule had addressed him from the scaffold, and uttered a prophecy, of which history, as well as fireside tradition, has preserved the very words.—"God," said the dying man, pointing his finger with a ghastly look at the undismayed countenance of his enemy, "God will give him blood to drink!"

In this passage readers briefly meet the titular house. The narrator's history of the house, and of the dispute over the plot of land on which it sits, tells us a great deal about the dispute and about the families involved in it—their histories, their social positions, and their values. Additionally, it tells us a great deal about the society in which Matthew Maule and Colonel Pyncheon lived. Careful readers will also discern something of the narrator, his attitudes, and his sympathies as they examine his narrative of the dispute, and since Hawthorne's preface claims that the purpose of his romance is to "connect a by-gone time with the very Present that is flitting away from us," you might discern some cultural commentary about Hawthorne's own time in this passage.

This passage deals only briefly with the house itself, and it does so in the process of introducing another home, that of Matthew Maule. The language that describes each house tells us a good deal about the owners of the two homes and of their relative social positions. While the Pyncheon house acquired a name of its own, the House of the Seven Gables, Maule's dwelling was a "cottage," "a hut, shaggy with thatch." This "rude hovel" was the "first habitation erected by civilized man on precisely the same ground" as the House of the Seven Gables. Similarly, "Pyncheon-street formerly bore the humbler appellation of Maule's Lane, from the name of the original occupant of the soil, before whose cottage-door it was a cow-path." The narrator seems intent on peeling back one layer of civilization in order to expose a previous layer. In so doing, he emphasizes that the property has undergone what in modern terms is often labeled "gentrification." As in modern times, issues of social class and social power seem to underlie this process.

In order to emphasize class issues that underlie the evolution of Maule's Lane into Pyncheon-street, the narrator provides even more history of the tract of land and the disputants who struggled for ownership of it. "A natural spring of soft and pleasant water," which the narrator calls "a real treasure," drew Matthew Maule to this parcel of land. Here, "with his own toil," Maule "had hewn out the primeval forest, to be his garden-ground and homestead," which was "somewhat . . . remote from what was then the centre of the village." In contrast, Colonel Pyncheon found that this tract of land "had become exceedingly desirable" only after the growth of the town. Consequently, this "prominent and power-ful personage . . . asserted plausible claims to the proprietorship of this, and a large adjacent tract of land, on the strength of a grant from the legislature." How would you characterize the value that each man finds in the property? What do your conclusions say about the value system of Maule and of Pyncheon? What does the language and the imagery associated with Maule's establishment imply about him and about his relationship with his land? How is Pyncheon's claim to the land differ-ent from Maule's claim? Maule, the narrator says, was "stubborn in the defence of what he considered his right." Given the nature of this dispute, why would Hawthorne emphasize that Maule believed that this tract of land was his by "right"?

The dispute came to an end only after Maule was executed for witch-craft, and this charge of witchcraft allowed the House of the Seven Gables and Pyncheon-street to obscure the foundations of Maule's cottage and Maule's Lane, for the execution "blasted with strange horror the humble name of the dweller in the cottage, and made it seem almost a religious act to drive the plough over the little area of his habitation, and obliterate his place and memory from among men." In the ensuing paragraph the narrator says that it was only after the witchcraft frenzy had subsided "it was remembered how loudly Colonel Pyncheon had joined the general cry to purge the land from witchcraft; nor did it fail to be whispered, that there was an invidious acrimony in the zeal with which he had sought the condemnation of Matthew Maule." How do these comments rein-scribe the importance of class and social position in the final resolution of this property dispute?

Despite the narrator's claim that "It would be bold . . . and possibly unjust to venture a decisive opinion" as to the merits of Colonel Pyn-cheon's claims to the land, most readers recognize a democratic flavor in his recounting of the Maule/Pyncheon dispute. He shapes his story and chooses his language to reflect favorably on the rights of the hard-working, lower-class Maule, emphasizing that this was a "controversy between two ill-matched antagonists—at a period, moreover, laud it as we may, when personal influence had far more weight than now." At best, Colonel Pyncheon has taken advantage of his enemy's misfortune and used it to justify his own actions. At worst, he has used his wealth and his political and social power to execute his personal enemy and advance his own social position and power. Labeling Maule "one of the martyrs to that terrible delusion" (the Salem witch trials), while it accurately reflects modern historical understandings of the event, only adds to this impression. Similarly, the narrator's reminder that "the influential classes, and those who take upon themselves to be leaders of the people are fully liable to all the passionate error that has ever characterized the maddest mob," serves to reinforce his democratic message.

Further, astute readers will note that the narrator also provides the history of his own particular version of the Maule/Pyncheon dispute. He remarks: "No written record of this dispute is known to be in existence. Our acquaintance with the whole subject is derived chiefly from tradition." Why does the narrator draw attention to the narrative history behind his recounting of these events? Further, why does he draw the distinction between "written record" and "tradition"? How do these two types of history differ? Examine how the following paragraph seems to pick up on this theme again, noting that "history as well as fireside tradition" recorded Maule's curse upon Colonel Pyncheon. Once again, why does Hawthorne draw attention to two types of historical memory, two types of storytelling—history and fireside tradition? How are the two different? Which, according to the narrator, seems more authoritative? More accurate? The narrator continues to emphasize the role of tradition when he remarks that "when the frenzy of that hideous epoch had subsided, it was remembered how loudly Colonel Pyncheon had joined in the general cry, to purge the land from witchcraft; nor did it fail to be whispered, that there was an invidious acrimony in the zeal with which he had sought the condemnation of Matthew Maule. It was well known, that the victim had recognized the bitterness of personal enmity in his persecutor's conduct toward him . . ." The phrasing is particularly interesting here. Notice how the narrator uses the passive voice—"it was remembered;" "nor did it fail to be whispered;" "It was well known." Who remembered, who whispered, and who knew these details? Why do you think the narrator chooses not to provide these particulars? (*Can* he provide these particulars?) What does this passive phrasing, along with the verbs "remembered," "whispered," and "known," suggest about this particular portrait of Colonel Pyncheon? What do the narrator's phrasing and his word choice suggest about the narrator's sympathies, leanings, and values?

Finally, if Hawthorne's preface claims that the purpose of this romance is to "connect a by-gone time with the very Present that is flitting away from us," how does this particular history reflect upon Hawthorne's present? How does it comment upon his own society and culture? The narrator emphasizes the distance between his own time and the events that ended Matthew Maule's life as well as his family's right to his land. He reminds the reader that the controversy took place "at a period . . . when personal influence had far more weight than now," and he notes that Maule's execution for witchcraft "affects the mind differently, in our day, from what it did a century and a half ago." And yet, he claims that this history "should teach us, along with its other morals, that the influential classes, and those who take upon themselves to be leaders of the people, are fully liable to all the passionate error that has ever characterized the maddest mob." Is this moral, then, one of which Hawthorne's contemporary audiences must be reminded? Is his own culture—far more democratic that that of colonial Salem—liable to the same misuses of power and position? Is this one of the morals that readers will find embedded in *The House of the Seven Gables?*

TOPICS AND STRATEGIES

The paragraphs below suggest possible paper topics for essays on *The House of the Seven Gables*. Remember that the topics discussed are quite broad; they give you a general framework to guide you as you read, reread, and analyze the novel. Use these topics as springboards. You will need to narrow the focus of your writing, constructing an analytical thesis and bearing in mind the proposed length of your paper.

Themes

Because the lens of *The House of the Seven Gables* focuses on the historical past as well as on Hawthorne's own time, the novel provides a great many themes. It brings issues of social class into focus almost instantly, but Hawthorne also considers questions of art and the artist's role in society and questions about social progress among other topics.

Sample Topics:

1. **Social class:** In Chapter 3, Hepzibah, explaining her fear of actually opening her cent shop, tells Holgrave: "But I was born a lady, and have always lived one—no matter in what narrowness of means, always a lady!" Asking her to move beyond traditional notions of social class, Holgrave responds: "These names of gentleman and lady had a meaning, in the past history of the world, and conferred privileges, desirable, or otherwise, on those entitled to bear them. In the present—and still more in the future condition of society—they imply, not privilege, but restriction." Examine *The House of the Seven Gables* as a commentary on social class. What does the novel say about class relations and about the class system in America? How is this theme related to notions of work and labor that appear in the text?

   In order to write about this topic, you will need to consider both the action that takes place in the present time of the novel and the history that Hawthorne paints in the first chapter. Clearly, he exposes the role of the class system in the feud between the Maules and the Pyncheons. What role does class have in the dispute and the "resolution" of that dispute in the 17th century? You can also find useful information in Holgrave's story of Alice Pyncheon. Does the class system of 17th-century Salem affect the class system of the 19th-century Salem that Hawthorne portrays in the novel? How and why? As you analyze the class system of 19th-century Salem, you should find Jaffrey's character and position particularly helpful. Hepzibah, too, should provide interesting material for analysis. You should think about her position in society as well as her attitudes. Similarly, you should examine the social philosophies of Holgrave, Clifford, and Uncle Venner.

2. **Capitalism, commerce, and consumption:** The early part of the novel spends a good deal of time considering Hepzibah and her decision to set up the cent shop. In chapter 3, Hepzibah tortures herself with a comparison of her little shop and the shops in cities: "So many and so magnificent shops as there were! Groceries, toy-shops, dry-goods stores, with their

immense panes of plate-glass, their gorgeous fixtures, their vast and complete assortments of merchandize, in which fortunes had been invested; and those noble mirrors at the farther end of each establishment, doubling all this wealth by a brightly burnished vista of unrealities! On one side of the street, this splendid bazaar, with a multitude of perfumed and glossy salesman, smirking, smiling, bowing, and measuring out the goods! On the other, the dusky old House of the Seven Gables, with the antiquated shop-window under its projecting story, and Hepzibah herself . . . behind the counter, scowling at the world as it went by!" Consider the novel's commentary on capitalism, commerce, and consumption. What does Hawthorne seem to say about the business of business in 19th-century America?

Examining the language and the commentary in the quote above is a good place to begin an investigation of commerce in the novel. In chapter 2, some townspeople assess Hepzibah's "commercial speculations," and Dixey says "Poor Business!" What seems to be necessary for good business? Where do we see the elements of good business? You might want to consider if good business is always successful business in the novel's logic. Examine the scenes that take place inside the cent shop as well, and compare Hepzibah and Phoebe's skills as shopkeepers. What does this comparison tell you about the business of selling? Does either woman seem to bear a resemblance to the "glossy salesmen" of the previous quote? Why or why not? Further, you might want to consider little Ned Higgins, Hepzibah's first customer, who is, quite literally, portrayed as a consumer. Think too of the emphasis placed on the arrangement of goods in these early chapters on the cent shop. Why is arrangement so important? What does that importance say about the qualities of successful business in Hepzibah's world?

3. **Art and the artist:** Like Hawthorne himself and many of his characters, Holgrave is an artist. He is a storyteller, a writer, and a photographer. Examine Holgrave's stories and his photographs. What does Hawthorne suggest is the role of the artist in

society? What fears does Hawthorne express about artists and their roles in society?

In order to analyze the novel's discussion of art, you will need to examine Holgrave's photographs and his storytelling. Clearly, his photographs seem to have a special ability to reveal the truth, but Hawthorne does a good deal more with Holgrave's art. It seems that art also has the possibility for misuse. Holgrave himself says that he "misuse[s] Heaven's blessed sunshine by tracing out human features, through its agency" (*The House of the Seven Gables,* chapter 3). In what ways can art be misused? Does the novel demonstrate any such misuse and/or does it comment upon the misuse of art? Is it fair to say that there is an ethical dimension to art? As you grapple with this issue, you should be sure to examine the reactions of the other characters to Holgrave's art as well as their reaction to Holgrave. Such an exploration should provide you with a good deal of material for analysis.

4. **Storytelling:** In his preface, Hawthorne's discussion of romance considers the relationship between history and fiction, and he says, "The point of view in which this Tale comes under the Romantic definition, lies in the attempt to connect a by-gone time with the very Present that is flitting away from us." In other words, his story is drawn from and made of the fabric of history. Consider the relationship between history and story in the novel. What does Hawthorne say about the roles of history and of story and of the relative truth of each?

Like Hawthorne, Holgrave is a published storyteller, as he tells Phoebe before he recounts his story of Alice Pyncheon. And, like Hawthorne, Holgrave weaves his tales from the threads of history. Nor are written, published narratives the only kinds of story that the novel discusses. What other types of storytelling are discussed in *The House of the Seven Gables?* What qualities mark these narratives? Besides examining the construction of story and its role in society, the novel also frequently mentions history and historical record. How does the book compare the composition, accuracy, and function of historical writing with those of story? What kinds of points does Hawthorne seem to be making about history, story, and their relationship?

5. **Progress:** While Hawthorne's work considers the relationship between past and present, it also comments about the future and the hope for human progress. Consider, for example, Holgrave's comment to Hepzibah on the role of the upper class in the past, present, and the future cited in the above discussion of social class. Does Hawthorne seem to be hopeful about the direction in which society is moving? Does he believe in the notion of human progress? What, does he seem to argue, is necessary for human progress and advancement?

As well as being an artist, Holgrave is a reformer, and you will need to examine his characterization very thoroughly if you are to write a paper on this topic. Holgrave frequently discusses his beliefs about reform and social progress. Both Uncle Venner and Clifford discuss the future of humanity, and you will need to analyze their philosophies as well as their characters and their roles in society. How do you balance all the different philosophies of human progress in the novel? What role does the narrator play in helping you sort out the novel's position on progress and reform? Does the narrator seem to be the voice of Hawthorne? Why or why not? Finally, although Phoebe does not share Holgrave's tendency to preach about progress, she is a representative of youth in the novel. Similarly, her marriage to Holgrave will help resolve the historical tension between the Maules and the Pyncheons. Both she and Holgrave seem to embody, at least in part, the novel's hope for the future. Examine Phoebe's relationship with the notion of progress in the novel.

Character

The House of the Seven Gables presents fully drawn portraits of five characters, and each of these characters could form the basis of a strong essay. As you construct an essay on a particular character, be sure that you consider all aspects of the character and his or her role in the text. Examine the character's language as well as other characters' assessment of him or her. Evaluate any changes your character undergoes, and consider how he or she affects the development of the plot.

Sample Topics:

1. **Holgrave as a character:** As Phoebe and Holgrave discuss the latter's interest in Clifford, Holgrave remarks: "Men and women, and children, too, are such strange creatures, that one never can be certain that he really knows them . . . What a complex riddle—a complexity of complexities—do they represent!" (*The House of the Seven Gables*, chapter 12.) Holgrave, himself, presents such a complex riddle to the reader. He might aptly be described as the novel's hero. As an artist and a reformer, he seems to embody a great many positive characteristics. His daguerreotypes apparently have the ability to reveal the truth about character, and his progressive philosophies reveal a belief in "the better centuries that are coming." And yet, his portrait is not wholly positive. Holgrave, himself, says that he "misuse[s] Heaven's blessed sunshine by tracing out human features, through its agency" (*The House of the Seven Gables*, chapter 3), and Phoebe is, at first, quite unsure of the artist because she considers him "lawless." What are Holgrave's strengths as an artist, a reformer, and a man? What are his shortcomings? Does Holgrave grow or change over the course of the novel? How and why? What seems to be Hawthorne's point in this complex sketch of his hero?

   As you analyze Holgrave's character and his role in the novel, you must examine numerous aspects of his character. Obviously, chapter 12 provides a good starting place for your analysis. Beyond this, you must be sure to examine Holgrave's art, his artistic methods, his philosophies, and his relationships with other characters. Pay close attention to what Hepzibah, Phoebe, and the narrator have to say about him. Similarly, try to assess Holgrave's motivations and his personality. Consider his relationship to his family, the past. Why is he living in the House of the Seven Gables in the first place? Does he inherit any of the traits associated with the Maules? What are they? Does he use these traits as his ancestors have done? Why or why not?

2. **Phoebe as a character:** Phoebe Pyncheon enters the narrative in chapters 4 and 5. A good deal of time is spent introducing Phoebe and demonstrating her effect on the House of the Seven Gables. By chapter 5's end, the narrator remarks: "It really seemed as if the battered visage of the House of the Seven Gables, black and heavy-browed as it still certainly looked, must have shown a kind of cheerfulness glimmering though its dusky windows, as Phoebe passed to-and-fro in the interior." Examine closely the description of Phoebe's effects on the house and its inhabitants. What skills, qualities, and values of Phoebe's allow her to have such a dramatic effect? How do these same qualities affect the course of the narrative and the book's final resolution? What argument does Hawthorne seem to be making through Phoebe's portrait and her role in the narrative?

You might begin to focus this question through an analysis of the language and imagery that is consistently associated with Phoebe in this chapter and throughout the book. The novel is almost unrelenting in linking particular patterns of imagery with her. What does this language imply or connote about Phoebe? Further, as in the portrait of Hepzibah, Hawthorne uses the terms "lady" and "woman" in the novel's description of Phoebe. How and why are these terms used in relation to her? Does Phoebe, finally, seem more a "lady" or a "woman"? Why? What qualities does the novel associate with "ladies" and what qualities does it associate with "women"? You might want to compare the skills and qualities of Phoebe with those of Hepzibah. What is responsible for the differences between these two Pyncheon women? Are their differences attributable strictly to age? As you assess Phoebe's role within the novel, you must also examine her relationship with Holgrave. Examine their interaction and their dialogue closely. Does Phoebe have an effect on Holgrave? If so, how is this effect related to the changes she brings to the House of the Seven Gables?

3. **Hepzibah as a character:** The early chapters of the novel clearly present Hepzibah as an example of the "hereditary noble [who] sinks below his order." Hawthorne, writing from the democratic perspective of mid-19th-century America, seems to have little sympathy for the old social order or the gentry who sat atop it. And yet, the narrator of *The House of the Seven Gables* treats Hebzibah with far more sympathy than satire and remarks: "Our miserable old Hepzibah! It is a heavy annoyance to a writer, who endeavors to represent nature . . . in a reasonably correct outline and true coloring, that so much of the mean and ludicrous should be hopelessly mixed up with the purest pathos which life anywhere supplies to him." In Hepzibah he clearly sees some of life's "purest pathos." What qualities of Hepzibah allow her to escape from the harsh commentary and satire that he heaps on Jaffrey, another representative of the old Pyncheon family?

This topic asks you to consider Hepzibah's characterization thoroughly. In what ways is she a true Pyncheon? Does she display any qualities that differentiate her from the other typical Pyncheons of either the past or the present? Consider the language and the imagery associated with Hepzibah, especially her scowl. What does the narrator's treatment of her scowl tell us about Hepzibah? Clearly you should consider the contrast presented in chapter 15. You should also evaluate Hepzibah's relationship with the other characters in the novel. What do her relationships with Clifford, Phoebe, Holgrave, Jaffrey, and Uncle Venner tell us about her? Similarly, examine Hepzibah's relationship with the House of the Seven Gables itself. What does Hepizbah's relationship with the hereditary Pyncheon home tell us about her? What effect has the home (and the family) had upon Hepzibah?

4. **Clifford as a character:** If Holgrave presents a riddle for the reader, Clifford presents an enigma. He seems an embodiment of regression in this novel that focuses on progress and overcoming the past. Though elderly, Clifford is repeatedly portrayed as childlike; his "mysterious and terrible Past" sends this childlike old man back to his childhood home. In chapter 10, the narrator describes the home's garden as "the Eden of a thunder-smitten Adam, who had fled for refuge thither out of the same dreary perilous wilderness, into which the original Adam was expelled." At the same time, the novel associates Clifford with the "visionary and impalpable." For a character so removed from the realities of the here and now, Clifford seems to possess a great deal of wisdom. How do you reconcile Clifford's dissociation from the real world with the insights that he provides at crucial moments in the text?

You might begin to focus this topic through a thorough investigation of the novel's descriptions of Clifford as childlike. In what ways is Clifford like a child? In what ways is he not like a child? Is it possible for a child to be wise? You might think of Clifford's new life as a sort of second childhood. How might that understanding be enhanced by the description of the Pyncheon garden as "the Eden of a thunder-smitten Adam, who had fled for refuge thither out of the same dreary perilous wilderness, into which the original Adam was expelled"? Certainly this passage figures the house and the garden as a kind of enclosed escape from the world around them. What is the effect of describing this refuge though the analogy of Eden and of Adam? How might Adam's second experience of Eden be different than his first? Why? Further, how would you describe Clifford's relationship with the world beyond the House of the Seven Gables? Does this relationship grow or change? Why or why not? Explore Clifford's likes and dislikes. What does Clifford enjoy? What does he fear or dread? Examine, in particular, chapters 11 and 17 to gain some insight into Clifford's character.

5. **Jaffrey as a character:** In chapter 1, the narrator says that "In almost every generation, nevertheless, there happened to be some one descendant of the family, gifted with a portion of the hard, keen sense, and practical energy, that had so remarkably distinguished the original founder." Hawthorne makes it quite clear that Judge Jaffrey Pyncheon is one of those descendents. At the same time, the novel emphasizes that Jaffrey is very much a man of his own time and generation. He is the "Pyncheon of today." Examine Jaffrey's characterization closely. If he is, in fact, a version of old Colonel Pyncheon adapted to his contemporary world, how does his portrait offer commentary on the values and the character of 19th-century America?

Hawthorne offers numerous portraits of Jaffrey throughout the course of his book—there are Holgrave's daguerreotype portrait of Jaffrey, the narrator's descriptions and commentary, different characters' reactions to the judge, and rumors and gossip. Examine all of this and determine how to interpret each. Taken together, what do they seem to say about Jaffrey's character and about the society that embraces such a character and grants him respect and social position? Look closely at the imagery and language associated with Jaffrey—his smile, his gold, his watch, his imposing physical presence. Look too at the markings of his social position—his job and his public works. Evaluate the skills that Jaffrey has. What qualities, besides his family name and status, enable him to achieve his social rank? How do all these aspects of Jaffrey's characterization help to paint a more complex portrait of both the judge and his world?

History and Context

While Hawthorne clearly draws on elements of New England's history in constructing the background of his story, his own times might provide the best avenue for a historical analysis of the text. As the paragraphs below suggest, the novel is clearly influenced by the 19th-century attitudes about domesticity and women's roles.

Sample Topics:

1. **Domestic ideology:** Nineteenth-century America saw the rise of the "Cult of True Womanhood" and its attendant philosophy of domesticity. This philosophy figured the home as a sanctified sphere that provided a corrective refuge from the outside world, which was dominated by the values of capitalism and commerce. These "separate spheres" were built upon the gender roles of the time. The proper role of the middle-class woman in the 19th century was managing the home and raising children. The world outside was the man's world. Consider *The House of the Seven Gables* as a commentary on this domestic ideology. Does the novel seem to be shaped by these beliefs or does it challenge notions of domesticity and true womanhood?

   You should probably begin an exploration of this topic with some historical reading that provides you with more insight into the cult of true womanhood and domestic ideology. Barbara Welter's article "The Cult of True Womanhood: 1820–1860," which appeared in the journal *American Quarterly* 18 (1966), should prove a good starting place. (A large portion of Welter's article is available at: http://www.pinzler.com/ushistory/cultwo.html.) Similarly, Gillian Brown's *Domestic Individualism* should provide helpful background as well as giving you some insight into *The House of the Seven Gables*. The Norton Critical Edition of *The House of the Seven Gables* provides useful information in its contextual unit on "Houses." As you examine the text from this particular perspective, you will need to examine Phoebe and the changes she brings to the House of the Seven Gables. What skills does Phoebe have that allow her to make this change? How do her skills compare to those described by Welter in her article?

Compare and Contrast Essays

Hawthorne's second novel provides plenty of material for compare and contrast essays. Like *The Scarlet Letter*, *The House of the Seven Gables* clearly considers the artist and his role in society, and it provides two artist figures for comparison. Hawthorne also explores topics and character traits considered in his other works, and any of these could provide a starting place for a compare and contrast essay that analyzes the author's treatment of these themes and traits.

Sample Topics:

1. **Reform:** Holgrave, with his notions of reform, seems to prefigure the character of Hollingsworth in *The Blithedale Romance.* While Holgrave has other interests and is as much an artist as a social reformer, Hollingsworth seems completely focused on his vision of reform. Compare Holgrave with Hollingsworth in order to ascertain Hawthorne's thoughts about human progress.

   To address this topic, you will need to explore the philosophies of each of the men and assess their characters. *Blithedale* links the philosophies of reform and social progress of some of its characters directly to some of the historical proponents of these ideas. In *The House of the Seven Gables,* various characters share their philosophical beliefs, though the novel is far less specific in tying them to specific thinkers and movements of Hawthorne's day. Do the philosophies of Holgrave share anything with those of Hollingsworth? How are their beliefs similar and how are they different? How would you compare Hollingsworth and Holgrave as men? What personality traits set them apart from each other? You may find it interesting to compare the language Hawthorne uses in reference to each of these characters. Look especially at the language of change, mutability, and flexibility. What does this language tell you about each of the men? How does it comment on their characters and their philosophies?

2. **Sunshine:** In a letter to his friend and publisher, James T. Fields, Hawthorne spoke of the darkness of *The House of the Seven Gables*: "It darkens damnably toward the close, but I shall try hard to pour some setting sunshine over it." Despite the dark, decaying house at the center, the novel includes a fair share of sunshine. Phoebe, whose name mean "bright" or "shining one"

is continually associated with sunshine and brightness, and Holgrave's daguerreotypes, he points out, are made from sunshine. Compare Hawthorne's use of sunshine in this novel to his use of it in another text. Does sunshine seem to serve the same function and embody the same meanings in the two texts?

Perhaps your first task in addressing this question will be to determine how Hawthorne uses sunshine in this novel. While it is fairly easy to trace and analyze Phoebe's connection to sunshine, Holgrave's "misuse" of sunshine may complicate your interpretation. Further, you may want to think about the relation between sunshine and the other imagery that surrounds Phoebe. How do they inform and enrich each other? The character of Pearl in *The Scarlet Letter* might provide a particularly interesting subject for comparison here. Notice how often Pearl is associated with sunlight. Yet Pearl and Phoebe are very different characters with strikingly different roles in their respective narratives. What conclusions can you draw from such a comparison?

3. **Magic and witchcraft:** *The House of the Seven Gables* is full of mentions of magic and witchcraft—Matthew Maule is convicted of being a witch and is executed; the Maules are reputed to have mesmeric powers; Hepzibah speculates that Holgrave "practiced animal-magnetism, and, if such things were in fashion now-a-days, should be apt to suspect him of studying the Black Art, up there in his lonesome chamber"; and Phoebe has the gifts of "homely witchcraft" and "natural magic" (*The House of the Seven Gables,* chapter 5). Examine Hawthorne's use of magic and witchcraft in this novel and compare it to his treatment of the topic in another work.

There are a number of different ways to treat this topic. If you begin with the history of Matthew Maule and consider Hawthorne's linkage of Maule's fate with the historical Salem witchcraft trials, you will have a particular focus for your investigation. Hawthorne addresses Puritan beliefs about witchcraft and the effects of these beliefs in a number of texts, including *The Scarlet Letter* and "Young Goodman Brown." Phoebe's magic is, of course, of a very different nature. You might compare Phoebe's brand of white magic with that of the character of Hilda in *The Marble Faun*. While the latter novel does not use the language of witchcraft so overtly as does *The House of the Seven Gables*, Hilda clearly shares some qualities with Phoebe, and she seems to be one of Phoebe's artistic descendants.

4. **Hawthorne's artists:** While Holgrave is clearly figured as an artist in the text, so too is Clifford. Clifford is a lover of beauty, and he is associated in the novel with both beauty and delicacy. Compare these two artist figures in *The House of the Seven Gables*. How are they different and how the same? What accounts for the differences between these two artist figures? Together, what do they say about the role and position of art in Hawthorne's world?

   You may find it difficult to see Clifford as an artist rather than an aesthete, but examine the text to see how you might consider Clifford an artist figure. How would you describe Clifford's art? How does it compare to Holgrave's art? Consider, too, his relationship with the world around him. How is it like or unlike Holgrave's relationship with the world? Alternately, you might wish to compare one of the artist figures from *The House of the Seven Gables* with another of Hawthorne's many artist figures. A comparison of Clifford and Owen Warfield from "The Artist of the Beautiful" should prove particularly fruitful.

5. **Labor, work, and dependence:** As Holgrave works to convince Hepzibah of the good of opening the cent shop and becoming a "true woman" rather than a "lady," he says "you will at least have the sense of healthy and natural effort for a purpose." Holgrave espouses the value of working for a living instead of depending on the strength of the family's wealth or position. A good

bit of the novel seems to speak of the value of self-help. After Hepzibah receives her first cent for little Ned Higgins's gingerbread, the narrator tells us of her exhilaration: "The healthiest glow, that Hepzibah had known for years, had come now, in the dreaded crisis, when, for the first time, she had put forth her hand to help herself" (*The House of the Seven Gables,* chapter 3). Compare Hawthorne's statements on labor and self-help in *The House of the Seven Gables* to his treatment of this theme in other works. What point is he making?

Hephzibah's exhilaration is short lived, but this is just one instance of the novel's consideration of the value of labor versus dependence. Examine the novel's other treatments of this theme. Hawthorne's discussion of his experiences in "The Custom-House" provides an excellent source for comparison here. Analyze his comments on the effects of Customs on its workers, and consider his commentary on dependence versus using one's own strength. Such an investigation should share a lot of ground with your examination of this theme in *The House of the Seven Gables.*

Bibliography and Online Resources for *The House of the Seven Gables*

Anthony, David. "Class, Culture, and the Trouble with White Skin in Hawthorne's *The House of the Seven Gables.*" *Yale Journal of Criticism* 12 (1999): 249–68.

Baym, Nina. *The Shape of Hawthorne's Career.* Ithaca, NY: Cornell UP, 1976.

Bell, Michael Davitt. *Hawthorne and the Historical Romance of New England.* Princeton, NJ: Princeton UP, 1971.

Bell, Millicent. *Hawthorne's View of the Artist.* Albany: SUNY P, 1962.

Bellis, Peter J. *Writing Revolution.* Athens: U of Georgia P, 2003.

Bloom, Harold, editor. *Nathaniel Hawthorne: Comprehensive Research and Study Guide.* Bloom's Major Novelists. New York: Chelsea House, 1998.

Brown, Gillian. *Domestic Individualism: Imagining the Self in Nineteenth-Century America.* Berkeley: U of California P, 1990.

Carton, Evan. *The Rhetoric of the American Romance: Dialectic and Identity in Emerson, Dickinson, Poe, and Hawthorne.* Baltimore: Johns Hopkins UP, 1985.

Castiglia, Christopher. "The marvelous queer interiors of *The House of the Seven Gables*." In *The Cambridge Companion to Nathaniel Hawthorne*. Ed. Richard H. Millington. Cambridge: Cambridge UP, 2004. 186–206.

Crews, Frederick C. *The Sins of Fathers: Hawthorne's Psychological Themes*. New York: Oxford UP, 1966.

Diamond, David B. "'There Is Nothing But Love Here': Toward a Recovery from Massive Psychic Trauma in *The House of the Seven Gables*." *Nathaniel Hawthorne Review* 28 (2002): 61–68.

Dollis, John. "Domesticating Hawthorne: Home Is for the Birds." *Criticism* 43 (2001): 7–28.

Dryden, Edgar. *Nathaniel Hawthorne: The Poetics of Enchantment*. Ithaca, NY: Cornell UP, 1977.

Eaton, Cathy, and Melissa Pennell. "The Three Female Characters in *The House of the Seven Gables* by Nathaniel Hawthorne." Hawthorne in Salem. Available online. URL: http://www.hawthorneinsalem.com/Literature/Hawthorne&Women/ThreeFemaleCharacters/Introduction.html. Downloaded June 7, 2006.

Friedman, Robert S. *Hawthorne's Historical Romances: Social Drama and the Metaphor of Geometry*. London: Harwood Academic Press, 2000.

Gilmore, Michael T. *American Romanticism in the Marketplace*. Chicago: U of Chicago P, 1988.

Gollin, Rita K. "Hawthorne and the Visual Arts." *A Historical Guide to Nathaniel Hawthorne*. Ed. Larry J. Reynolds. New York: Oxford UP, 2001. 109–33.

Hawthorne, Nathaniel. *The House of the Seven Gables*. Norton Critical Editions. Ed. Robert S. Levine. New York: Norton, 2005.

Herbert, T. Walter. *Dearest Beloved: The Hawthornes and the Making of the Middle-Class Marriage*. Berkeley: U of California P, 1993.

Herbert, T. Walter. "Hawthorne and American Masculinity." *The Cambridge Companion to Nathaniel Hawthorne*. Ed. Richard H. Millington. Cambridge: Cambridge UP, 2004. 60–78.

Hunter, Gordon. *Secrets and Sympathy: Forms of Disclosure in Hawthorne's Novels*. Athens: U of Georgia P, 1988.

Johnson, Claudia Durst. "The Secular Calling and the Protestant Ethic in *The Scarlet Letter* and *The House of the Seven Gables*." Hawthorne in Salem. Available online. URL: http://www.hawthorneinsalem.com/ScholarsForum/NEHHawJohnsonlecture.html. Downloaded June 7, 2006.

Male, Roy R. *Hawthorne's Tragic Vision*. New York: Norton, 1957.

Mancall, James N. *"Thoughts Painfully Intense": Hawthorne and the Invalid Author.* New York: Routledge, 2002.

Martin, Robert K. "Haunted by Jim Crow: Gothic Fictions by Hawthorne and Faulkner." In *American Gothic: New Interventions in a National Narrative.* Eds. Robert K. Martin and Eric Savoy. Iowa City: U of Iowa P, 1998. 129–42.

Michaels, Walter Benn. "Romance and Real Estate." *The American Renaissance Reconsidered.* Eds. Walter Michaels and Donald Pease. Baltimore: The Johns Hopkins UP, 1985. 156–82.

Millington, Richard H. "The Meanings of Hawthorne's Women." Hawthorne in Salem. Available online. URL: http://www.hawthorneinsalem.com/Literature/Melville/LiteraryLinks/MMD1210.html. Downloaded June 7, 2006.

Noble, Marianne. "Sentimental Epistemologies in *Uncle Tom's Cabin* and *The House of the Seven Gables.*" *Separate Spheres No More: Convergence in American Literature, 1830–1930.* Ed. Monika Elbert. Tuscaloosa: U of Alabama P, 2000. 261–281.

Pease, Donald E. *Visionary Compacts: American Renaissance Writings in Cultural Context.* Madison: U of Wisconsin P, 1987.

Powell, Timothy. *Ruthless Democracy.* Princeton, NJ: Princeton UP, 2000.

Reynolds, Larry H., ed. *A Historical Guide to Nathaniel Hawthorne.* New York: Oxford UP, 2001.

Trachtenberg, Alan. "Seeing and Believing: Hawthorne's Reflections on the Daguerreotype in *The House of the Seven Gables.*" *American Literary History* 9 (1997): 460–81.

Welter, Barbara. "The Cult of True Womanhood: 1820–1860." *American Quarterly* 18 (Summer 1966): 151–74.

Williams, Susan S. *Confounding Images.* Philadelphia: U of Pennsylvania P, 1997.

Wineapple, Brenda. *Nathaniel Hawthorne: A Life.* New York: Knopf, 2003.

THE BLITHEDALE ROMANCE

READING TO WRITE

IN THE midst of a spring snowstorm in April 1841, Nathaniel Hawthorne moved to the utopian socialist community of Brook Farm
in West Roxbury, Massachusetts. Apparently hoping that Brook Farm
would provide both an amenable environment for his writing and a suitable home for his fiancée, Sophia Peabody, Hawthorne was mistaken on
both counts. The intensive labor and long days required to keep the farm
afloat kept his pen idle. In June 1841, he wrote to Sophia, "[T]his present
life of mine gives me an antipathy to pen and ink, even more than my
Custom House experience. . . . in the midst of toil, or after a hard day's
work in the gold mine [Hawthorne's ironic reference to the manure pile],
my soul obstinately refuses to be poured out on paper." He left Brook
Farm briefly in September and returned as a boarder, hoping to find a
respite from the labor and a renewed interest in his pen. In November,
though, Hawthorne left Brook Farm and returned home.

The only one of Hawthorne's novels to use a first-person narrator, *The
Blithedale Romance* explores the fictional utopian community of Blithedale and is drawn, at least in part, from the novelist's own experiences
at Brook Farm. "I shall take the Community for a subject, and shall give
some of my experience and observations at Brook Farm," he wrote to a
friend in 1851. In his preface, Hawthorne offers his days at Brook Farm as
a suitable grounds for romance. They were "certainly the most romantic

episode of his own life—essentially a day dream, and yet a fact—and thus offering an available foothold between fiction and reality." And yet, he claims, "His whole treatment of the affair is altogether incidental to the main purpose of the romance; nor does he put forward the slightest pretensions to illustrate a theory, or elicit a conclusion, favorable or otherwise, in respect to Socialism." Instead his aim in the novel is to "establish a theatre, a little removed from the highway of ordinary travel, where the creatures of his brain may play their phantasmagorical antics, without exposing them to too close a comparison with the actual events of real lives." Despite these claims, the novel's reception has been complicated by the fact that its narrator, Miles Coverdale, like Hawthorne, is a writer who travels to an experimental community in the midst of an April snowstorm. Similarly, critics have noted that Hawthorne draws heavily from his own journals and letters from his days at Brook Farm in his construction of *Blithedale*. While conflating an author's biography and his fiction, his narrator and his own voice, is always a dangerous interpretative practice, Hawthorne's own experiences clearly underlie much of *The Blithedale Romance*. At the same time, it is clear that his characters and their fictional drama take on their own life and are the true subjects of the novel. Analysis of *Blithedale* over the years has tended to focus on four broad areas: connections to Hawthorne's biography and to Brook Farm; the portrait of the community of Blithedale; the actions of the three main players of the novel's plot—Zenobia, Priscilla, and Hollingsworth; and Coverdale's position as narrator. The last of these elements has generated a good deal of scholarship and understandably so, since everything readers learn of Blithedale is channeled though him. It is impossible to reach any conclusions about the community at Blithedale or about the interaction of the three major characters without first determining what you think both about Coverdale and his assessments of those around him. Similarly, because he is an artist, a "minor poet," his portrait might reflect upon Hawthorne's beliefs about his own role as artist. Coverdale complicates a good deal about Blithedale, both for his fellow characters and for Hawthorne's readers. Consider the following passage that begins chapter 9:

> It is not, I apprehend, a healthy kind of mental occupation, to
> devote ourselves too exclusively to the study of individual men and

women. If the person under examination be one's self, the result is pretty certain to be diseased action of the heart, almost before we can snatch a second glance. Or, if we take the freedom to put a friend under our microscope, we thereby insulate him from many of his true relations, magnify his peculiarities, inevitably tear him into parts, and, of course, patch him very clumsily together again. What wonder, then, should we be frightened by the aspect of a monster, which, after all—though we can point to every feature of his deformity in the real personage—may be said to have been created mainly by ourselves!

Thus, as my conscience has often whispered to me, I did Hollingsworth a great wrong by prying into his character, and am perhaps doing him as great a one, at this moment, by putting faith in the discoveries which I seem to make. But I could not help it. Had I loved him less, I might have used him better. He—and Zenobia and Priscilla, both for their own sakes and as connected with him—were separated from the rest of the Community, to my imagination, and stood forth as the indices of a problem which it was my business to solve. Other associates had a portion of my time; other matters amused me; passing occurrences carried me along with them while they lasted. But here was the vortex of my meditations around which they revolved, and whitherward they too continually tended. In the midst of cheerful society, I had often a feeling of loneliness. For it was impossible not to be sensible that, while these three characters figured so largely on my private theatre, I—though probably reckoned as a friend by all—was at best but a secondary or tertiary personage with either of them.

This passage raises many issues and questions that careful readers may have already found themselves pondering as they read Miles Coverdale's account of his early days at Blithedale. Many of these probably surround Coverdale himself. What kind of a self-portrait does he create here? What do you think of him? What do you think about his interest in Hollingsworth, Priscilla, and Zenobia? While he says that "it is not . . . a healthy kind of mental occupation, to devote ourselves too exclusively to the study of individual men and women," the rest of the passage discusses his continued study of Hollingsworth, Zenobia, and Priscilla. Indeed, the whole of the book chronicles his intent observations of these three. Do you see in Coverdale's propensity for observation, or in his observations themselves, any sign of an "[un]healthy mental occupation"? His recognition that such scrutiny of others is unhealthy does not seem sufficient motivation to cease his observation. Indeed, he says, "But I could not help it." Why can he not help studying these three so intently? Would it be fair to say that Coverdale is obsessed with these three characters? If so, why is he so obsessed? What explains his intent focus on his three friends? Why does he feel the need to put them "under [his] microscope"?

It is telling to look at the language he uses to describe his fascination with these three. They "stood forth as the indices of a problem which it was my business to solve." What does it mean to view the intimate dealings between three of your "friends" as "the indices of a problem"? What does this say about his relationship with Zenobia, Priscilla, and Hollingsworth? Further, in what way are their affairs his "business"? Two chapters later, Coverdale hopes that "the design of fate" will allow him "into all Zenobia's secrets" as he is poised to overhear her conversation with Westervelt. Are her secrets, too, his "business"? Or, might we conceive of the word "business" in a more concrete way? As a writer, it is his "business," his method of earning an income, to observe life and to transcribe it into his writing. Does he mean to use the word in this way? You should also look closely at the language he uses to describe his fascination with the "problem" his friends present. They are the "vortex of [his] meditations around which they revolved, and whitherward they too continually tended." What connotations do the image of a vortex carry? How do those connotations work to color your impression of Coverdale and his fascination with his friends? Yet another suggestive phase is his confession that his three friends "figured so largely on my private theatre." How does this description of the lives of his friends as his "private theatre" reflect upon Coverdale himself? What does it imply about his relationship with these three? About the extent of his sympathy and engagement with them? Further, is it telling that Coverdale acknowledges that he could be considered "at best but a secondary or tertiary personage with either of them"? Does that description ask you to reconsider his statement that he could "probably [be] reckoned as a friend" by each of them? Does that sufficiently explain the "loneliness" that he feels? Does Coverdale sound like someone you would like to have as a friend? Why or why not?

Still another series of questions that this passage generates surround Coverdale's portraits of Hollingsworth, Zenobia, and Priscilla. In the first paragraph he tells us that such close scrutiny of another creates "a monster," a patchwork creation that "may be said to have been created mainly by ourselves!" If this observation is, indeed, accurate, how does it reflect upon the portraits of Hollingsworth, Zenobia, and Priscilla that Coverdale presents in *Blithedale?* How much should we trust his characterizations and his assessments, how much "faith" should we put into his "discoveries"? If the figures he presents to us are, indeed, little more than patchwork monsters, how are we to gain an accurate picture of his friends and their affairs?

Finally, Coverdale tells us that Hollingsworth, Zenobia, and Priscilla "stood apart from the rest of the Community, to my imagination." And yet, all three were integral parts of the Blithedale community. Although Coverdale seems to render the affairs of his three friends as separate from the affairs of Blithedale, how separate are they? To what extent do the interactions of these three characters reflect back on Blithedale, the titular subject of the novel? Asking questions like these about Coverdale and his relationship with Blithedale and with his three friends can shed a great deal of light on the workings of the novel as a whole. Examining Coverdale and his musings should help you to develop paper topics that explore the themes, characters, philosophies, and history of *The Blithedale Romance.*

TOPICS AND STRATEGIES

Your assessment of Coverdale as the lens through which the reader views all of Blithedale and its members is an important first step in finding your way into the novel and assessing Hawthorne's themes and characters. The historical circumstances of the novel's background can also be helpful in forging productive paper topics. Remember that the topics suggested below are broad; you will need to focus and refine them.

Themes

Along with Coverdale, Hollingsworth, Zenobia, and Priscilla, the Blithedale community might also be considered a character in *The Blithedale Romance.* Analysis of the character of the Blithedale community, though, is more productively incorporated into an analysis of the main theme of the novel, human community. As you read Coverdale's musings on Blithedale and its members, think about how the actions and interactions of the characters reflect upon the nature of human community in the novel. Since one of the goals of Blithedale is "the reformation of the world," a related theme is the question of human progress and the notion of reform. While this chapter considers that topic under the heading of Philosophy and Ideas, you could easily consider it as one of the novel's themes. If you choose to write about one of these themes, be sure to carefully analyze how the other elements in the work, especially the characters and their interactions, help to shape or comment upon that theme.

Sample Topics:

1. **Human Community:** Part of the aim of the Blithedale community is "the reformation of the world." They imagine their "new arrangement of the world" as a "paradise," an "Arcadia" built upon the "blessed state of brotherhood and sisterhood, at which [they] aimed" (*The Blithedale Romance,* chapter 2). And yet, even before the end of his first evening at the farm, the language that Coverdale uses to describe this "Blessed state of brotherhood and sisterhood" seems to cast doubt on the viability of the enterprise. What, finally, seems to be the novel's assessment on the value and viability of human community?

   You will need to examine a good many factors to focus this topic and shape a thorough response. Perhaps the most important element to evaluate is the nature of the relationships among the four major figures in the book. These characters provide our clearest glimpse into how this "blessed state of brotherhood and sisterhood" functions at Blithedale. Do they seem to treat one another according to the principles you would expect in a utopian human community? Similarly, you should examine the language of insubstantiality that surrounds Blithedale throughout the novel. In the passage previously quoted, Coverdale accuses the members of Blithedale of "making a play-day" of the endeavor. Note how often he uses the language of play, of acting and theater, and of dreaming as he describes Blithedale and the life of its inhabitants. How does this language reflect upon the effectiveness and the viability of human community? As you analyze the nature of the community at Blithedale and the language that describes that community, be sure to keep in mind that all we see is filtered though Coverdale. How much do you trust his reporting and his evaluation of what he observes? Does he seem to speak for Hawthorne, or does it seem that Hawthorne wants readers to find some space for their own evaluations of Blithedale? Despite Hawthorne's claim that the novel was in no way meant to comment upon socialism, the whole of the novel clearly examines the viability of human community. Examining these elements should help you shape a strong paper about the conclusions that Hawthorne draws.

Character

The drama of *The Blithedale Romance* is dependent upon the interactions of its major characters, and Coverdale remains intent on observing his friends and their interactions. As you analyze character and character development in the novel, always remember that you are seeing through Coverdale's eyes. Your assessment of the others is always dependent on your assessment of him.

Sample Topics:

1. **Coverdale's role:** Coverdale's position in the novel is complicated. He is a character in the novel and a member of the Blithedale community. But he remains at a distance from most of the action and the drama of the plot. The story line revolves around the drama of Hollingsworth, Zenobia, and Priscilla. They are "the indices" of the novel's plot, and Coverdale remains a "secondary or tertiary personage." He observes his friends, draws conclusions about them, and narrates their story. An artist, he turns their affairs into art. Toward the novel's end in chapter 26, Zenobia says to Coverdale, "Ah, I perceive what you are about! You are turning this whole affair into a ballad." How are we to assess Coverdale as a character? As a narrator? Why does Hawthorne choose to make his narrator a poet, a writer?

   As the introductory section of this chapter noted, you must grapple with Coverdale and his role in the novel before you address any other topic. But grappling with Coverdale is not easy. A paper that assesses his role might approach this topic in a number of ways. You might choose to deal with Miles Coverdale the character. You might choose to deal with Miles Coverdale the narrator, or you might combine the two to consider the portrait of the artist that Hawthorne creates in Coverdale. A study of Coverdale's role as narrator should consider his reliability. How much do you trust his portraits of his friends? Why? Are these characters little more than the patchwork monsters Coverdale describes in chapter 9? After a particularly lengthy description of Hollingsworth, Coverdale asserts, "Of course, I am perfectly aware that the above statement is exaggerated, in the attempt to make it adequate. . . . Let the reader abate whatever he deems fit." How should the reader make those kinds of decisions? Do you have any insight into what has influenced or affected the particular portraits Coverdale draws of Zenobia, Hollingsworth, and Priscilla? Similarly, be sure to note how much of the narrative action Coverdale actually sees or overhears. How much does he actually know? How might his knowledge—or lack thereof—affect the narrative that he shapes for us? How might Coverdale's name give us some clues about his role as narrator? Finally, you might consider how Coverdale reflects Hawthorne's beliefs about the artist. Any consideration of Coverdale must consider his propensity for watching and observing others while remaining somewhat separated from them. He is a largely solitary observer, and his "hermitage" at Blithedale is a wonderful symbol of these qualities. It is, he says, "an observatory, not for starry investigations, but for those sublunary matters in which lay a lore as infinite as that of the planets" (*The Blithedale Romance*, chapter 12). Examine the text closely and analyze Coverdale's propensity for watching and observing. How does this serve to characterize Coverdale? How might you read Coverdale as a kind of commentary on the artist or, perhaps, on Hawthorne himself?

2. **Hollingsworth as a character:** From the first, Hollingsworth seems a particularly fraught character. Coverdale tells us, "But

there was something of the woman moulded into the great, stalwart frame of Hollingsworth; nor was he ashamed of it, as men often are of what is best in them, nor seemed ever to know that there was such a soft place in his heart." Within a page, though, Hollingsworth responds, "And you call me tender! . . . I should rather say, that the most marked trait in my character is an inflexible severity of purpose." Throughout the text, Hollingsworth is marked by such contradictions. Further, he seems to inspire contradiction in others. What are we to make of his character? How would you finally assess Hollingsworth?

Any paper that analyzes Hollingsworth must take into account his philanthropic goal for the reformation of criminals. This plan seems to consume his life, and he is single-minded in his pursuit of it. Examine his philanthropic plan closely. Does it reveal him to be community-minded, sympathetic, and giving, as we often assume philanthropists are? Further, consider his relationships with the other characters in the novel. He proves to be a tender and effective nurse to the ailing Coverdale, providing "more than brotherly attendance" (*The Blithedale Romance*, chapter 6). Both Zenobia and Priscilla fall in love with him. How would you assess his interaction with the two women? What do Hollingsworth's relationships tell about his character? What do you make of the transformation he undergoes at the end of the novel? What is responsible for that transformation? Does this transformation reflect growth on the part of Hollingsworth? Why or why not? Be sure to examine the language that Coverdale uses to characterize Hollingsworth. How does this help to shed light on his character? Is his former job as a blacksmith relevant to his characterization?

3. **Zenobia as a character:** Like Hester Prynne, Beatrice Rappaccini, and Miram of *The Marble Faun,* Zenobia is one of Hawthorne's so-called "dark ladies" who embodies beauty, passion, sensuality, sexuality, and abundance. Like Hester and Miriam, Zenobia espouses a feminist philosophy. But like Coverdale and Hollingsworth, her true nature is difficult to pin down. In chap-

ter 1, we learn that Zenobia is "her public name; a sort of mask in which she comes before the world." Toward the end of the novel Coverdale muses, "To this day, however, I hardly know whether I then beheld Zenobia in her truest attitude, or whether that were the truer one in which she had presented herself at Blithedale. In both, there was something like the illusion which a great actress flings around her." Does the novel give insight into the truth of Zenobia's nature? If so, how would you define the "true" Zenobia, and what do you think has shaped her into the woman she becomes?

A paper examining Zenobia must consider many elements of her character, and there are a number of ways to focus a topic around Zenobia. You must, of course, analyze her relationships with the other characters. Many critics see her treatment of Priscilla as a true test of her character, though it is impossible to assess Zenobia without considering her relationship with Hollingsworth. A strong woman who boldly professes a feminist philosophy, she, nonetheless, apparently falls in love with Hollingsworth despite his rather virulent anti-feminist ravings in chapter 14. Examine this apparent contradiction as well as her response to Hollingsworth's comments. How do you interpret Zenobia's response? Further, examine her suicide in chapter 27. Why does Zenobia drown herself? Do you agree with Coverdale that she kills herself because of her love for Hollingsworth? Why or why not? Finally, you should pay close attention to the language and the patterns of imagery used to describe Zenobia. Of particular interest are the organic images associated with her, especially her association with flowers. What do these say of her character? Still more important are her continual associations with the theater. Coverdale repeatedly emphasizes that she is like an actress, and he associates her with the stage and with drama. What do you make of these associations?

4. **Priscilla as a character:** Examine Priscilla's role carefully. She is often associated with insubstantiality; she is, Coverdale says,

"shadowlike" (*The Blithedale Romance*, chapter 9). Stemming from her role as the "veiled lady," there are rumors of her sibylline, or prophetic, abilities. Indeed, Coverdale frequently notes that at many times she appears to be listening to distant voices. Despite these qualities, the novel never seems to imply that she is connected to the supernatural or witchcraft. In contrast, Zenobia is often associated with witchcraft and enchantment. Why does Priscilla, with her "sibylline" qualities, escape such associations?

To assess Priscilla's character and her presentation, you must compare her portrait to Zenobia's and you need to sort out Coverdale's feelings about both women. Like Hilda and Miriam from *The Marble Faun*, Priscilla and Zenobia are opposites who represent very different types of womanhood. Further, Coverdale's response to the two women tells us much about his perceptions of women. What do you make of his final confession that he was in love with Priscilla? Does his confession come as a surprise to you? Why or why not? Why would Coverdale claim to love Priscilla rather than Zenobia? Further, you should explore Priscilla's role as the veiled lady. How might this role serve as a metaphor for Priscilla? How might it explain Coverdale's confession?

5. **Westervelt as a character:** While Westervelt is a relatively minor character, he has important ties to both Priscilla and Zenobia and is intimately involved with the "problem" that Coverdale seeks to solve. What is his role in the novel?

Like Chillingworth of *The Scarlet Letter*, Westervelt's role seems largely allegorical. The imagery that surrounds him partakes of the language of substance and shadow, reality and unreality, that permeates the novel. How are Westervelt's descriptions telling? What do Coverdale's choice of images tell us about Westervelt? Examine, too, Westervelt's own speech and actions, especially his response to Zenobia's suicide. What does he seem to represent?

History and Context

Because this novel grew from Hawthorne's own history, *The Blithedale Romance* provides many opportunities for exploring historical context. Remember, though, your job is not historical sleuth, unearthing references to Brook Farm or Margaret Fuller in the text. Your job is to use historical research to illuminate the text. How does knowing about Hawthorne's time at Brook Farm allow you to understand the artistry of *The Blithedale Romance* more fully?

Sample Topics:

1. **Brook Farm:** In his preface to *The Blithedale Romance*, Hawthorne takes great pains to distance Blithedale from the historical Brook Farm. "In short," he says, "his present concern with the Socialist Community is merely to establish a theatre, a little removed from the highways of ordinary travel, where the creatures of his brain my play their phantasmagorical antics, without exposing them to too close a comparison with the actual events of real lives." Despite this claim, Hawthorne drew heavily from his own personal writings while at Brook Farm in his composition of the novel. Is Hawthorne disingenuous in his claims? Does his experience at Brook Farm, as his preface states, seem "incidental to the main purpose of the novel"?

   You must take Hawthorne's claims here seriously; the fictitious drama of *Blithedale* is not woven from the daily fabric of life at Brook Farm. Nevertheless, you might find that Hawthorne's observations and conclusions about Brook Farm inform and expand your reading of the novel. This is especially true if you are considering Hawthorne's philosophies about progress or the nature of human community. In order to develop your topic, you should look at biographies of Hawthorne. You might also find it helpful to read from his letters and his notebooks. (Information about where to find them is in the bibliography at the end of this chapter.) The Bedford Cultural Series edition of *The Blithedale Romance* provides excellent primary sources on "Prospects for Change," "The Idea of Community," "Life at Brook Farm," and "Women's Roles and Rights." It includes letters and journal entries from Hawthorne.

2. **Margaret Fuller and *The Blithedale Romance*:** Over the years, many readers and critics have tried to connect Zenobia to the 19th-century writer Margaret Fuller. Fuller, with whom Hawthorne was acquainted, was an outspoken advocate of women's rights and was, briefly, a resident at Brook Farm. Like Zenobia, Fuller also died by drowning. (Fuller, though, did not take her own life but died in a shipwreck.) To what extent do Fuller and her philosophies seem to be represented in *The Blithedale Romance*? How valid are comparisons between Fuller and Zenobia?

To explore this question, you should research Fuller's life and her beliefs. There are many books and biographies available on Fuller, and you can also locate information online from a number of reputable sources. The Bedford Cultural Edition of *The Blithedale Romance* provides good source material on Fuller and on women's rights. You might want to read Fuller's *Woman in the Nineteenth Century* to learn more about her thoughts on women's rights. Similarly, you should thoroughly examine Zenobia's feminist philosophies. Does she espouse views similar to those of Fuller? Are there other ways in which Zenobia seems to reflect Fuller? Are there ways in which the two seem different? Explain and explore these questions to shape a response.

Philosophies and Ideas

The philosophical and ideological concerns of *The Blithedale Romance* are closely tied to its historical context. *Blithedale* addresses some of the ideological concerns of Hawthorne's day more directly than any of his other works, and in drawing portraits of an experimental socialist community, an outspoken feminist, and a social reformer, he brings these ideological concerns to the forefront.

Sample Topics:

1. **Progress and reform:** Despite Hawthorne's claim in the preface to *The Blithedale Romance* that he "does not put forward the slightest pretensions to illustrate a theory, or elicit a conclusion, favorable or otherwise, in respect to Socialism," the

novel spends a great deal of time grappling with the idea of human progress. Both the community at Blithedale and Hollingsworth's plan for prison reform are examples of forward-looking projects that aim to benefit society. Both, it seems, are undertaken in the name of human progress. In the final chapter of the book, a somewhat jaded Coverdale says, "As regards human progress (in spite of my irrepressible yearnings over the Blithedale reminiscences,) let them believe in it who can, and aid in it who choose!" What attitude, finally, does *The Blithedale Romance* take toward the idea of human progress?

While this topic clearly shares territory with an investigation into the theme of human community, it asks you to broaden your focus a bit. To consider the novel's attitude toward human progress you would need to explore not only the viability of the community at Blithedale, but also analyze Hollingsworth, his plan for prison reform, and its effects. You would do well to examine chapter 7 where Coverdale reads from many of the progressive writings embraced by the residents of Blithedale and where he and Hollingsworth debate the philosophies of Charles Fourier (whose beliefs were eventually adopted by the residents of Brook Farm). You can find good historical information on Brook Farm, Fourier, "The Idea of Community," and "Prospects for Change" in the Bedford Cultural Edition of *Blithedale* and on the Web.

2. **Feminism and women's rights:** Zenobia is an outspoken advocate of women's rights. Coverdale records her philosophies throughout the novel, beginning with their first meeting at Blithedale. In chapter 14, Coverdale tells us that Zenobia "declaimed with great earnestness and passion . . . on the injustice which the world did to women, and equally to itself, by not allowing them, in freedom and honor, and with the fullest welcome, their natural utterance in public." Further, the novel seems to offer Zenobia and Priscilla as two completely different "models" of womanhood. In chapter 14, Zenobia sadly says of Priscilla, "She is the type of womanhood, such as man has spent

centuries in making it." By contrast, comparing Priscilla and
Zenobia, Westervelt says that the latter, "even with her uncom-
fortable surplus of vitality, is far the better model of womanhood" (*The Blithedale Romance,* chapter 11). What, finally, does
the novel seem to advocate about the position and the rights of
women?

You will need to thoroughly consider the characterizations of
both Priscilla and Zenobia. Analyze Zenobia's feminist philosophies as well as Priscilla's responses to them. Further, explore
the responses of Hollingsworth and Coverdale to both women.
As you sort through this maze of opinions and attitudes, be
sure to keep in mind that every character you meet—Zenobia, Westervelt, Hollingsworth, Priscilla, and Coverdale—has
a particular agenda and holds a particular worldview. This
should help you assess how much stock to place in their words
and actions.

Language, Symbols, and Imagery

The Blithedale Romance is not so laden with symbols as *The Scarlet Letter* or "The Minister's Black Veil," but in Hawthorne's use of veils we find
a familiar image. Conversely, *Blithedale* is filled with the language of the
stage. Analyzing Hawthorne's use of such referential language illuminates his themes and his characters, and it tells us a great deal about his
thoughts.

Sample Topics:

1. **The language of theater:** As this chapter has frequently noted,
   The Blithedale Romance is rife with the language of theater, acting, and drama. In the preface, Hawthorne describes his concern
   with Brook Farm in the novel as "a theatre, a little removed from
   the highway of ordinary travel." In chapter 9, Coverdale views
   the interactions of his friends as "my private theatre." Zenobia is
   frequently referred to as an actress. Additionally, the novel frequently refers to the whole enterprise at Blithedale as a kind of
   drama. As the community prepares to begin their experiment,
   someone asks, "Have we our various parts assigned?" Further,

the novel frequently talks of "scenes," "drama," and "tragedy." What is the apparent purpose—or purposes—of this profusion of theatrical language? How does it reflect on the themes of the novel or the development of the individual characters?

This language is so prevalent throughout the novel that it seems to function in a number of different ways. You will need to really focus a paper on this topic. Reading this language as a commentary on the viability of the enterprise at Blithedale should prove productive. Similarly, this language goes a long way toward characterizing Miles Coverdale and his role as narrator. Focusing on stage language and Coverdale alone could easily support a substantial paper. Finally, you might even take a more philosophical approach to this question and consider what this language says about the "truth" of individual identity and character. Examining Zenobia (or even Priscilla) in this light might prove especially helpful.

2. **Veils, veiling, and masks:** Veils, veiling, masks, masking, and masquerade all connect to create the dominant pattern of imagery in *The Blithedale Romance.* Examine the veils and masks, literal and metaphoric, that populate the novel. What is their effect? Why does Hawthorne use them?

Because all these images are so prevalent in the novel, this question, too, will require you to focus. One of the most obvious focuses for a paper on veils is to study Priscilla's role as "the veiled lady" along with Zenobia's story, "The Silvery Veil" in chapter 13. What does the veil—and her position and performance—seem to tell us about Priscilla? What kind of commentary does Hawthorne seem to be providing about her? What is the role of Zenobia's story? How accurately does it reflect Priscilla's situation or her role in the novel? Alternately, you might consider the connection between veils and narrative. You could begin with Zenobia's story. How does "The Silvery Veil" itself function as a kind of veil? What connections does it bear to Coverdale and his writing? Is Coverdale's name suggestive here? Further, does this connection between veils and narrative connect back to Hawthorne and romance writing? Yet another approach might explore some of the issues discussed under the theme of community. Take note of the Blithedale community's connections to masks, both literal and metaphoric. This exploration ties back to the language of theater. Look especially at the community's masquerade and the theatrical masque. How do these images reflect on the community?

Compare and Contrast Essays:

While *The Blithedale Romance,* with its first-person narrator, is in many ways quite different from Hawthorne's other romances, it still partakes of some of the themes, images, and philosophical concerns that occupied the author throughout much of his life. It provides fertile ground for compare and contrast essays. Keep in mind that your purpose in these essays is not just to point out similarities and differences, but to draw conclusions about their significance.

Sample Topics:

1. **Reform and progress:** Hollingsworth is not the only character in Hawthorne's fiction who is labeled as a reformer. Compare Hollingsworth to another of Hawthorne's reformers. What does Hawthorne seem to be saying about reform and the idea of human progress through these characters?

   This paper could begin with the kind of questions posed in the discussion of Hollingsworth's character and in the discussion of the idea of progress in the novel. Holgrave from *The House of the Seven Gables* provides the most likely character for comparison with Hollingsworth, though the two are, in many ways, quite different.

2. **Hawthorne's dark women:** As the discussion of Zenobia's character noted, she shares many qualities with some of the other women that are often called Hawthorne's dark ladies—Hester Prynne, Miriam from *The Marble Faun,* and Beatrice Rappac-

cini. Compare Zenobia to another of these women. What does Hawthorne's characterization seem to say about these women? How does he seem to feel about these women?

Depending on the comparison that you choose to draw, your paper might take a number of approaches. All these characters are similar in their beauty and their sensuality. Hester, Miriam, and Zenobia all share a belief in what we might call feminism. Zenobia, Beatrice, and Hester are all marked by the language of nature. The organic imagery—particularly references to flowers and plants—associated with Beatrice and Zenobia is particularly striking. What does this imagery seem to say about the characters? Does its resonance seem to apply largely to the characters' ideas, personalities, or their physical beings? Why is this significant?

Alternately, you might compare the women who present striking contrasts to these dark women. Just as Hawthorne seems to present Zenobia and Priscilla as alternate "models" of womanhood, he does something similar with Miram and Hilda in *The Marble Faun*. You might compare his use of these two pairs of women. You could also compare Hilda and Priscilla. Phoebe Pyncheon, too, could be added to this latter list.

3. **Coverdale as an artist:** Coverdale is one of Hawthorne's many artist figures. Choose another artist figure to compare with Coverdale. What does Hawthorne seem to be saying about the nature of the artist and the nature of art?

You have many possibilities to choose from here, and many of the characters appear initially to be quite different from Coverdale. While you might initially think of Holgrave or Owen Warland from "The Artist of the Beautiful," characters like Roger Chillingworth, Dr. Rappaccini, or Aylmer from "The Birth-Mark" would also allow for strong papers. Think of what qualities Coverdale shares with these latter characters. Similarly, there are grounds for comparing Westervelt and Coverdale. In chapter 12, Coverdale asserts a kind of identity between the two when he discusses the influence of

Westervelt and says, "And it was through his eyes, more than my own, that I was looking" at Hollingsworth and Zenobia. Further, both Westervelt and Coverdale "present" Priscilla to the public view. How are their enterprises similar? How are they different?

4. **Veils and veiling:** Choose another work in which Hawthorne uses the theme or the symbol of veils and veiling and compare that use to *Blithedale*.

"The Minister's Black Veil" uses a veil symbolically, and this could provide room for comparison with *Blithedale*. If you consider Hawthorne's statement in "The Custom-House" that, despite his "autobiographical impulse," he will "still keep the inmost Me behind its veil," this suggests still other possibilities for this question. How does the act of writing or storytelling function as a kind of veil for Hawthorne? For Coverdale? For Zenobia?

Bibliography and Online Resources for *The Blithedale Romance*

American Transcendentalism Web. Available online. URL: http://www.vcu.edu/engweb/transcendentalism/. Downloaded August 2, 2006.

Baym, Nina. *The Shape of Hawthorne's Career.* Ithaca, NY: Cornell UP, 1976.

Bell, Michael Davitt. *Hawthorne and the Historical Romance of New England.* Princeton, NJ: Princeton UP, 1971.

Bell, Millicent. *Hawthorne's View of the Artist.* Albany: SUNY P, 1962.

Bellis, Peter J. *Writing Revolution.* Athens: U of Georgia P, 2003.

Berlant, Lauren. *The Anatomy of National Fantasy: Hawthorne, Utopia, and Everyday Life.* Chicago: U of Chicago P, 1991.

Brodhead, Richard. *Hawthorne, Melville, and the Novel.* Chicago: U of Chicago P, 1973.

———. "Veiled Ladies: Toward a History of Antebellum Entertainment." *American Literary History* 1 (1989): 273–94.

Brown, Gillian. *Domestic Individualism: Imagining the Self in Nineteenth-Century America.* Berkeley: U of California P, 1990.

Bumas, Shaskan E. "Fictions of the Panopticon: Prison, Utopia, and the Out-Penitent in the Works of Nathaniel Hawthorne." *American Literature* 73 (2001): 121–45.

Carton, Evan. *The Rhetoric of the American Romance: Dialectic and Identity in Emerson, Dickinson, Poe, and Hawthorne.* Baltimore: Johns Hopkins UP, 1985.

Cary, Louise D. "Margaret Fuller as Hawthorne's Zenobia: The Problem of Moral Accountability in Fictional Biography." *ATQ* 4 (1990): 31–48.

Castronovo, Russ. *Necro Citizenship: Death, Eroticism, and the Public Sphere in the Nineteenth-Century United States.* Durham, NC: Duke UP, 2001.

Christianson, Frank. "Trading Places in Fancy: Hawthorne's Critique of Sympathetic Identification in *The Blithedale Romance.*" *Novel: A Forum on Fiction* 36 (2003): 244–63. Available online. URL: http://www.findarticles.com/p/articles/mi_qa3643/is_200304/ai_n9205352. Downloaded August 2, 2006.

Crews, Frederick C. *The Sins of Fathers: Hawthorne's Psychological Themes.* New York: Oxford UP, 1966.

Dryden, Edgar. *Nathaniel Hawthorne: The Poetics of Enchantment.* Ithaca, NY: Cornell UP, 1977.

Flynn, Kelly. "Nathaniel Hawthorne Had a Farm: Artists, Laborers, and Landscapes in *The Blithedale Romance.*" In *Reading the Earth.* Ed. Michael P. Branch. Moscow: U of Idaho P, 1998. 145–54.

Fuller, Margaret. *Woman in the Nineteenth Century.* Available online. URL: http://www.vcu.edu/engweb/franscendentalism/authors/fuller/woman/html.

Gable, Jr., Harvey L. "Inappeasable Longings: Hawthorne, Romance, and the Disintegration of Coverdale's Self in *The Blithedale Romance.*" *New England Quarterly* 67 (1994): 257–78.

————. *Liquid Fire: Transcendental Mysticism in the Romance of Nathaniel Hawthorne.* New York: Peter Lang, 1998.

Gordon, Jessica. "History of Brook Farm." American Transcendentalism Web. Available online. URL: http://www.vcu.edu/engweb/transcendentalism/authors/fuller/. Downloaded August 2, 2006.

Hawthorne, Nathaniel. "The American Notebooks of Nathaniel Hawthorne." Nathaniel Hawthorne (1804–1864) home page. Available online. URL: http://www.eldritchpress.org/nh/pfanb.html. Downloaded August 6, 2006.

Hawthorne, Nathaniel. *The Blithedale Romance.* Bedford Cultural Editions. Ed. William E. Cain. Boston: Bedford Books, 1996.

Herbert, T. Walter. *Dearest Beloved: The Hawthornes and the Making of the Middle-Class Family.* Berkeley: U of California P, 1993.

Hunter, Gordon. *Secrets and Sympathy: Forms of Disclosure in Hawthorne's Novels.* Athens: U of Georgia P, 1988.

Lawrence, D. H. "Hawthorne's Blithedale Romance." *Studies in Classic American Literature.* New York: T. Seltzer, 1923. Available online. URL: http://xroads.virginia.edu/~HYPER/LAWRENCE/dhlch08.htm. Downloaded July 8, 2006.

Levine, Robert S. *Conspiracy and Romance: Studies in Brockden Brown, Cooper, Hawthorne, and Melville.* New York: Cambridge UP, 1989.

———. "Sympathy and Reform in *The Blithedale Romance.*" *The Cambridge Companion to Nathaniel Hawthorne.* Ed. Richard H. Millington. Cambridge: Cambridge UP, 2004. 207–29.

Male, Roy R. *Hawthorne's Tragic Vision.* New York: Norton, 1957.

Mancall, James N. *"Thoughts Painfully Intense": Hawthorne and the Invalid Author.* New York: Routledge, 2002.

McCall, Dan. *Citizens of Somewhere Else: Nathaniel Hawthorne and Henry James.* Ithaca, NY, and London: Cornell UP, 1999.

Miller, John N. "Eros and Ideology: At the Heart of Hawthorne's Blithedale." *Nineteenth-Century Literature* 55 (2000): 1–21.

Millington, Richard H. "American Anxiousness: Selfhood and Culture in Hawthorne's *The Blithedale Romance.*" *New England Quarterly* 63 (1990): 558–83.

———. "The Meanings of Hawthorne's Women." Hawthorne in Salem. Available online. URL: http://www.hawthorneinsalem.com/Literature/Melville/LiteraryLinks/MMD1210.html. Downloaded June 7, 2006.

Mitchell, Thomas. *Hawthorne's Fuller Mystery.* Amherst: U of Massachusetts P, 1998.

Newfield, Christopher, and Melissa Solomon. "'Few of Our Seeds Ever Came Up at All': A Dialogue on Hawthorne, Delany, and the Work of Affect in Visionary Utopias." In *No More Separate Spheres.* Eds. Cathy N. Davidson and Jessamyn Hatcher. Durham, NC: Duke UP, 2002. 377–408.

Pearce, Roy Harvey. *Hawthorne Centenary Essays.* Columbus: Ohio State UP, 1964.

Pease, Donald E. *Visionary Compacts: American Renaissance Writings in Cultural Context.* Madison: U of Wisconsin P, 1987.

Ponder, Melinda M. *"The Blithedale Romance." Essex Institute Historical Collections.* Special issue on "The Presentation of Hawthorne's Romances" 127 (1991): 50–68.

———. "Hawthorne and 'the sphere of ordinary womanhood.'" Hawthorne in Salem. Available online. URL: http://www.hawthorneinsalem.com/Scholars Forum/Hawthorneandwomanhood.html. Downloaded June 7, 2006.

Reynolds, Larry J., ed. *A Historical Guide to Nathaniel Hawthorne.* New York: Oxford UP, 2001.

"[Sarah] Margaret Fuller." American Transcendentalism Web. Available online. URL: http://www.vcu.edu/engweb/transcendentalism/authors/fuller/. Downloaded August 2, 2006.

Schriber, Mary Suzanne. "Justice to Zenobia." *New England Quarterly* 55 (1982): 61–78.

Swann, Charles. *Nathaniel Hawthorne: Tradition and Revolution.* Cambridge: Cambridge UP, 1991.

Tanner, Laura E. "Speaking with 'Hands at Our Throats': The Struggle for Artistic Voice in *The Blithedale Romance.*" *Studies in American Fiction* 21 (1993): 1–19.

Tatar, Maria M. *Spellbound: Studies on Mesmerism and Literature.* Princeton, NJ: Princeton UP, 1978.

Tharpe, Coleman W. "The Oral Storyteller in Hawthorne's Novels." *Studies in Short Fiction* 16 (1979): 205–14.

Wineapple, Brenda. *Hawthorne: A Life.* New York: Knopf, 2003.

Yellin, Jean Fagan. "Hawthorne and the American National Sin." In *The Green American Tradition: Essays and Poems for Sherman Paul.* Ed. H. Daniel Peck. Baton Rouge: Louisiana State UP, 1989. 75–97.

THE MARBLE FAUN

READING TO WRITE

HAWTHORNE COMPOSED his last completed romance while living in Italy and England, and it was published in 1860. In England, it bore the title *Transformation;* the American edition was titled *The Marble Faun.* Like *The Blithedale Romance, The Marble Faun* draws a great deal from Hawthorne's private notebooks. Whole sections of his Italian notebooks seem to be transcribed straight into his last novel. He records his reactions to Rome and its artwork and interweaves these with the fictional narrative of his four characters, Miriam, Hilda, Kenyon, and Donatello. Hawthorne's time in Rome was turbulent. While there, his eldest daughter, Una, nearly died after contracting malaria and suffered through a protracted convalescence. He had mixed feelings about the city, its history, and its inhabitants. At home, America was spiraling toward civil war. All these elements leave their mark on *The Marble Faun,* and the book is complex and often contradictory. To appreciate the novel's merits, you must keep in mind this multifaceted history and be alert to the ways that the travelogue informs the purpose and meaning of the romance. Skim through Hawthorne's descriptions of Rome or the artwork at your own peril, for careful readers quickly see how integral these descriptions are to the texture of the romance.

Miriam and Hilda's discussion of Beatrice Cenci in chapter 7 provides an excellent example of this interweaving of history and romance. Generally perceived as a tragic figure, the historical Beatrice, a 16th-century Italian noblewoman, was imprisoned and, she claimed, raped by her father. As a result of Francesco Cenci's cruel treatment of Beatrice and her stepmother, the two women, along with Beatrice's brothers, had her father murdered. Beatrice and her conspirators were put to death in 1599. As Miriam and Hilda discuss Guido's portrait of Beatrice and Hilda's copy of the work, their conversation touches upon many of the major themes of the novel.

> "Here it is then," said Miriam. . . . "Everywhere we see oil paint-ings, crayon sketches, cameos, engravings, lithographs, pretend-ing to be Beatrice. . . . But here is Guido's very Beatrice. . . . And now that you have done it, Hilda, can you interpret what the feel-ing is that gives this picture such a mysterious force? For my part, though deeply sensible of its influence, I cannot seize it."
>
> "Nor can I, in words," replied her friend. "But while I was paint-ing her, I felt all the time as if she were trying to escape from my gaze. She knows that her sorrow is so strange and so immense that she ought to be solitary forever, both for the world's sake and her own; and this is the reason we feel such a distance between Bea-trice and ourselves, even when our eyes meet hers. It is infinitely heartbreaking to meet her glance, and to feel that nothing can be done to help or comfort her; neither does she ask help or comfort, knowing the hopelessness of her case better than we do. She is a fallen angel—fallen, and yet sinless; and it is only this depth of sorrow, with its weight and darkness, that keeps her down upon earth, and brings her within our view even while it sets her beyond our reach."
>
> "You deem her sinless?" asked Miriam. "That is not so plain to me. If I can pretend to see at all into that dim region whence she gazes so strangely and sadly at us, Beatrice's own conscience does not acquit her of something evil, and never to be forgiven!"
>
> "Sorrow so black as hers oppresses her very nearly as sin would," said Hilda.
>
> "Then," inquired Miriam, "do you think that there was no sin in the deed for which she suffered?"
>
> "Ah!" replied Hilda, shuddering. "I really had quite forgotten Beatrice's history, and was thinking of her only as the picture seems to reveal her character. Yes, yes; it was terrible guilt, and

inexpiable crime, and she feels it to be so. Therefore it is that the forlorn creature so longs to elude our eyes, and forever vanish away into nothingness! Her doom is just!"

"Oh, Hilda, your innocence is like a sharp steel sword!" exclaimed her friend. "Your judgments are often terribly severe, though you seem all made up of gentleness and mercy. Beatrice's sin may not have been so great: perhaps it was no sin at all, but the best virtue possible in the circumstances."

At first, the women's discussion seems to focus on aesthetic questions, on the merit of Guido's painting and of Hilda's copy. The reader might first ask what makes Guido's portrait such a masterpiece with such "mysterious force." Why has this particular portrait generated such a demand for copies in the Roman picture shops? (Hawthorne was echoing a historical fact here. The portrait generated a great deal of interest among visitors to Rome in the 19th century. You can see a copy of the portrait online at http://gallery.euroweb.hu/html/s/sirani/b_cenci.html). Beyond this, though, the two women begin to discuss the artistic merit of the copies of the painting. How is the aesthetic merit of a copy of a painting assessed? What qualities seem essential in producing copies of great works of art? Why is Hilda's copy so superior to all the others that Miriam sees in the picture shops? Such questions of art, artistry, and aesthetic merit pervade this text, and some critics argue that one of Hawthorne's main themes in the novel concerns the relationship between art and life, between illusion and reality. If this is so, the novel's many discussions of art and artistry certainly reflect back on Hawthorne's attitude toward his own written art. This discussion of Guido's Beatrice, then, opens the door to the exploration of one of Hawthorne's major concerns in the novel.

This passage, though, moves far beyond issues of artistic merit and purpose. As Hilda and Miriam discuss Guido and Hilda's work, their discussion moves from art to life. They begin by trying to interpret the painting and soon find themselves debating the guilt or innocence of the historical Beatrice. In their individual responses to the historical Beatrice, both women reveal a good deal about their characters. Additionally, the story of Beatrice asks the reader to consider another of the novel's main concerns—the effect of evil or sin upon innocence. Beatrice is the innocent who is initiated into evil through her father's treatment, and as such she embodies the novel's thematic concern with humanity's fall from innocence.

To begin, you might question Hilda's convoluted and contradictory response to Beatrice. Hilda claims that Beatrice "knows that her sorrow is so strange and so immense that she ought to be solitary forever. . . . nothing can be done to help or comfort her; neither does she ask help or comfort, knowing the hopelessness of her case better than we do." To those familiar with Beatrice's story, the reason for her sorrow seems evident. Readers, however, might question why Hilda believes that Beatrice's experience necessarily leads to her isolation. Why is her case "hopeless"? Why can "nothing be done to comfort her"? Is Beatrice beyond human sympathy? Further, we might ask if Hilda sees Beatrice's sorrow as rooted in her rape or in the act of parricide. As first, Hilda's assessment of Beatrice seems to hinge around the incest, for she declares, "She is a fallen angel—fallen and yet sinless." Here, Hilda seems to read Beatrice as a violated innocent, a young woman who lost her innocence, but who was not culpable for her own fall. And yet, Hilda quickly changes her assessment. She soon argues that she had been describing her "only as the picture seems to reveal her character." Once she considers Beatrice's history she declares, "Yes, yes; it was a terrible guilt, an inexpiable crime." What has caused this reassessment on Hilda's part, and to what "crime" does she refer? Does she see Beatrice as culpable in her own rape, or is the parricide the "inexpiable crime"? How do you react to Hilda's judgment of Beatrice? How does Hilda's judgment help to develop her character at this point in the novel? Do you agree with Miriam that Hilda's "innocence is like a sharp steel sword" and that she is "terribly severe"?

Miriam's assessment of Beatrice's sin, though, is quite different from Hilda's, and you might ask how her attitudes about Beatrice reflect upon her character and her worldview. Initially, when Hilda judges Beatrice as "sinless," Miriam believes that Beatrice is haunted by her "own conscience." Why might Miriam believe that Beatrice is tormented not by her father's sin, but by her own conscience? How does each of these women's interpretation of the painting reflect back upon her own character?

Further, you might consider how this discussion reflects on the theme of humanity's fall. Consider Hilda's "theology" when she proclaims Beatrice "a fallen angel—fallen and yet sinless." Here Hilda seems to envision a theological impossibility. According to Christian theology—including the Puritan theology that Hilda repeatedly claims as her own—humanity is fallen and, therefore, sinful. No human can be without sin. Why would Hilda initially strive to see Beatrice as sinless, despite the fact that her Puritan upbringing would deny that very possibility? What does this tell us about her belief in innocence? Why is Hilda so quick to back away from her initial assessment?

Once Hilda does her about-face and passes judgment on Beatrice's "terrible guilt" and "inexpiable crime," Miriam proposes yet another possibility: "Beatrice's sin may not have been so great: perhaps it was no sin at all, but the very best virtue possible in the circumstances." What does Miriam's attempt to rename Beatrice's "sin" as "the very best virtue possible in the circumstances" tell about her worldview? How might you describe the worldviews of Hilda and of Miriam when you compare their assessment of Beatrice? What parameters does this discussion establish for the novel's discussion of the fall? How might your analysis of this discussion aid your examination of Donatello, yet another of the fallen innocents in *The Marble Faun?*

While this conservation about a painting from 1662 might at first appear irrelevant to the novel's plot and main thematic pursuits, careful readers can discover a wealth of information about the novel's characters and themes that can help guide their reading of the novel. Such close analysis should allow you to generate a number of thoughtful essay topics about *The Marble Faun.*

TOPICS AND STRATEGIES

Descriptions of other works of art abound in *The Marble Faun,* and many of these descriptions also shed light on the themes and characters that populate the novel. You will find that the characters and their interactions provide starting places for other topics, as do the novel's setting and its tie to Hawthorne's own history. This section of the chapter provides you with some broad topic suggestions to consider as you shape a paper on *The Marble Faun.*

Themes

The opening section of this chapter pointed toward two of the major themes of *The Marble Faun,* art and the fortunate fall. The novel deals with other themes as well. Just as Hawthorne grappled with his experiences in Rome, the four characters of his romance are transformed by their encounters in Rome. The "eternal city" forces the characters to confront the past as they think about the city's history and as they draw connections between its history and their own. Similarly, their confrontation with the past also leads them to think about the future and the course of human history. *The Marble Faun* continually questions and challenges the relationship between past, present, and future. Nearly all of these themes are connected with the idea of the fortunate fall, which the novel self-consciously presents as its focus.

Sample Topics:

1. **The fortunate fall:** In the penultimate chapter of the novel, Kenyon finally poses a question that reflects upon most of the action of *The Marble Faun.* Contemplating the change in Donatello, Kenyon asks Hilda, "Is sin, then—which we deem such a dreadful blackness in the universe—is it like sorrow, merely an element of human education, through which we struggle to a higher and a purer state than we could otherwise have attained? Did Adam fall, that we might ultimately rise to a far loftier paradise than his?" What does *The Marble Faun* say about the idea of "the fortunate fall"?

   Many scholars see the fortunate fall as the central theme of the novel, though they are far from reaching critical consensus about its treatment of this theme. In order to sort out your beliefs about Hawthorne's use of the fortunate fall in *The Marble Faun,* you will need to analyze a number of complex elements. You must examine the experiences of Donatello very closely. As the discussion of his character later in this chapter indicates, the novel offers Donatello as the quintessential "innocent" whose encounter with evil and whose subsequent sin transforms him.

   Consider Miriam's assessment of Donatello's history in chapter 47. Since both Kenyon and Hilda also comment on Donatello's transformation and the doctrine of the fortunate fall at various points in the novel, you must consider their comments. You must also decide how much weight to give the opinions of each of these characters. Does one character or another seem to speak for Hawthorne? Does he invest one or more of the characters with moral authority in the novel? Does the moral voice of the characters seem to align itself with that of the author? How do you know? Where do you locate the narrator's voice in this discussion of the fortunate fall, and how closely do you align the narrator's voice with Hawthorne's? These are questions that you will need to pursue, and the novel provides no clear and easy answers. In addition, you might find it useful to analyze the novel's treatment of Kenyon's bust of Donatello. Does it shed any light on the transformation of Donatello himself? How does the novel use this work of art? While a good bit of the discussion of the fortunate fall in the novel centers around Donatello, you would do well to remember that Hilda is another of Hawthorne's innocents. She, too, encounters sin in the course of the novel. Assess her reaction to sin as well as her assessment of the idea of the fortunate fall. How does this analysis affect your reading of the novel? Where else does *The Marble Faun* grapple with this philosophy?

2. **The burden of the past:** In his preface to *The Marble Faun*, Hawthorne claims that he has set his romance in Italy rather than in America because "of the difficulty of writing a romance about a country where there is no shadow, no antiquity, no mystery, no picturesque and gloomy wrong . . . as is the case with my dear and native land." In other words, he claims that unlike America, Rome has a past. Kenyon seems to echo his sentiment in chapter 33, when he says to Donatello, "You should go with me to my native country. . . . In that fortunate land, each generation has its own sins and sorrows to bear. Here, it seems as if all the weary and dreary Past were piled upon the back of the Present." Repeatedly, the novel presents readers with images and musings about the burden that the past imposes on the present.

What, finally, does *The Marble Faun* argue is the effect of the past upon the present?

This is a broad question, and it shares some territory with the theme of the fortunate fall as well as with the theme of the course of human history. Examine how many ways Hawthorne casts and recasts the idea of the past burdening the present in this novel. Clearly, you must study his treatment of Rome in the book. He constantly characterizes Rome as both burdened by and enriched by its long history. Examine the language that surrounds Rome very carefully. Similarly, Miriam seems to share much with the "eternal city." How might we consider her as burdened by her past? What imagery does Hawthorne use to express her relationship with her past? How is it similar to the imagery he uses to present Rome's past? What are the effects of these patterns of imagery? By contrast, consider Hilda's relationship with her past. She is an American and she is an orphan. How do these two facts affect her relationship with history?

You might also address this question a bit more philosophically. Hawthorne's preface contrasts Rome and America. Their relationships with the past, he claims, are quite different. Do you agree with the preface and with Kenyon that America in 1860 was free from the burden of the past? Does the novel as a whole seem to support this assertion? Why or why not? Clearly, this approach asks you to examine Rome, Miriam, Hilda, Kenyon, and the decision of the latter two characters to return to America at the novel's end.

3. **Art:** *The Marble Faun* focuses on the activities of three artists—Kenyon, Miriam, and Hilda. The other major character, Donatello, is a young Italian who is compared to the Faun of Praxiteles, and who is sculpted by Kenyon. Further, the novel presents Rome as a world full of artists and famous art. Frequently, the characters or the narrator discuss the artistic merit of various works of art and of various artists. Can *The Marble Faun* be read as a statement about art? How does the novel

define "good" art, and what does it seem to say about the art's purpose and its relationship with reality?

This question will need to be focused, and there are a number of different directions that you might take. You should closely analyze the numerous discussions about the quality of works of art and the more abstract discussions that address the qualities of "good" art. Remember Miriam's reaction to Hilda's copy of Guido's Beatrice. What makes Hilda's copy worthy of such praise? What differentiates it from the other copies Miriam speaks of? You could broaden this investigation to analyze Hilda's abilities as a copyist. What makes Hilda such an effective and admired copyist? Any investigation into the quality of Hilda's copies must necessarily lead to a question about the very nature of Hilda's art. Why does Hilda choose to copy the works of others rather than to create original art? What artistic merit is there in copying the works of others? If you are investigating the question of what makes "good" art according to the novel, you should also examine the art and the philosophies of Kenyon and Miriam. Analyzing the "success" of each of these artists as well as their relationship with their art should prove useful as well. Additionally, there are a number of individual works of art in the text that merit your close attention, including the Faun of Praxiteles, the portrait of Beatrice Cenci, Kenyon's bust of Donatello, Kenyon's Cleopatra, the paintings and sketches that Donatello examines in Miriam's studio, and the famous statue of the Laocoön that Kenyon examines in chapter 43.

In *The Shape of Hawthorne's Career*, critic Nina Baym suggests yet another way to approach this question when she argues that in *The Marble Faun* Hawthorne proposes "that great or serious art was no longer possible." Do you agree that the novel makes such a pessimistic statement about art? Further, how might you broaden this question to include Hawthorne's statements on the viability of his own written art? Clearly, his preface to the novel seems to express some cynicism about the reception that his book would receive.

4. **Progress and the course of human history:** As Kenyon discusses the history of Monte Beni with old Tomaso, the narrator describes the artist's musing on progress and the course of human history:

> Not that the modes and seeming possibilities of human enjoyment are rarer, in our refined and softened era . . . but that mankind are getting so far beyond the childhood of their race, that they scorn to be happy any longer. A simple and joyous character can find no place for itself among the sage and somber figures that would put his unsophisticated cheerfulness to shame. The entire system of Man's affairs, as at present established, is built up purposely to exclude the careless and happy souls. . . .
>
> It is the iron rule in our days, to require an object and a purpose in life. It makes us all parts of a complicated scheme of progress, which can only result in our arrival at a colder and drearier region than we were born in. (*The Marble Faun*, chapter 26.)

Later, in chapter 27, Kenyon argues, "We all of us, as we grow older . . . lose somewhat of our proximity to nature. It is the price we pay for experience." What, does the novel argue, is the trajectory of human history? Are we traveling farther away from nature as Kenyon argues? Does Hawthorne seem to be hopeful or pessimistic about the path of human history? Why?

While this theme is closely related to the theme of the fortunate fall, it approaches some of the same issues quite differently and removes the theological grounding. Instead, it grounds the text in Hawthorne's own historical context. Indeed, Kenyon sounds a bit like some of the British romantic poets and thinkers and like American transcendentalists like Ralph Waldo Emerson when he describes humans' path away from nature. In order to shape a response to this question you should examine the two most childlike and "innocent" characters in the novel—Donatello and Hilda. You should think about them in a more realistic and less allegorical sense then you did in the investigation of the fortunate fall. Both encounter evil and their innocence is challenged. How does each respond? How are they alike and how different in their response to sin and to sorrow? Which of these two characters seems more prepared to live in the "modern" world? Why? Additionally, examine the language of paradise, Arcadia, and "the Golden Age" that the novel uses repeatedly. How are Arcadia and Eden different from the modern world that the four characters inhabit? How are these differences relevant to Hawthorne's point?

Character

The Marble Faun was published in England under the title *Transformation*. Many readers see this as a more appropriate title, for each of the characters is transformed by his or her experience in Rome. As you shape a paper about any of the characters you should chart the growth and change in the character you are focusing upon. How do you feel about the individual transformation of the character? Why?

Sample Topics:

1. **Kenyon as a character:** Playing on his work as a sculptor, Kenyon calls himself "a man of marble." When Miriam is thinking about confessing to Kenyon, she recasts this playful language when she accuses Kenyon of being "as cold and pitiless as your own marble." Do you agree with Miriam's assessment of Kenyon as cold? Many readers identify Kenyon as the voice of Hawthorne in the novel. Do you agree with this interpretation? If so, do you believe that Hawthorne uses Kenyon to comment on his own role as artist-writer?

    This topic asks you to evaluate Kenyon's characterization and to follow his history as an artist. Evaluate his abilities and insights as an artist. Is he a good artist? If so, what qualities does he have that allow him to be a good artist? Miriam's assessment of Kenyon's Cleopatra and the novel's discussion of Kenyon's bust of Donatello tell us a great deal about his artistic abilities and skills and of his qualities as an individual.

Examine his relationships with the other characters. What role does he play in his relationships with Miriam, Donatello, and Hilda? What do you think of his decision to marry Hilda at the novel's end and to return to America? Do you agree with the narrator's assessment toward the end in chapter 46 that Kenyon "could hardly, we fear, be reckoned a consummate artist, because there was something dearer to him than his art"?

2. **Miriam as a character:** At the novel's end, Hilda and Kenyon see Miriam across the Pantheon: "she looked toward the pair, and extended her hands with a gesture of benediction. . . . They suffered her to glide out of the portal, however, without a greeting; for those extended hands, even while they blessed, seemed to repel, as if Miriam stood on the other side of a fathomless abyss, and warned them from its edge." Why does the novel seem to banish Miriam to "the other side of a fathomless abyss"? What is her role in the novel? What does she represent? Is her banishment at the end of the novel just? Why or why not?

Miriam is the most complex character in the novel, and she shares a great deal with Hawthorne's other dark ladies—Hester Prynne, Beatrice Rappaccini, and Zenobia from *The Blithedale Romance.* In order to thoroughly evaluate her role in the novel and her banishment at the end, you must carefully assess both her character and her attitudes. Additionally, you should examine the images and the language associated with her throughout the novel. She is associated with rich colors, the exotic and the foreign, with Rome, and with her model. How do all these associations help to develop her character? Look, too, at her artwork. What does it tell us about Miriam? About her history and her relationship with her past? Many readers see her as one of the more engaging characters in the novel and believe that Hawthorne—or his narrator—abandons her at the end. Do you agree? Why or why not?

3. **Hilda as a character:** Throughout the novel, Hilda sees the world and its moral imperatives in simple black and white. She

claims that she is "a poor, lonely girl, whom God has set here in an evil world, and given her only a white robe, and bid her wear it back to Him, as white as when she put it on" (*The Marble Faun*, chapter 23). She continually clings to this simple plan for her life. When Kenyon, discussing the crime of Donatello and Miriam, speaks of the "mixture of good there may be in things evil," Hilda responds, "But there is, I believe, only one right and one wrong." By the novel's end, Kenyon, who seems to have wavered in his interpretation of Donatello's sin and on the theory of the fortunate fall, succumbs to Hilda's worldview that pronounces the fortunate fall as a creed that makes "a mockery . . . not only of all religious sentiments, but of moral law." He exclaims, "Forgive me, Hilda! . . . I have neither pole star above nor light of cottage windows here below to bring me home. . . . Oh, Hilda, guide me home!" Does the novel seem to present Hilda as the appropriate guide? Why or why not?

Critics have been divided about Hilda since *The Marble Faun* was published. Many see her as the embodiment of goodness, purity, and morality, others see her as stuffy, hypocritical, and narrow-minded. To develop your own reading of Hilda, you must closely examine the language and the imagery that surrounds her. She is continually associated with whiteness, with purity, with her tower, with the Virgin Mother, and with her doves. Is Hilda pure and good? Consider, too, the other characters' assessments of Hilda's moral pronouncements. Is she, as Miriam suggests in chapter 7, "sharp" and "severe"?

Comparing Hilda's response to sin and to sorrow with Donatello's might also help you develop your interpretation of her character and her role in the novel. These two innocent characters respond quite differently. What accounts for their differences? Does Hawthorne seem to embrace one of their worldviews as more appropriate? As more realistic?

4. **Donatello as a character:** Donatello's transformation is, arguably, the transformation to which the novel's British title refers, and it is impossible to analyze his character without some dis-

cussion of the fortunate fall. Does Donatello's transformation construct an argument for the theory of the fortunate fall?

This question shares a good deal of territory with the thematic discussion of the fortunate fall. In order to develop this particular angle, you will need to study Donatello's transformation in great detail. Look at his characterization early in the novel and compare it to Donatello after he has killed the model. How do you assess his character at each stage of development? Additionally, you will need to analyze the numerous discussions the other characters have about Donatello's transformation and about the idea of the fortunate fall. As noted above, Miriam clearly links Donatello with the story of the fall of man in chapter 42. How do you assess the interpretations of the various characters and that of the narrator? You will also need to study Dontatello's bust. What do the bust and the characters' reactions to it tell us about Donatello?

History and Context

In addition to its use of Beatrice Cenci, the novel's Roman setting provides plenty of opportunity for exploring history and context. It is particularly worthwhile to explore Hawthorne's own experiences in Rome and to see their effect upon the romance. As in *The Blithedale Romance*, Hawthorne explores the position of women in his culture. This, too, provides fertile ground for interpretation.

Sample Topics:

1. **Hawthorne and Rome:** Hawthorne drew heavily from his notebooks during the composition of *The Marble Faun*. Consequently, the novel reflects the author's own opinions and observations about Rome, Italian culture, and the art that he observed in Italy. How do the author's private writings, especially his meditations on Rome, shed light on the action, character, and themes of *The Marble Faun*?

   Hawthorne's *French and Italian Notebooks* are published and widely available. Browsing through them, you can quickly see just how much Hawthorne used them in the novel. Whole sections are lifted word for word. Most interesting are his meditations on Rome. Hawthorne seems to vacillate between love for the city and a kind of revulsion. As he does in the preface and in the novel, he also spends a good deal of time comparing Italy to America. These comparisons reveal a great deal about Hawthorne's attitudes toward antebellum America. What relationship does Hawthorne see between Rome and America? The notebooks' passages on Rome also allow readers to develop a clearer understanding of the author's use of Rome as a setting within the novel, helping to clarify the city's symbolic significance in the text.

2. **Womanhood/women's roles:** Although Miriam is not so clearly identified as a proponent of women's rights as Zenobia is in *The Blithedale Romance,* she too seems to push against the boundaries of women's roles. In chapter 5, when Donatello is momentarily startled by her model, Miriam says, "Do not be afraid, Donatello. . . . It is a lady of exceedingly pliable disposition; now a heroine of romance, and now a rustic maid; yet all for show; being created, indeed, on purpose to wear rich shawls and other garments in a becoming fashion." This comment seems to invite an examination of the different "models" of womanhood offered throughout the text. Does *The Marble Faun* seem to offer a preferred model of womanhood, and does this act as a commentary on the position of women in society?

This question asks you to explore the characterizations of Miriam and Hilda thoroughly. You must analyze their characters, their actions, their philosophies, their interactions with others, and their art. What does this say about their positions in society and about the author's attitude toward each of the women? Remember, too, that such an exploration requires you to grapple with the difficult question of whether any of the characters or the narrator actually speak for Hawthorne or whether the author seems to keep himself at a distance from all the voices in the novel. You might also examine the women that appear in the artwork described in the novel. What light do they shed on this topic? You could potentially expand this question into a compare and contrast essay by comparing Hawthorne's treatment of Hilda and Miriam with his treatment of Priscilla and Zenobia in *The Blithedale Romance*.

Language, Symbols, and Imagery

As this chapter has already noted, *The Marble Faun* is rich with imagery. Particular patterns of color mark both Hilda and Miriam, and images of paradise and Arcadia envelope Donatello. Perhaps the most interesting and suggestive imagery in the novel, though, is that which describes Rome.

Sample Topics:

1. **The chasm:** In chapter 18, the four main characters stand in the Forum. Kenyon declares that they stand "precisely [on] the spot where the chasm opened into which Curtius precipitated his good steed and himself." As they speculate about the chasm and its import, Miriam remarks: "The chasm was merely one of the orifices of that pit of blackness that lies beneath us, everywhere. The firmest substance of human happiness is but a thin crust spread over it, with just reality enough to bear up the illusive stage scenery amid which we tread." In response, Hilda claims, "It seems to me that there is no chasm, nor any hideous emptiness under our feet, except what the evil within us digs. If there be such a chasm, let us bridge it over with good thoughts and deeds, and we shall tread safely to the other side." Despite Hilda's claims, *The Marble Faun* repeatedly incorporates the chasm and related imagery. How does Hawthorne use this imagery of the underground and that which lies beneath? What does it symbolize?

   This question asks you to consider images of the underground and images of layering that Hawthorne uses repeatedly throughout the text. Examine the very real space that lies beneath Rome, examine its contents, and examine its relationship with the world aboveground. You might find that this question shares some territory with the thematic question about the burden of the past in the novel.

Compare and Contrast Essays

Hawthorne comes back to many familiar themes in his last completed romance, and some of his characters share qualities with those of his earlier fiction, so *The Marble Faun* provides a rich ground for mining topics for compare and contrast papers. As you develop your topics, keep in mind that you will want to develop a thesis that draws some conclusions about the similarities and differences that you observe.

Sample Topics:

1. **The confrontation with evil/sin:** The novel presents both Donatello and Hilda as innocents who encounter evil, sin, and sorrow for the first time. Compare their experiences and their responses. How are they alike and how different? Do both characters grow as a result of their experiences? Why or why not? How might the comparison of their experiences help us to see Hawthorne's beliefs about the appropriate response to sin and to evil?

   This question asks you to explore some of the same questions posed in the discussion of the fortunate fall, as well as those posed about Hilda and Donatello's characterizations. As you draw comparisons, you must deal with the complicated question of the novel's attitude toward each character. Since so much of the commentary on both characters comes through the voices of the other characters as well as through the voice of the narrator, you will need to consider where Hawthorne seems to stand among this chorus of voices and assessments.

   You could also approach this question by considering some of Hawthorne's other characters who seem to experience evil for the first time. Young Goodman Brown and Robin Molineux provide possibilities, as does Giovanni from "Rappaccini's Daughter." Assess whether you believe that these characters grow as a result of their encounters and whether they seem to learn the proper lessons.

2. **"The world's law":** In chapter 13 of *The Scarlet Letter,* Hawthorne writes that "The world's law was no law" for Hester. Similarly, in chapter 23 of *The Marble Faun* Miriam questions the wisdom of "what men call justice." Compare Hester and Miriam in their philosophies and their positions in society. What qualities do they share? How are they different? What does Hawthorne seem to be saying about the necessity and the correctness of "the world's law"?

In chapter 19 of *The Marble Faun,* the narrator says that "The foremost result of a broken law is ever an ecstatic sense of freedom." Another way to shape this question about the world's law, then, might be to compare and analyze the reactions of some of Hawthorne's other characters in the wake of a broken law. Pearl, Donatello, and Dimmesdale are all viable possibilities for evaluation.

3. **The sins of the past:** In chapter 33 of *The Marble Faun,* Kenyon says to Donatello, "You should go with me to my native country. . . . In that fortunate land, each generation has only its own sins and sorrows to bear. Here, it seems as if all the weary and dreary Past were piled upon the back of the Present." The burden of the past upon the present is a common topic in Hawthorne. Compare its treatment in *The Marble Faun* and another of Hawthorne's works.

The House of the Seven Gables presents the most likely comparison. Generational guilt haunts both families in this novel and it haunts the titular house as well. Both *Seven Gables* and *The Marble Faun* deal with this theme extensively. Other works too might provide room for comparison. For example, in "Roger Malvin's Burial," the past obviously haunts the present.

4. **Confession:** Hawthorne frequently explores the interrelationship between sin and confession. In *The Marble Faun,* Miriam almost confesses her past to Kenyon. Similarly, desperate to relieve the sorrow and guilt she feels after she witnesses the

model's murder, Hilda, the self-proclaimed "daughter of the
Puritans," seeks out the confessional at St. Peter's to share her
"sin." *The Scarlet Letter* also asks us to consider the role of confession—both public and private—in the wake of sin. Dimmesdale, especially, seems to need some sort of confession in order
to end his suffering and guilt. Consider the role of confession in
these two novels. What does Hawthorne seem to argue about
the validity and the use of the confession of secret sin?

In *The Marble Faun*, this issue is caught up with Hawthorne's
assessment of the Catholic Church, and his feelings seem to
be quite complex. You could easily consider the question of
confession, though, without involving Hawthorne's attitudes
toward Catholicism. What is confession's role in assuaging
sin? How effective is confession? Are there times when it is
effective and others when it is not? If so, what separates these
instances?

Bibliography and Online Resources for *The Marble Faun*

Amoia, Alba. "Hawthorne's Rome: Then and Now." *Nathaniel Hawthorne Review*
22 (1998): 1–34.

Auerbach, Jonathan. "Executing the Model: Painting, Sculpture, and Romance-
Writing in Hawthorne's *The Marble Faun*." *ELH* 47 (1980): 103–20.

Bailey, Brigitte. "Fuller, Hawthorne, and Imagining Urban Spaces in Rome." In
Roman Holidays: American Artists and Writers in Nineteenth-Century Italy.
Eds. Robert K. Martin and Leland S. Person. Iowa City: U of Iowa P, 2002.
175–90.

Barnett, Louise. "American Novelists and the 'Portrait of Beatrice Cenci.'" *New
England Quarterly* 53 (1980): 168–83.

Baym, Nina. *The Shape of Hawthorne's Career*. Ithaca, NY: Cornell UP, 1976.

Bell, Millicent. *Hawthorne's View of the Artist*. Albany: SUNY P, 1962.

Burdick, Emily Miller. "Perplexity, sympathy, and the question of the human:
a reading of *The Marble Faun*. In *The Cambridge Companion to Nathaniel
Hawthorne*. Ed. Richard H. Millington. Cambridge: Cambridge UP, 2004.
230–50.

Carton, Evan. *The Marble Faun: Hawthorne's Transformations*. New York:
Twayne, 1992.

————. *The Rhetoric of American Romance. Dialectic and Identity in Emerson, Dickinson, Poe, and Hawthorne.* Baltimore: Johns Hopkins UP, 1985.

Crews, Frederick C. *The Sins of Fathers: Hawthorne's Psychological Themes.* New York: Oxford UP, 1966.

Dauber, Kenneth. *Rediscovering Hawthorne.* Princeton, NY: Princeton UP, 1977.

Dryden, Edgar. *Nathaniel Hawthorne: The Poetics of Enchantment.* Ithaca, NY: Cornell UP, 1977.

Fogle, Richard Harter. *Hawthorne's Fiction: The Light and the Dark.* Norman: U of Oklahoma P, 1952.

Fossum, Robert H. *The Inviolable Circle: The Problem of Time.* Deland, FL: Everett/Edwards, Inc., 1972.

Gollin, Rita. "Hawthorne and the Visual Arts." In *A Historical Guide to Nathaniel Hawthorne.* Ed. Larry J. Reynolds. New York: Oxford UP, 2001. 109–33.

Hamilton, Kristie. "Fauns and Mohicans: Narratives of Extinction and Hawthorne's Aesthetic of Modernity." In *Roman Holidays: American Artists and Writers in Nineteenth-Century Italy.* Eds. Robert K. Martin and Leland S. Person. Iowa City: U of Iowa P, 2002. 41–59.

Hawthorne, Nathaniel. *Passages from The French and Italian Notebooks.* Nathaniel Hawthorne (1804–1864) home page. Available online. URL: http://www.eldritchpress.org/nh/pffinb.html. Downloaded August 2, 2006.

Herbert, T. Walter. *Dearest Beloved: The Hawthornes and the Making of the Middle Class Marriage.* Berkeley: U of California P, 1993.

Levin, Harry. *The Power of Blackness: Hawthorne, Poe, Melville.* New York: Alfred A. Knopf, 1958.

Levine, Robert. "'Antebellum Rome' in *The Marble Faun.*" *American Literary History* 2 (1990): 19–38.

Male, Roy. *Hawthorne's Tragic Vision.* New York: Norton, 1957.

Marks, Patricia. "Virgin Saint, Mother Saint: Hilda and Dorothea." *Hawthorne and Women: Engendering and Expanding the Hawthorne Tradition.* Eds. John L. Idol, Jr. and Melinda M. Ponder. Amherst: U of Massachusetts P, 1999. 151–58.

Martin, Robert. "'An Awful Freedom': Hawthorne and the Anxieties of the Carnival." In *Roman Holidays: American Artists and Writers in Nineteenth-Century Italy.* Eds. Robert K. Martin and Leland S. Person. Iowa City: U of Iowa P, 2002. 28–40.

Martin, Terence. *Nathaniel Hawthorne,* rev. ed. Boston: Twayne, 1983.

Michael, John. "History and Romance, Sympathy and Uncertainty: The Moral of the Stones in Hawthorne's *The Marble Faun.*" *PMLA* 103 (1988): 150–57.

Millington, Richard. "Where Is Hawthorne's Rome?: *The Marble Faun* and the Cultural Space of Middle-Class Leisure." *Roman Holidays: American Artists and Writers in Nineteenth-Century Italy.* Eds. Robert K. Martin and Leland S. Person. Iowa City: U of Iowa P, 2002. 9–17.

Mitchell, Thomas. *Hawthorne's Fuller Mystery.* Amherst: U of Massachusetts P, 1998.

Newberry, Frederick. *Hawthorne's Divided Loyalties: England and America in His Works.* Rutherford, NJ: Fairleigh Dickinson UP, 1987.

Newbury, Michael. *Figuring Authorship in Antebellum America.* Palo Alto, CA: Stanford UP, 1997.

Person, Leland S. "Falling into Heterosexuality: Sculpting Male Bodies in *The Marble Faun* and *Roderick Hudson.*" *Roman Holidays: American Artists and Writers in Nineteenth-Century Italy.* Eds. Robert K. Martin and Leland S. Person. Iowa City: U of Iowa P, 2002. 107–39.

Proctor, Nancy. "The Purloined Studio: The Woman Sculptor as Phallic Ghost in Hawthorne's *The Marble Faun.*" *Roman Holidays: American Artists and Writers in Nineteenth-Century Italy.* Eds. Robert K. Martin and Leland S. Person. Iowa City: U of Iowa P, 2002. 60–72.

Reynolds, Larry J. *A Historical Guide to Nathaniel Hawthorne.* New York: Oxford UP, 2001.

Rowe, John Carlos. "Hawthorne's Ghost in James's Italy: Sculptural Form, Romantic Narrative, and the Function of Sexuality in *The Marble Faun,* 'Adina,' and *William Wetmore Story and His Friends.*" *Roman Holidays: American Artists and Writers in Nineteenth-Century Italy.* Eds. Robert K. Martin and Leland S. Person. Iowa City: U of Iowa P, 2002. 73–106.

Schiller, Emily. "The Choice of Innocence: Hilda in *The Marble Faun.*" *Studies in the Novel* 26 (1994): 372–92.

Sterling, Laurie. "'A frail structure of our own rearing': The Value(s) of Home in *The Marble Faun.*" *ATQ* 14 (2000): 93–113.

Stern, Milton. *Contexts for Hawthorne: The Marble Faun and the Politics of Openness and Closure in American Literature.* New York: Oxford UP, 1991.

Waggoner, Hyatt H. *Hawthorne: A Critical Study* Cambridge, MA: The Belknap Press, 1955.

Williams, Susan S. *Confounding Images.* Philadelphia: U of Pennsylvania P, 1997.

Wineapple, Brenda. *Hawthorne: A Life.* New York: Knopf, 2003.

INDEX